SO-BJN-292

MAN AND MASK

MAN *and* MASK

Forty Years in the Life
of a Singer

BY

Feodor Chaliapin

*

Translated from the French for the first time
By Phyllis Mégroz

GREENWOOD PRESS, PUBLISHERS
WESTPORT, CONNECTICUT

Originally published in 1932
by Alfred A. Knopf, New York

Reprinted from an original copy in the collections
of the Brooklyn Public Library

First Greenwood Reprinting 1970

Library of Congress Catalogue Card Number 70-109841

SBN 8371-4332-2

Printed in the United States of America

TO

MY CHILDREN

PREFACE

◆◇◆

Now that this book of memories is about to see the light, I think I ought to explain why I decided to devote my rare moments of leisure to writing it. It is usual, I know, for those who have achieved a certain amount of celebrity in any quarter of the globe to tell the world through their biographers (or by writing their memoirs) the history of their lives — the year in which they were born, the truth about their parents, the schools where they made their mark by brilliant scholarship or remarkable laziness, the name of their first love, and, finally, how they ascended the ladder of fame. As a rule, however, the literary tyro can be forgiven only one book, a fact that somewhat complicates my position. I committed my first literary offence many years ago, and so I am a little unnerved. When I was a child, I had a predilection for the apples in the next-door garden; the first time the gardener caught me, he forgave me, but when next he discovered me redhanded, he did not spare the rod. That is why I anticipate my friends saying:

"Another book? Why on earth have you written another book? Wouldn't it have been better if you had stuck to singing?"

Perhaps they would be right. Nevertheless, I have an excuse — the idea of this book was the outcome of an event whose appeal was irresistible, this event being the recent fortieth anniversary of my first appearance on the stage as a professional singer. The dawning of that anniversary made me feel a little sentimental. I looked into my mirror and discoursed somewhat weightily to my reflection:

" Most worthy and illustrious Feodor Ivanovitch, although, during your time, you've created many a ' scandal' behind the scenes, and made the lives of conductors a misery, one thing remains — during all those forty years you've put your whole soul into your singing. Forty years devoted to singing. Forty years of uninterrupted work which has often been raised by the kind gods who love you to the level of inspiration. Forty years of the divine fire, for art without the divine fire has never meant, can never mean, anything to you. Forty years — a whole lifetime of uncertainties, agonies, enthusiasms, dissatisfactions, and triumphs. Where have you not wandered, Feodor Ivanovitch, in the space of those years? Your feet have trodden the willow-bordered by-ways of your own Russia, side by side with the *laptis* [1] of the moujiks you love — those moujiks whose voices blend so exquisitely in the popular songs that reach your heart. Your feet have led you along the dusty roads of country towns where the people draw heart-breaking melodies from barrel-organs and make harmonicas manufactured in Germany quiver with sound. You have stood in the squares and boulevards of great cities, listening to re-echoing regimental music, and you have been carried along the steel highways of the world, your ears filled with the thunderous rhythm of the giant wheels. What music have you not heard? What music have you yourself not sung? "

As is only correct in such circumstances, the " speaker " made himself a present — a gold fountain-pen; I was so touched by the attention that I promised to gather together and relive the memories of those forty years and

---

[1] Primitive shoes of bark, worn by Russian peasants.

tell them to all who cared to listen, but primarily to myself and my children. . . .

I must admit that the ways of which I have spoken in my " oration " were not always easy, and that my art did not spring up in me, spontaneously and without difficulty, like a gift from Heaven. It is only at the price of a long struggle that I have attained perfection in it, and much pain and labour have gone to build up my natural gifts. I sincerely believe that a true history of my experiences towards this end would prove profitable to those of my young fellow-aspirants for operatic laurels who are pre-pared to throw themselves whole-heartedly into their work with no expectation of easily won success. Today, above all, now that art has fallen into the hands of theorists and illusionists, I dare hope that my ideas and impressions may prove of some interest to a larger circle of readers.

Another thing that has moved me of late years as deeply as the theatre is the thought of Russia. I own that I have never been particularly affected by the yearning for one's country which threatens (or perhaps builds up) one's happiness in a foreign land. Whether the reason for this springs from the fact that I have always been a wanderer, or from some totally different cause, I do not often feel that home-sickness. Yet, wherever I go, whenever I think of the ways of living, the customs of other people, thoughts of my own country rise ever-green in my memory. I recall the past, the good with the bad, purely personal happen-ings, and wider, universal, unrelated events.

And as I recall these things, a sense of sadness steals over me; I am conscious of a deep-rooted necessity to co-ordinate my thoughts of my own Russian people and my own Russia. All my impressions of them are confused, varying, multi-coloured. Sometimes sleep is broken by them; at other times I feel my eyes blazing with pride and my heart beating wildly. Oh, Russia, my country, how tempestuous, how ridiculous, but how wonderful you are!

Preface

I have torn myself away from Russia, I have left her for strange lands. My children, too, live out their lives in foreign cities. I took them away with me when they were babies, unable to choose for themselves. Why did I do this? What actuated me? I feel I must answer these questions, and that is why I am dwelling in this book on the last years I spent in Russia, the country that was no longer summed up briefly in the single word " Russia," but was known as the United States of Soviet Russia. . . .

The theatre was the magic crystal through which I saw Russia. Everything in this book is more or less bound up with my life in the theatre. My outlook on the world is neither political nor sociological; it is an actor's point of view, an actor's outlook, and from this angle I find that human beings — their individualities, their gestures, their make-up — are of supreme interest to me. It is this overwhelming interest that leads me into detailed descriptions of apparently insignificant happenings. I feel that details are very often a thousand times more colourful, more pregnant, and more vital than the structure itself. The amiable Commissioner of Police at Kiev who received me in his bath, up to his neck in water, and who, divested of any artificiality, offered me a glass of vodka at a most unseasonable hour; the eccentric Komissar in the north who telephoned me at three in the morning to say that he must come and drink my health immediately and regale me with smoked salmon that he had just received from Archangel — how can I pass them over unheeded? I find them just as interesting as the Grand Duke watching the performance at the Hermitage, just as interesting as the Prime Minister in his palatial residence and the Commander-in-Chief in his *wagon-lit*. They are all Russians, they all play parts, even though they are different parts, in the Masque of Russia.

I have spoken of my first book. I should like to explain briefly how this second book differs from it. In *Pages of*

Preface

My Life,[1] which I wrote a long time ago in Russia, I devoted much space to a description of my childhood, but gave only a very sketchy and superficial account of my career and artistic evolution. The events of which I speak in my first book refer principally to the years previous to 1905.

In this book I have endeavoured to give a complete picture of my life up to the present. I have avoided repetitions, and have only made mention of incidents that have been described in my first book because it is necessary to analyse their effect on my development. To sum up, my first book was unfinished, myself seen from the outside, while this one is intended to be an analytical autobiography of the man and the mask.

If an author may be allowed to speak of his work, I should like to say that I have done my utmost to set down the unvarnished truth. I present myself to my readers without make-up or disguise.

[1] Published by Harper & Brothers (New York, 1927).

CONTENTS

～～

Part I

RUSSIA

[xiii]

Contents

Contents

Contents

Contents

Contents

Contents

⌇⌇

Part II

IN THE POLITICAL AND REVOLUTIONARY
WHIRLPOOL

Contents

Contents

Contents

three o'clock in the morning to request the pleasure of drinking my health: His visit: My visit to Zinoviev

Chapter 20.   Dalski and his anarchism: My friends the Barons Stuart are arrested: I visit the Tcheka: I receive a promise: My friends are shot: Gorki goes to Moscow to beg Lenin to spare the lives of the Grand Dukes: His request is granted: A telephone call: Death of the Grand Dukes

Chapter 21.   My wife begs me to leave the country at all costs: Blockade: Dreams

Chapter 22.   Life becomes hideously " official ": All human feeling has disappeared: I fall ill: I am neglected, alone, poverty-stricken: I am surrounded by complete indifference: Escape . . .: My wife is recruited to do hard labour on the Neva in mid-winter: I visit the Komissar: I protest, and flatter him: A visit of inspection: I win my case: Five million roubles are demanded of me: Fresh requisitions: My triggers refuse to catch

Chapter 23.   I go to Moscow to visit Lenin: He helps me to save the treasures of the Marie Theatre: Work in the theatre: No need of art: Triumph of the backstage Soviet: The actors' rations become too meagre: I visit Trotski: His reply

Chapter 24.   Lounatcharski: Soldiers sack my flat in Moscow: My visit to Kamenev: A " charming" revolutionary: " War to the palace, peace to the cottage ": We talk politics

Chapter 25.   My relations with the Bolshevik leaders: The magistrate of Vilno implores me to save his son: Peters, the notorious head of the Tcheka: Dzerjinski: A mysterious encounter that occurs later in Berlin

Contents

Contents

෨ ෨

Part III

IN FOREIGN LANDS

ILLUSTRATIONS

✍ ✍

[xxv]

Illustrations

Part I
RUSSIA

CHAPTER I

*The wandering Russian: Varlaam: Ivan the Terrible: Boris
Godounov: Prince Galitski*

い の

WHEN I WAS young, I liked to go fishing. I would leave
the house and the civilization of the town behind me and,
armed with rod and bait, start out into the country. I
would spend long days on the water, and at night I would
find any sort of resting-place in a peasant's cottage. On
one of these expeditions I slept in a miller's *izba*. One
evening, as I was going back to the *izba* for the night, I saw
a figure stretched out in a corner wearing a threadbare
grey garment and gaping felt boots, although it was summer. A beggar's pouch covered his face, a stout staff pro-
truded from under an arm, and in the midst of it all he
was sound asleep.

I lay down opposite the door on a heap of hay which
had been piled up for me. But I was wakeful, and tossed
restlessly, longing for day to dawn. At daybreak the
fish rise eagerly. At last it began to grow light. As soon as the
night faded, the grey figure with the worn felt shoes began
to stir uneasily and stretch itself to an accompaniment of
grunts; presently the visitor sat up, yawned, crossed himself, got to his feet and made for the door. On the threshold
he turned to the wash-basin, a primitive affair hung by a
string at one end of the entrance. From my heap of hay I

watched his movements with interest; he poured water on his hands, soaked his white beard, rubbed it, and dried it on his *chlamys*. Next he took his staff, crossed himself again, bowed in three directions, and departed.

I should have liked to talk to the old man, but there had been no time, he had already gone. I was strangely moved and was conscious of a strong desire to see him once again. He had some curious attraction for me. I knelt on the hay and, leaning my elbows on the window-sill, opened the casement. His figure was a long way distant. As he moved still farther off, it became smaller and smaller until it finally disappeared, remaining, however, to my eyes and my mental vision extraordinarily clear and distinct.

The old man was a pilgrim, a *strannik*. From time immemorial such wanderers have existed in Russia, nomads, homeless and hearthless, possessing no earthly ties, following no trade, driven onward by some nameless thought. Leading the life of gypsies, and yet not of the gypsy clans, they roamed over the vast territories of Russia, from village to village, from country to country. They were to be seen going from one tavern to another, dragging themselves to the fairs, entering a hostel for a brief moment. They rested and slept when and where they chose. Nobody knew the meaning of their pilgrimages. I am convinced that had any of them been asked whither he was going, and why, not one could have answered. Not one of them would have known. Not one of them had ever considered the reason of his wanderings.

All these pilgrims appeared to be in search of something. Their minds seemed to be filled with a confused idea of an unknown country where life would be kinder and more just. Perhaps they were escaping from something. Perhaps they were escaping from nothing more tangible than *toska,* that nostalgia that only Russians experience, utterly indescribable, utterly incomprehensible, and often without motive.

[4]

Varlaam

In *Boris Godounov,* Moussorgski has pictured the Wandering Russian with extraordinary force in the old man Varlaam. I have never seen an entirely satisfying presentment of Varlaam in the Russian theatre, and I myself have never been quite able to create a perfect Varlaam, although I *feel* him and can explain him. But Moussorgski, with passionate intensity, has succeeded in expressing the illimitable soul-sickness of the pilgrim, who is a kind of monk without a monastery, or, more simply still, a sacristan of old. So overwhelming is Varlaam's *toska* that he must either hang himself or laugh till he dies during the frenzied orgy. Moussorgski has given a wonderful interpretation of Varlaam's bitter laughter, laughter beneath which one senses the deepest tragedy. When Varlaam invites Grichka Otrepiev to drink and jest with him, and the stripling says coarsely: " Drink, but take heed of thyself," what depth of bitterness is in his reply: " Of *myself?* What use in taking heed of *myself?* . . ." Leaning heavily on the table, he breaks into a wild strain in a minor key. This is no song, but a cry of grief disguised.

Usually Varlaam is represented in the Russian theatre as a drunken sot who swallows down great gulps of vodka. His fear of the law is generally interpreted as being the outcome of a guilty conscience — he has committed a crime, and therefore is in terror of arrest, reasons the actor. As though Varlaam would dread the thought of prison. Isn't he already in prison, isn't his whole life a prison? Quite possibly he is a criminal. Quite possibly he has committed a crime. In any case he is a swindler. But that is not the essential Varlaam.

His " What use in taking heed of *myself?* " means: " I realize perfectly that I am morally rotten. . . ." His soul is tortured by the thought of his worthlessness. Go where he will, he is surely doomed — it is unimportant whether he is finally smothered in a snowfall or drowned in a pool. He knows that wherever he may go he is of no use to anyone. A beggared wastrel is no good to the world. . . .

And so Varlaam roams from monastery to monastery, yields to temptation on the Solovki Isles, strays from town to town, bounds along in the train of religious processions, and runs panting behind a wonder-working ikon. He holds a taper in his cupped hand so that the wind shall not extinguish it, and, like the deacons, shrieks in a hoarse, half-stifled voice: " Crush the filthy serpent with its twelve wings beneath your heel. . . ."

He stinks of sweat and oil and incense. His white beard is wildly tangled, and is twisted into two corkscrew ends. Swollen and bloodless, with the startling exception of his veined, discoloured nose, he is an assiduous visitor at the Flea Market. There he goes in his grisly grey rags thread-bare down to the cord about his waist, with an affair that looks like a skull-cap on his head. There he is in that cor-ner, stuffing himself — if he has enough money — with the leavings of tripe from an earthenware pot, on the top of which an old woman usually squats to keep her wares warm beneath layers of drawers and petticoats. There he is, babbling explanations to a pothouse audience of the whys and wherefores of his latest expulsion from a monastery.

" I had a bout of the h-hiccups . . . I hic-hiccuped in the hostel. I was d-drunk, and I stripped — hic — and I st-started to hop about in the nave, when along c-came the Reverend Father on his way to — hic — matins. . . ."

He is driven away.

When Varlaam crosses himself, he is exorcizing his own soul-sickness and the uncleanness of life rooted within him. But nothing can rid him of these stains, singing and dancing will not help him. His only consolation is to read aloud or intone the words of the Evangelist:

" Come unto Me, all ye that are weary and heavy-laden, and I will give you rest."

He knows that he is not weary, but he sincerely believes that he is heavy-laden. . . . Then he proceeds to dull his mind with a self-administered drug: he persuades himself that somewhere, even though it be at the ends of the earth, there is a land where the just and wise hold sway, a land where the wretched can dwell unmolested. . . .

I do not know if beings like Varlaam need exist, and if so, whether we should attempt to alter them. I can only say this: such beings are one of the most remarkable, even though one of the most unhappy, features of Russian life. Had they not existed, life would have seemed emptier to Moussorgski and also to us. . . .

Toska is a bottomless abyss. Yet when I think of the characters I have created on the Russian stage, I am conscious not so much of the characters themselves as of an all-pervading sense of the Russian temperament that is all extremes. In *Khovantchina* it is religious fanaticism, and how profound and powerful is that fanaticism! A normal mind could not possibly comprehend that perfect serenity which enables men to die for their belief. They stand on the sheer rampart, utterly oblivious of the stairway by which they might descend to safety. They batter their heads against the wall, unconscious of pain. . . . In Rimski-Korsakov's *Pskovitaine* I take the part of Ivan the Terrible. He, the Tzar, cares nothing that the river runs red with blood, so illimitable is his knowledge of his power over others, so unshakable is his belief in his own sovereignty. . . .

There is tremendous strength in Boris Godounov, the part I would sooner play than any of the others of my repertory. In spite of his despotism, the wretched king is like a wounded lion surrounded by jackals and hyenas, who finally succeed in destroying him. For a time, instinctively feeling his power, and dreading it, the boyars prowl about him with hang-dog glances and gnashing teeth. But only for a time. When the moment is ripe, the treacherous and cowardly crowd tears the lion to pieces. Here again the Russian temperament is overwhelmingly manifest in the seditious licence of the boyars, as it is in the boundless autocracy of Ivan the Terrible. It appears also in the lawlessness and drunkenness of Prince Galitski, one of the chief characters of Borodin's admirable opera *Prince Igor*. Galitski's excesses are as extreme as his cynicism. It seems as though the Russian temperament is entirely devoid of moderation.

CHAPTER II

The legend of Stenka Razin: Russian mentality: Contradictions and extremes

လာ လာ

MOST CHILDREN, THE world over, I expect, love to play at brigands. The game has a kind of romantic fascination, an element of adventure and danger. Russian children have always had a particular predilection for this play, and I doubt whether in any other country brigands are so cherished in the youthful imagination. Perhaps this is because there have always been numbers of brigands in Russia, whose lives, according to popular belief, have always been lived against a background of endless, gloomy forests and rushing rivers. A scarlet belt and a scarlet shirt, care-free songs, a wild and reckless existence — that is the Russian small boy's picture of a brigand.

Perhaps, too, this predilection for brigands has its roots in those far-off times when the people were oppressed by their overlords and the officials of the Tzar, for then the brigand appeared as the protector of the downtrodden. Who is the most-loved brigand in Russia? None other than the Tzar-brigand, Stenka Razin. Magnanimous and cruel, savage and despotic, Stenka revolted against those in authority, and rallied the poor and rebellious beneath his banner.

[9]

Stenka Razin

It is curious that the legend of Stenka Razin still retains the following incident in all its wild abandonment of savagery. The story runs that Stenka, " joyous and drunken," lifted the Persian Princess, his beloved, over the side of his barque and flung her into the Volga — " A gift from a Cossack of the Don," as the well-known ballad puts it. Thus did he tear from his breast a segment of his bleeding heart, flinging it overboard into the rippled waters. . . . Now you can see what sort of a man he was, this much-loved Russian brigand.

Naturally, I am far from considering Stenka Razin as the symbolic prototype of all Russia, but one could hardly visualize Russian mentality or the destiny of Russia without evoking him. Let us admit that if he does not symbolize the whole of Russia, he has a curiously close affinity with the Russian Volga. . . . There are moments when your Russian feels the surge of " Razinism " within him, and at such times he is capable of extraordinary acts. This is so true that sometimes I wonder if all of us, Reds, Whites, Greens, or Blues, have not been so demoniacally possessed by Razinism that we lost all consciousness of ourselves in a gigantic game of brigands. Have we not also been guilty of lifting the lovely Princess over the side of the ship, of flinging her to the waves with a heroic gesture — only the Princess was no Persian Princess, but our own mother, Russia — " A gift from a Cossack of the Don."

Today, one meets many people ready to admire this ultra-romantic gesture, which seems to them both superb and tragic. As a rule, I am keenly sensitive to tragic beauty, which I love, but in this Russian drama there is something which fails to strike the right chord. I see many other things, as well as the romantic, in our desire to " play brigands," things in which romanticism is out of place. Side by side with poetry and beauty, there are painful and sickening contrasts in the Russian mentality. Intolerance,

FEODOR CHALIAPIN

jealousy, fury, and cruelty — the rest of humanity is subject, no doubt, to these vices, but so strange is our Russian character that good and bad alike take on giant proportions with exceptional intensity. Not only are our passions and impulses like our snowstorms, in which a man grows giddy and is lost; not only is our *toska* overwhelming, sticky, and glutinous, even our temperamental apathy clogs our very heart, filling us with a sensation of such tragic emptiness that it transcends the melancholy of any European country.

Russian mentality knows no moderation. Its soul-conflicts and emotions are of extreme violence, and for that reason Russian life is made up of contradictions and contrasts. There are contradictions in every human intelligence, and without them there would be no natural lights and shades. There are opposing forces in every mind, but in a normal state these forces, paradoxically, do not destroy one another. The shaded outline of a range of hills does not shatter the harmony of a landscape; on the contrary, it adds to its beauty; but a jagged chain of mountain-tops upsets the entire composition. We may realize that these mountains only *appear* to be harsh and out of the picture, simply because their peaks are not level; in spite of this realization, we receive an impression that an earthquake has occurred.

Whether it is because the Russians are still rather primitive or because they are still a young people, the fact remains that their contradictions are far more harsh and violent than those of most mentalities. Russian mentality is broad, but the Russian way of life is niggling and paltry, narrow and bickering enough, Heaven only knows. The Russian heart is infinitely pitiful and tender, but at the same time what gross, and often completely aimless, cruelty and tyranny are to be found in Russian life. The Russian soul is extraordinarily sensitized, but what brutality and

[11]

Russian Mentality

hurtful suspicion and vulgarism are to be found in the human relationships! It is only too true that neither in good nor in evil can the Russian steer a middle course:

Among the ordered stars till strength is gone
He, like a crazy comet, rushes on.

CHAPTER III

The genius of Russia: Harmony

⧼⧽

I<small>N</small> S<small>PITE</small> O<small>F</small> everything, however, the genius of Russia echoes down the ages like a starry carillon of bells.

I cannot bear patriotic pæans of praise. Whenever I begin to talk glowingly about Russia, I immediately feel I am like a certain general who always exclaimed without rhyme or reason: "If I give a Turk a bowl of rye gruel and butter to eat, he's bound to die three hours later in horrible convulsions on the pavement, with everybody staring at him."

"But, your Excellency, *you* eat it and nothing happens to you."

"*I?* From the age of seven, my dear sir, *I've* been able to digest nails!"

As I have already remarked, I dislike flattering comparisons. But there are times when they are warranted, and the genius of Russia can only be likened to an astral melody quivering in the sky.

For example, note how subtly and exquisitely Poushkin, our national genius, can give an effect of light and shade. In *L'Invité de pierre*, the Spanish beauty cries:

"Come — open the balcony window — how still is the night!
The warm air's redolent of lemon- and laurel-trees,
See, over the deep blue of heaven, the moon sheds her light.
The long-drawn cries of the watchmen echo and fade . . .

Harmony

But far away in Paris, in the north,
Perhaps the beauty of night is cloud-overlaid,
Chill, grey rain patters, and the wind howls forth. . . ."

Far away, in Paris, *in the north.* . . . And those lines
were written in Russia, at Mikhailovskoie in the province
of Novgorod, probably on an icy day, deadened and
blanketed with swirling heaps of snow. . . . Yet from
thence Poushkin transports himself to Madrid, and his
conception of Paris is of a distant and *northern* city. . . .

I do not know whether Poushkin was a musician. I am
inclined to think he was not. There is no indication of
such a gift in his lyrical works or in his letters. He was not
a musician, and yet how sensitive he was to the very soul
of music. Every word that he wrote about music in *Mozart
and Salieri* is of the highest significance. How deeply he
felt Mozart — not only Mozart's counterpoint, melody, and
harmonic modulations, but the essence, the very meaning
of Mozart's genius. Do you remember Mozart's words to
Salieri:

"If only the whole world could feel the power of harmony. . . . But it is impossible for the world to feel it,
for under that divine influence, the world would cease to
be; humanity could not endure the paltriness of existence"?

These were the only possible words that could express
Mozart. Poushkin does not make him say: "the power of
melody," that would be utterly inadequate; instead, he
writes: "the power of *harmony,*" because he knows that
whatever music the stars ring out, whatever of their music
echoes in our ears, the very essence of this starry melody is
harmony.

All the contradictions of Russian existence and character, many examples of which occur in this book, find
their ultimate reconciliation in the profound and harmonious words of creative Russian genius.

[14]

CHAPTER IV

Reality and Imagination

ᔫᔫ

I HAVE OFTEN WONDERED why the theatre has so completely obsessed me. The explanation is simple enough. The actual life about me was negative and devoid of imagination, and I was always aware of its vulgarity and coarseness.

Most people must experience this reaction in the course of their lives, but the atmosphere of the Soukonnaia Sloboda [1] of Kazan, where fate had placed me, was particularly gross. Possibly I could not have defined it, probably I could not have given it a name, but I was extremely conscious of its influence. Something deep within me told me that the life I was living was not the life that mattered. My first contact with the world of the theatre moved me profoundly because it confirmed my instinctive realization that life could be other than I knew it — lovelier and nobler.

I did not know the actors who took part in *Medea* and *The Russian Wedding*, but to me they appeared like beings from a higher planet. They were dressed so magnificently (at least, I thought so — in all likelihood, they were nothing of the kind). They wore the splendid caftans of the old-time boyars, boots of scarlet leather, and

---

[1] The poor quarter of Kazan

[15]

sarafans of emerald-green. But what fascinated me most of all was the words they declaimed. It was not the actual words themselves that thrilled me — they were ordinary, everyday words that I knew perfectly well — no, it was the glowing and jewelled sentences that were made up of these words. They gleamed with luminous ideas; their exquisite cadences held new forms of thought. Most wonderful of all, the ring of these familiar words filled me with a newly-experienced emotion.

I have dwelt with some insistence on my first over-whelming impressions of the theatre, because my later feelings, matured by my experience of art and life, were not substantially different in essentials. Although everything has suffered change — years, towns, countries, conditions, and outward forms — the basic emotion is unaltered. I am filled with the same flood of wonder at the protean transformations of life through art — the simplest sentiments, the most everyday words, are remade, renewed under its enchantment.

I remember how profoundly I was moved when, during the time that I was singing at the Marie Theatre, I heard my own opinion voiced by a quite unlettered woman. Mention of her brings back one of the loveliest ties of my youth. Glorious, fascinating Elizabeth — her life in the house of an under-stationmaster in the depths of a boring little Russian province was dull and weary enough. She was as magnificently formed as Venus, and, like Venus, totally unlearned. But Elizabeth's chief attraction lay in the fact that she was a Russian woman, as simple as she was good. A wayside flower.

When we were together, and by the light of an oil lamp shaded by a newspaper, I would read aloud Lermontov's well-known verses: " A golden cloud lay on the bosom of a giant rock "; she would listen to me with wide-open eyes and, completely carried away, would say:

" What marvellous men you writers and actors are!

Reality and Imagination

You use words that I hear every day of my life, but nobody can put them together like you. Cloud, rock, bosom, giant — absolutely ordinary words, and yet how beautiful they sound when they're strung into a sentence. They make me want to cry. Oh, the exquisite patterns that you make of words! "

It was my very own thought proceeding from Elizabeth's lips. In my boyhood I had thought and felt exactly as she thought and felt. In the Soukonnaia Sloboda, I had listened to words spoken with varying intonations, but none of them had ever awakened an echo in me, whereas in the theatre the same words uttered by an actor became clothed in meaning and beauty. . . . Add to this the effect on me of limelight, scenery, mysterious curtain, and the barrier separating the unsophisticated inhabitants of the Soukonnaia Sloboda from the heroes in scarlet leather boots — it far transcended my powers of imagination. I was more than wonder-stricken, I was emotionally shattered.

From that moment, although I was very young at the time, I was possessed by a deep-rooted determination, that held no hint of wavering, to devote myself entirely to art. Since then it has often occurred to me that other things besides commonplace words can be transformed into poetry, and that our customary actions, the familiar everyday little actions of our Soukonnaia Sloboda, can also be construed into a poem fraught with meaning. To make this possible we must cultivate our creative imagination and artistic will-power in life, as in art.

My first adoration and idol, Iachka, the buffoon and popular clown: First dreams of the stage: My first appearances: My first costume and my first make-up

✄

Medea and *The Russian Wedding* were not my first glimpses of the theatre, and not altogether the first spark to the fuel of my ambitions. It was one cold December, when I was eight years old, that I singed my wings in the flame of the footlights. I was taken to a Christmas fair and for the first time saw Jacob Ivanovitch Mamonov, an actor known in the neighbourhood of the Volga as Iachka, a mummer and a clown.

Iachka was blessed with an extraordinary physiognomy, perfectly in keeping with his fooling. Although not old, he was inclined to be corpulent, and this gave him a somewhat commanding presence. Besides this, he had stiff bristling moustaches as black as pitch, and grotesquely fierce eyes, so that altogether he was a figure of superstitious terror to the small boys in the audience. But the terror he inspired was a pleasurable emotion. He frightened us, but he also had an irresistible attraction for us. Everything about him was fascinating; his hoarse, roaring voice, his spontaneous movements, and the joyful flow of jests and buffooneries that he let loose on the open-mouthed listeners.

Iachka

" Houp-la, my hearties, pick up your kit and come along up to me, you blockheads, you numskulls! " he would yell at the crowd from the stairway of his booth with its book-muslin trappings.

His clowning and punning and heavy humour were altogether to the public taste. Each of his sallies provoked shouts of laughter. His improvisations seemed very daring to them. While he was presenting his troupe of assistants and pushing them on to the stage — they consisted of his wife, his son, and a few additional players — Iachka held up a grotesque puppet, intended to represent the Governor, and yelled:

> *" Hey, you dummies, move about,*
> *Now then, Governor, hoof it out! "*

During the icy-cold weather Iachka would amuse for hours on end an uncritical audience who shook the walls with their laughter. Literally spellbound, I watched him with fascinated eyes. I stood for hours in front of his booth until my very marrow was frozen, and still I could not tear myself away from the enchanting sight. Sometimes Iachka was enveloped in a mist of his own breath, and then he seemed to me to be a supernatural being, a sorcerer, a magician.

How feverishly and impatiently I waited each morning for his booth to open! With what adoration I gazed at him! And how astounded I was when, after he had finished all his side-splitting numbers, I saw him sitting at the Palermo Inn, a tankard of beer and some slices of black bread in front of him, with a deadly serious, almost tragic expression on his face! It was curious to see the fun-maker, the tireless jester, wearing so sorrowful a look. In those days I did not know how many things may be hidden behind the glitter of the footlights. . . .

Iachka was the first person I had ever met who impressed me by a marvellous readiness of wit. He was never at a

[19]

loss with his buffoonery, and, with a nightcap on his head, he would crack endless jokes. And I remember wondering:

"How does he keep on and on without hesitating or stammering? It's just as though he had learnt it all off by heart!"

Moreover, I was certain that Iachka had no awe of anyone, not even the police! Didn't he brandish at arm's length a dummy that was supposed to be the Governor?

I stood and froze in his company, and when the day ended and the show was over, I was miserable. When I got home, I thought: "Oh, what a man he is! If only I could be like him!" But instantly I felt a pang:

"How ever could *you* be like him? You'd spoil it all before you'd spoken a word, and then everybody would hiss you!"

In spite of this, I went on dreaming of being like Iachka. I helped the small boys who lived in my road to make something that might have been a booth, in the back yard. Then I began to do some turns, which I felt were more or less successful, but the minute a passer-by or a country-woman stopped to watch, I lost countenance, and inspiration failed me. To the horrified amazement of my companions, I was quite unable to get out another word. . . .

Under the spell of Iachka, a certain idea became obstinately fixed in my mind, and this was that it would be pleasant for a short while not to be myself any longer. The result was that when the master asked me a question, I couldn't answer. I deliberately gaped like an idiot. . . . At home, the notion came into my head that it would be fun to steal one of my mother's skirts and turn it into a sort of clown's costume; this I did, and a paper cap on my head, a beard and moustache added to my face by means of a little burnt cork, completed the effect. I was always borrowing the play-bills of the shows I had seen Iachka give, and I fully believed that all that man's genius could do was set forth on the printed sheet. There was nothing worth while outside its scope.

I would play at being Iachka and would feel for a moment that I was no longer myself. It was a very soothing sensation.

Iachka, I thought, had no further pinnacles to attain. Today, after half a century, I think rather differently. . . .

At the time of my greatest successes, even in the rôle of Boris Godounov, I feel as though I am only on the border-line of a magical, indescribable, unattainable world. The road has been long — how long! . . . I want to tell you now about some of the halting-places on the way. Perhaps there is somebody who will find my story of use.

CHAPTER VI

Russia's passion for music: Popular songs and religious canticles

∽ ∽

Oɴᴇ ᴛʜɪɴɢ ᴛʜᴀᴛ strikes me as being particularly significant in the life of Russia is the fact that my singing has
always been encouraged by simple Russian artisans, and
that my apprenticeship to music was served in the choir
of a Russian church. There is a strong hidden affinity
between Russian church-music and the songs of the Russian people. Russians sing before they can talk; they learn
to sing in their cradles. This, at least, was the case when
I was a boy. Tragedy was innate in the soul of the people,
and their songs were full of wild melancholy and des-
perate gaiety. Why, then, have they exchanged those songs
for the unbearable triteness and banality of *tchastouchki*?
Is it because their lives are happier, or rather because,
having lost all heart, they stand on the Devil's Bridge,
midway between hope and despair? Perhaps the real reason lies in their newly-acquired sophistication, which mani-
fests itself in the shiny rubber overshoes, and the woollen
scarves that they wrap round their throats, regardless that
it is summer, the sun is shining, and the birds are twitter-
ing. Perhaps the reason is to be found in the corsets that
the village beauties tighten beneath their dresses; or perhaps it lies in the wretched German accordions the factory-
hands fondle so lovingly on Sundays. How beautifully they

[22]

used to sing in those lost days! At nightfall they sang in meadows and haylofts, by the windings of rivers and brooks. They were inspired by the spirit of song, and the consciousness of lyric joy was ever present.

In Russia the voice of love is raised at dawn, and rings in the shadowy darkness. Often during the dreary days and nights and twilights, when the mists hang low, and roofs, hedges, and trees are faintly sparkling with frost, the deep tones of a bell chime forth and re-echo the song. The shadows quiver, and the whisper of a divine annunciation seems to steal into the very essence of one's being.

I know that many people of overwhelming intelligence have proclaimed that Religion is Opium for the People, and that the Church is a corrupting influence. I do not wish to enter into a discussion of this statement, because my point of view is that of an actor, and not that of a statesman or a philosopher. I feel, however, that if religion does contain an anodyne, that anodyne is music.

Although I am not religious in the accepted sense, I have the feeling of being momentarily lifted out of myself and no longer of the earth earthy whenever I enter a church and hear the Kyrie Eleison.

Is there anything in the world so beautiful as the " Blessed art Thou, O Lord our God," and the Russian *panikhida* with its pure and noble melancholy? Is there anything so beautiful as the Orthodox Requiem?

I do not know, and have never wanted to know, what subjects are raised, what laws are made by synods. Whose Christ is the most transcendent? Is He the Christ of the Catholics, or the Protestants, or the Orthodox Church? I have no idea where, and by whom, such contentions are upheld. I cannot even tell whether such contentions are necessary. Perhaps it is inevitable. I only know that the Lament at the Tomb expresses man's suffering and despair throughout the ages. . . .

If all the tears of joy and grief that have been shed in

[23]

churches could be crystallized, what strange stalactites they would form. The twin elements of joy and grief are so mystically mingled in the liturgy of the Russian Church that their fusion is imperceptible; none can tell whether he is draining the cup of ecstasy or of sorrow. The hours of strife and peace in a man's life are many, but his real resurrection is in the spiring melody of song and the ascending harmonies of choral chants.

I start singing in a church choir: My nervousness, and its disastrous results: I turn to lay-singing: My first part: I am paralysed by nervousness: Dreadful check to my ambitions: I lose my work: Despair

ৡৡ

Reverting to the beginning of the previous chapter, the first words of encouragement I heard came from a young blacksmith who lived near us in a Tartar courtyard.

" Sing, Feodor, sing," he would say to me. " Singing will make you happier. A song's like a bird — open the cage and out it will fly! "

There was also a coachmaker, a neighbour of ours, who was kind to me. Many a summer night, when I was tired of singing, I lay in one of his broughams or carriages, soothed by the fragrance of leather and varnish.

Then there was a furrier who gave me five kopeks every time I ran an errand for him with his soft, clinging pelts. He, too, would say:

" Sing, Feodor, sing! "

To tell the truth, I needed very little inducement. Singing somehow came naturally to me. Sometimes I used to sing duets with my mother, who had a charming voice. Although it was untrained and unsophisticated, it was pretty, and we could often harmonize well-known Russian airs. As I have already said, singing came naturally to me, and any form of music pleased and delighted me.

One winter's day I was sliding on wooden skates on the Place de Kazan, near the magnificent old church of Saint Varlaam. I was frozen with cold and wanted to warm myself; this profane wish led me into the church.

It was the hour of evening prayer. I heard the chanting of the choir. For the first time in my life I listened to the harmonious blending of several voices. This was none of the simple part-songs I had sung with my mother, it was the perfect unison of sound. (Although I was unable to explain it to myself then, what I received was an impression of an indescribable whole.) I found it breath-takingly beautiful. Drawing near the choristers, I was dumbfounded to discover that they were all youngsters of my own age. They each held in front of them a sheet of paper covered with cabalistic signs; they kept their eyes fixed on these signs, and their lips gave utterance to the loveliest notes. I was so astounded that I gaped idiotically. I listened for I do not know how long, and went home in a kind of dream.

"They're all boys, like me," I said to myself. "They can sing, and yet they're no different from me. Why shouldn't I sing in a choir? Perhaps I could make music like that come out of my throat." I could sing louder than anyone in the house, much louder than my mother. I must be a soprano!

Not long afterwards chance favoured me, and I joined a church choir. I remember my ecstasy when I learnt that there was such a thing as written music, and that the notes were indicated by certain signs, of which I had never heard until then. I learnt them, just like all the other choristers! I also was able to utter agreeable sounds by keeping my eyes fixed on the sheet of paper with its magical hieroglyphics! Beloved Iachka, in those moments I was unfaithful to thee and thy enchanted booth, so fascinating with its pictures of far countries and imaginary animals. . . .

Perhaps I might long have enjoyed the pleasure that springs from choral singing, had I not discovered to my downfall that we choirboys did not always sing in unison, and that at certain moments in the midst of a chant the rest were silent while a single voice was raised. As soon as I realized this, I tried my hardest to be the solo singer, no matter whether it was in the hymn of the cherubim or in one of Bortnianski's canticles; to sing alone while all the others listened was now my only ambition. But I was doomed to failure. Whenever I was chosen to sing solo, and it was my turn to begin, my heart began to thump in an extremity of fright. Terror made my voice almost inaudible, and I stumbled into mistake after mistake, in spite of the fact that my ear was trained and that I was making rapid progress in my music. Soon I became aware that the choirmaster was grinding his teeth at me, forbidding me to sing another note. . . .

" I'm disgraced again," I thought, and this added to my fright, a sensation that refused for many years to leave me. When I was fourteen or fifteen years old, having managed to insinuate myself through the stage-door of the municipal theatre, I was entrusted with a " leading part." To the question in the play: " What are you holding? " I had only to say: " A piece of string," and I did say: " A piece of string," but in so quavering and shaky a voice that not only was it unheard by the audience, but it was quite unintelligible to the actor who had been so anxious to know what it was that I held in my hand! The stage-manager drew the regrettable conclusion that my professional capacity was extremely limited, and not long afterwards his opinion was confirmed.

I had been given another part, this time that of a policeman in a French detective farce. I was pushed on to the scene, but had such a violent attack of stage-fright that I could not utter a single word. I was overcome with horror! They had impelled me on to the stage with moderate gentleness, but the energy with which I was propelled off it was lacking in any such refinement!

My ardour for the theatre, however, was not cooled by these contretemps, and my ambitions continued to flourish unchecked. I was not cast down; in my secret soul I cherished a dim hope of succeeding, in spite of the realization that I lacked the necessary attributes.

Presently I made a new discovery, a discovery to whose charms I was faithful for a long time.

This discovery was — operetta.

CHAPTER VIII

I discover operetta: I make the acquaintance of opera: I make my first appearance in the chorus of Meyerbeer's The Prophet: *I am captivated by the enigmatic character of Mephistopheles: My first season at Oufa as an opera-singer*

ᔥ ᔥ

THE FIRST TIME I saw a theatre, complete with an or-chestra, a chorus, and actors who broke off in the midst of dialogue to warble melodies and waltzes, I was dumb-founded with amazement.

"This is astounding!" I thought. "These marvels of men can sing and act, they're not in the least self-conscious, and they don't stammer over their words when they're singing in unison or alone. . . . What acting! Iachka isn't a patch on them."

All their costumes were new to me. It was not only that their caftans and leather boots were superior to any I had seen, but their appearance was fairy-like, with scarlet and emerald trappings, silver breastplates, golden spangles, waving feathers, and shining swords. The whole setting was extremely distinctive, and I need hardly say that I was completely dazzled by the beauty and novelty of it all.

But an even more overwhelming surprise was in store for me. The municipal theatre where I had distinguished myself with the " piece of string " was taken by an operatic company under the management of Peter Mikhailovitch

Medviediev, himself a talented actor and a more than able manager. Meyerbeer's *The Prophet* was to be given, and the play-bills announced that the stage would be temporarily transformed into an ice-rink. Naturally, this was an irresistible attraction to the Kazan public, myself included. The advertised sensation took place, and you can imagine what an extraordinary contrast there was between the tropically heated auditorium and the realistically wintry stage. Up in the gallery I sweated, as I watched the actors performing complicated evolutions on the " ice " (they were probably on roller skates). I must admit that the emotions I felt at my first opera were begotten, not by the lovely music or the grandeur of the story, not even by the thrilling ice-rink; instead of being moved by pure artistic appreciation, my vanity was flicked on the raw. To my great surprise, I noticed that amongst those taking part in the opera were the very choirboys with whom I had sung. There were eleven of them, all with voices of different timbre, and when the conductor waved his white-gloved hand, they lined up with the rest and sang:

" *The Prophet, garlanded, appears. . . .*"

I longed for the end to come, so that I might elucidate the mystery of their appearance in the opera.

" How on earth did you manage it? " I asked them afterwards. " How did *you* learn operatic singing? Why didn't you tell me about it? Why didn't you let me join with you? "

" You? Pooh! You'd be struck dumb again! " the eldest of them remarked coolly. " Still, if you like, you can come with us. This is what you've got to sing — get it into your head."

He hummed it to me. There were only a few bars, and I did my best to learn them. Presently one of them, ready to initiate me into my duties as a member of the chorus, took me behind the scenes, but, to my great disappointment, there was no costume I could wear. I was left stranded in the wings, but from this point of vantage I sang lustily with the chorus, determined not to forget the simple melody. It is, of course, very wrong to rejoice in another's misfortunes, but when one night I was told that one of the chorus was ill, and that I might wear his clothes and take his place, I own that I had no thoughts to spare for the invalid. On the contrary, I said to myself: " My prayers have been answered! " My prayers *had* been answered. As a chorister, who knows how many times I had gazed on the image of Jesus, or on a picture of the saints, and murmured:

"Grant, O Lord, that I may one day become a singer . . ."?

I felt a new pleasure whenever anything was added to my theatrical experience. After the opera I realized the nature of a symphony concert. Great was my wonder to find that it had nothing in common with drama, operetta, or opera. Forty musicians in stiff shirts and black ties sat on the stage and played, most likely, Beethoven, Handel, and Haydn. I listened curiously, and thought: " It may be good, but it's not so good as an operetta. An operetta's much better than a symphony concert, it's even better than opera. For one thing, it's so gay and sparkling; the actors are amusing, and the music's light and easy to understand." What annoyed me in opera was the fact that the music drowned the voices, and such beautiful voices into the bargain. . . .

The first opera to overcome my prejudices was Gounod's *Faust*. Faust's heroic love, Siebel's artless and touching affection, won my heart. Their sort of love was evidently very different from the love I saw about me in the Soukonnaia Sloboda, but, in spite of its quality, that was not what chiefly fascinated me. It was the supernatural element in *Faust* that enthralled me. Picture my stupefaction when I saw huge flames streaming over the stage.

"Oh God, the theatre's on fire!" I thought, but as I was springing up to go, a sinister scarlet figure suddenly appeared in the heart of the flames. This apparition bore the semblance of a man, and had a cap with twin plumes, a sharp-pointed beard, mustachios that curled upward, and beetling brows that sloped towards his ears!

I was so terrified that I could not stir a limb. In fact I nearly died of fear when I saw the glitter of flames in his eyes. Every time he blinked, I saw a flash of fire.

"Oh Jesus, it's the Devil himself!" I thought, and mentally I made the sign of the Cross. Much later I learnt that the sparks from his pupils were prosaically contrived by means of tiny metal disks glued to his lids. But at that time, the mystery was still a mystery to me, and consequently I was filled with awe.

"I shall never be able to do things like that," I told myself. "You've got to be born to it. . . ."

The fire-flashing glances completely obsessed me. When, in the interval, I saw the apparition in the flesh drinking a glass of vodka and, surprisingly, eating bilberry jam, I stared piercingly into his eyes and tried to discover the source of the sparks they sent forth. But the more I stared, the less I saw. Yet there he was in the buffet, in a dark coat, without so much as a crimson tie! I could only conjecture that he must supply himself with fiery glances before going on the stage. . . .

I was quite fifteen years old and had enough sense to have grasped how the effect was produced. But I was shy; I dared not approach the gods who performed such miracles before the footlights, dared not enter a well-known singer's dressing-room to see how he made himself up. Had I thought of questioning the dresser, he would certainly have told me, but the truth was that I did not really want an explanation. The fiery glances had fascinated me, they had absorbed all my interest. I did not care whether the music was good, or whether the acting was good; even the story of *Faust* did not matter — those glittering sparks seemed to me the apex of art. . . .

It was at this time that I first began to consider the meaning of the theatre. That it could be a serious vehicle for higher thought never entered my head; I had only one conception, and that, I believed, was indisputable. This was that the theatre was an entertainment, a diversion slightly more complex than Iachka's side-show, but nothing more than a diversion. What about opera? The same thing applied to opera. What about symphony concerts? They came under exactly the same classification. Operetta was an exception, inasmuch as it was a brighter, more amusing form of entertainment.

It was under the influence of these ideas that at seventeen I joined the chorus of the Oufa light-opera company, complete with contract and salary. I found lodgings in a washerwoman's hovel — a dirty little underground room, whose windows were below the level of the pavement. My view consisted of the feet of passers-by and the scuttering claws of distracted hens. My bed was made up of wooden planking on which lay a mattress sparsely stuffed with straw. I cannot remember whether there were any sheets, but I know that there was a multi-coloured patchwork counterpane. In a corner of the room a much-cracked, fly-blown mirror hung on the wall. This was all the luxury I could expect for my twenty roubles a month.

I felt both proud and glad to think that all I did was for a worthy cause — for the cause of art. I took my work very seriously, alternately making myself up as a peasant and a Spanish grandee. . . .

These two types, the peasant and the grandee, formed my entire repertoire. But, apparently, even in my modest capacity as one of the chorus, I succeeded in calling attention to my musical and vocal attributes. One day, when a leading baritone had suddenly, on the eve of the production, refused to play the part of the officer in Monuiszko's *Halka,* and none of the other principals could take it, the manager, Semenev-Samarski, asked me if I would fill the gap. In spite of my extreme nervousness, the offer was so tempting that I accepted. For the first time in my life I had a real part! I quickly learnt it, and braved the audience.

In spite of a lamentable lapse (I sat down *beside* my chair) Semenev-Samarski was pleased with my singing and my sincere attempt (which was as good as it was bad) to create the picture of a Polish officer. He increased my salary by five roubles, and gave me other parts. To this day I consider it a lucky sign if an actor happens to sit *beside* his chair on his first appearance in public. . . . During the course of my career, however, in spite of this superstition, I have always kept a wary eye on my property chair, for fear not only that I should sit *beside* it, but that I might seat myself in a chair intended for someone else. . . .

During my first season I added to my repertoire the rôle of Fernando in *Trovatore* and that of the Stranger in *Askold's Tomb.*

Success added to my determination to devote myself to the stage. I began to wonder how I could contrive to play in Moscow. But when the season ended, although it had been triumphant from an "artistic" point of view, it had not left me with enough money to undertake the journey. I could not go to Moscow. Moreover, the musical coterie at Oufa, who had applauded my appearances, were interested in me, probably because I was young and showed promise, and they persuaded me to remain. They offered to send me to the Moscow Conservatoire, and meanwhile they found me a vacancy in the Zemstvo. But I ask you: can a young man with his head full of ideals sit quietly at a desk, copying out interminable lists of defaulting taxpayers? Be that as it may, one summer evening I stole quietly away from Oufa. Then began an era of trials and difficulties; I joined companies that were on the point of disbanding, and had to seek another company; I tried in turn Little Russian comedy, vaudeville, and French operetta companies. As my musical repertoire consisted of three songs: *Meadows, They Suspect the Truth,* and Kozlov's romance *Had I but Known,* I could not consider giving a concert! There followed a period of misery, and I led that wretched, wandering life in the Caucasus that I have described in my first book. Chance brought me to Tiflis, a city that was to prove providential to me.

Tiflis: A fateful encounter: Ousatov, my first singing-master: His influence on me: My artistic senses are aroused: I discover a new life in the world of the theatre: Ousatov and his conception of singing: La Donna e mobile *and Moussorgski: My first success: I sing bass in the Tiflis Opera Company*

ᔓ ᔓ

DURING THE SUMMER of 1892 I was working as a clerk in the Accounts Department of the Transcaucasian Railway Company. I had had great difficulty in finding this post. It kept me from utter destitution, and I clung to it so desperately that, for the time being, my dreams of the theatre faded. Only those who have suffered similar hardships will be able to understand this state of mind.

The theatre had been my childhood's ruling passion and my boyhood's dream; I had tasted the sweets of success and the insidious poison of the stage at Oufa; I had been thrilled by the thunderous murmur of an audience before the lifting of the curtain; I had felt the glamour of the footlights (though they consisted at that time of some dozen oil lamps); I could not help knowing that I had a voice and musical ability. But when the starving animal that was myself saw the chance to snatch at a crust of bread and a bowl of *chtchi*[1] in a hovel where I could at least find shelter from the cold and rain, I was frightened to budge. I clung to my wretched "comforts" and lay low.

[1] Cabbage soup.

I doubt whether I could have borne this renunciation of my dreams for long — probably I should have been filled with utter loathing for my existence, and the *bourlak* [1] in me would have driven me to escape (as had already happened at Oufa) and pursue my visions of the theatre. . . . As it was, however, what wakened me out of my lethargy and set me on the true path came, not from within me, but from without.

My fellow-clerks had heard me sing, and they urged me to go at once for an audition to a man named Ousatov, a singing-master in Tiflis. For a time I refused steadily, then I wavered, and finally yielded to their advice.

Dmitri Andreivitch Ousatov, a brilliant musician, had once sung tenor at the Grand Theatre in Moscow, and now taught singing in Tiflis. He heard me sing and, with the enthusiasm of a true artist who loves his profession, showered words of encouragement on me. Not only did he teach me for nothing, he also enabled me to live.

This good man and excellent master played a considerable part in my artistic career. My life as a conscious artist dates from my first meeting with him. Although I was not then fully aware of the admirable quality of his teaching, its influence over me was none the less great. He shaped my first serious ideas of the theatre, gave me an insight into the nature of music, refined my taste, and — most valuable of all, in my opinion — helped me to a clear understanding and interpretation of different kinds of music.

In addition to all this, he taught me, of course, all that singing-masters usually teach. He pronounced the mystic words heard in every singing-class. That is to say, he taught me how to control my vocal cords. Sound should, in fact, rest lightly but firmly on the breath and be able to run freely up and down, like the bow over the strings of the 'cello, for example. Just as the bow, caressing the

[1] There is no exact translation of this word; it means literally "one who tows boats along the Volga."

[37]

string, does not always produce a single note, but, thanks to its quick movement over all four strings, brings out varied sounds, so the voice, making use of skilful breathing, should be able to produce different sounds with ease. Whether the notes produced by the bow or the fingers of the musician be short or long, each of them should be equally clear. So it should be with the voice. So much so that all the instructions given to the student of singing are to the end that he may make the bow glide over the strings — that is to say, control his vocal cords. This is the essential of good singing. But Ousatov did not teach the technique of singing alone, and therein lay the difference between him and the majority of teachers then and now.

But how must breathing from the chest, the sternum, the abdomen — in short, the diaphragm — be controlled so as to express a musical situation, the mental state of a character, with the appropriate intonation? I am speaking here not of *musical* intonation, of the production of such and such a note, but of the *colour* of the voice, which, even in an ordinary conversation, assumes various shades. Obviously, it is impossible to say " I love " and " I hate " in the same tone of voice. In each case there will be a different intonation — the *colour* of which I am speaking. Neither technique, therefore, nor singing-lessons, nor a song itself, is enough to create a true artist. And Ousatov demonstrated this clearly by giving examples.

He would seat himself at the piano, while we gathered round him, and play various excerpts, pointing out the differences between an opera of the Italian school and one which was typically Russian. Although he certainly did not overlook the merits of the former, he said that simple melody, intelligible to all, predominated in it. It would appear, he explained, that this type of music had been composed for a people endowed with musical gifts who, when they had heard and memorized an opera, would henceforth sing its charming airs in the sad or joyful moments of their lives. Russian music, including that of Moussorgski, is the entire antithesis of this school. The melody is there, but it is of an entirely different character. In Russian music, melody is the medium through which the atmosphere is suggested and the drama unfolded; it expresses both love and hate in a far more profound and penetrating manner.

"Take *Rigoletto*," he proceeded, "the music is pleasing, light and tuneful, and at the same time in keeping with the characters of the protagonists. Nevertheless, it is superficial and entirely lyrical." (And he would sing *Rigoletto*.)

"Now, gentlemen, listen to Moussorgski. This composer expresses the psychology of each of his characters through the medium of his music. In *Boris Godounov* two voices are heard, in two short musical phrases. One voice sings:

"'Mitiouk, Mitiouk, what are we growling about?' and Mitiouk replies:

"'How the devil do I know?'"

The music gives you a perfectly clear picture of the two boon companions. One is a red-nosed argufier with a hoarse voice and a weakness for drink, the other is dull of wit.

Ousatov sang us both phrases, and said:

"Now you see how music can react upon the imagination. You see how a silence and a pause are able to give the subtle effect of characterization."

Unfortunately, not all Ousatov's pupils were able to follow or feel the sense of what he was trying to tell them. Neither the composers, whose characteristic passages he expounded to them, nor the remarkable interpretation he gave them, could fire their imagination. I believe the class was quite indifferent to his explanations. It is very likely that I, too, owing to my youth and lack of knowledge, took in very little of what our master told us with such fervour and conviction. Nevertheless, his teaching had a profound effect on me. I began to understand that the admiration I had felt for the art of Oufa, and the happiness it had given me, were utterly worthless; I began to realize that true art is almost beyond reach. I had a sudden onrush of depression.

" What can I ever hope to do with my wretched little thread of voice, a provincial like me? " I thought. " What makes me call myself an artist? Who ever said I was one? I invented it myself. . . ."

Meanwhile I was getting more and more engrossed in Moussorgski. What an extraordinary man! Moussorgski's music, played or sung by Ousatov, had a powerful effect on me. It awoke curiously familiar echoes in me. Apart from all Ousatov's theories, Moussorgski suggested to my mind a strong concoction of the aromatic herbs of my native home.

I felt that his music was fundamentally Russian, and for that reason I could understand it.

But my class-mates — basses, tenors, and sopranos — chorused:

" Don't take any notice of what our worthy Dmitri Andreievitch Ousatov tells us. We all know he is eloquent, and all he says may be true, but *La Donna e mobile* is the right stuff for singers. Moussorgski, with his Varlaams and Mitiouks, is literally poison for the voice and singing."

I was somehow torn in two, and could not as yet see which half of me was in the right. Sometimes I was so racked with doubt that I lay sleepless. Which should I choose:

La Donna e mobile, or *In the big town of Kazan?* . . .

Something within me drew me instinctively towards Moussorgski. And when, shortly afterwards, I sang in the Tiflis Opera Company and achieved a certain popularity in the town, and became sought after to appear at benefit concerts, I would, with growing frequency, sing songs by Moussorgski. The audience did not care for them, but forgave them on account of my voice. Although I was only twenty years of age, I had attained a certain position on the stage. I was already singing the rôles of the Miller in *Rousalka,* Mephistopheles in *Faust,* Tonio in *Pagliacci,* and other bass parts in various operas. The lessons I had learnt at Oufa had proved not without profit. I was now aiming confusedly at something different, but what it was I scarcely knew myself. Moreover, I was still bound by conventions and was very far from being a " revolutionary " as regarded opera. Outward effects had not ceased to have an appeal for me. My first Mephistopheles at the Tiflis Opera House in 1893 did not disdain the glitter of spangles, and his eyes shot forth the most convincing flashes of flame.

CHAPTER X

*St. Petersburg: Disappointment: My success in one of Meyer-
beer's operas: I begin to be talked about: Philippov and his
soirées: I sing at his house, and triumph: I am asked to sing at
the Imperial Marie Theatre, thus reaching my dreamed-of
paradise*

ᗡᗡ ᗡᗡ

M Y SUCCESS IN the Tiflis Opera Company gave me a
flying start. I was spoken of as a singer with a great future,
and from now onward, my dream of reaching the capital
began to take shape. I could see a way out of my money
troubles, and during the season I had managed to save
up enough roubles to carry me to Moscow.

In Moscow I had the satisfaction of seeing that my performances at Tiflis had aroused the interest of various
entrepreneurs. An offer from Lentovski, then a well-known
impresario, to join his opera company for the summer season at the Arcadia Theatre, St. Petersburg, seemed to
point to a fortunate beginning of my career in the capital.
But in this I was disappointed; artistically and financially,
Lentovski's season was a bitter disappointment.

It was not until the following winter, when I was appearing with a company who had booked the Panaiev
Theatre on the Admiralty Quay, that I attracted the notice
of St. Petersburg audiences.

From the actor's standpoint, this was a bad house to
sing in, but it was extremely popular with the public. Our

repertory consisted of the more tuneful operas, those of
Meyerbeer in particular. I was given the rôle of Bertram
in *Robert le Diable*. In spite of my admiration for Meyerbeer's greatness, I cannot deny that the characters in this
opera are mere lay-figures. It is difficult for the singer to
infuse into them any semblance of life. Yet it was precisely in the part of Bertram that I won the public's favour. Not only were they charmed by my youthful voice
— musical connoisseurs had already discovered that it possessed a special, rather unusual timbre — but my rendering impressed them as being out of the ordinary. Probably
my acting was quite commonplace, but I had at least
broken away from the time-honoured conception of how
Bertram should be played, thus giving his curious personality a touch of strength quite beyond the scope of
the opera. People now began to speak of me as a singer
who must be heard. It was almost a foreshadowing of
coming triumph.

After my success in *Robert le Diable,* I was invited to
sing at several private houses. Let me say in parenthesis
that my first appearance in one of these salons made me
doubt the breeding of so-called society people. My suit
had not been made to measure, and was probably all
wrong in cut, whilst my manners were inclined to be
awkward; I overheard remarks to this effect from persons
who, obviously, were perfectly turned out, and whose
manners should have been above reproach.

An extraordinary personage was then living in St. Petersburg. This was Tertii Ivanovitch Philippov, Minister of
State Control. His leisure was devoted to music, especially
Russian choral singing, to which he was passionately addicted. His soirées were renowned throughout the capital,
and singers considered it a great honour to take part in
them. This honour fell to my lot in a quite unhoped-for
manner practically at the beginning of my first season in
Petersburg.

Philippov's Soirée

One of these soirées took place on January 4, 1895. All the distinguished musicians of the capital were present. A boy who had but recently arrived in the city played the piano; this was Josef Hofmann, who was eventually to become a famous virtuoso. Fedosova, the peasant woman, gave a superb rendering of traditional Russian ballads. Between the "wonder-child" and the remarkable old woman, I, the young beginner, appeared. I sang Sousanin's aria from *The Life of the Tzar,* and when I had finished, Madame Chestakova, Glinka's sister, who was among the audience, paid me the most overwhelming compliments. This soirée greatly influenced my future, for Philippov, in addition to the weight he carried in his official capacity, was also considered an authority on music. The fact that I had sung at his house made a considerable impression, and rumours of my achievement reached as far as the Imperial Theatres. I was invited to sing there, an invitation that I hastened to accept. After a private audition, held before a number of guests and musicians, the management gave me a contract to sign on February 1, 1895. My first appearance was fixed for the spring. So it came about that, less than a year after my arrival in St. Petersburg, I had realized the supreme ambition of every singer: I had been engaged by the Imperial Theatres. I was just twenty-one.

CHAPTER XI

The glory of the Imperial Theatres: Artistic education in Russia

∽ ∽

THE IMPERIAL THEATRES, whose many defects I shall
point out, were unquestionably surrounded by an atmosphere of glory. Russia had reason to be proud of them,
since the patron of these theatres was none other than the
Tzar of all the Russias himself. American millionaire,
Mæcenas, English subscriber, French shareholder, paled
into insignificance beside him. Although the Tzar probably never gave a thought to his theatres, his glory was
reflected in them, merely through the medium of his
bureaucrats.

To begin with, both actors and staff were generously
salaried. This enabled the former to live comfortably with
sufficient leisure for work and thought. The settings of
opera and ballet were magnificent. Nothing was stinted,
no expense spared. The lavishness of costumes and décor
far exceeded the wildest dreams of other managements,
and this was particularly the case at the Marie Theatre.

Possibly the Imperial Opera could not always boast of
having the finest singers in the world, but some of our
Russian singers were undeniably of the first rank. From an
artistic standpoint, the Imperial Dramatic Theatres glittered with a galaxy of talent. The Imperial Russian Ballet
was also of the highest order.

[45]

Apart from the theatres themselves, Petersburg and Moscow owned some remarkable Imperial Conservatoires, whose numerous offshoots in provincial towns provided Russian opera with perfectly schooled actors and out-standingly accomplished musicians. Dramatic academies also flourished. The School of Ballet had been sumptu-ously equipped. Children of both sexes became boarders at the earliest age, and received a full secondary-school education in addition to dancing.

What other country can boast such lavishly endowed institutions? In Russia they have existed for over a hun-dred years. This fully explains why no other nation can compare with Russia in the matter of technique and artistic foundation.

Although there must sometimes have been worthless productions in our theatres — bad singing, bad acting — the lack of artistry so often seen in the best theatres of Europe and America was absolutely inconceivable in our Imperial Theatres. It was hardly ever to be witnessed even on our provincial stages. . . . That is why the brilliant pianists, violinists, singers, and dancers to be met with in Europe so often prove to be those who have mastered their art in Russia.

It would be distasteful to me should the foregoing para-graphs be construed as a mere eulogy of everything Rus-sian. Doubtless this unpleasing trait is characteristic of a Russian; he loves to glorify all that is Russian. But I wish to avoid such a pitfall, and so have set down nothing but actual facts.

From what I have already said, you will be able to share the excitement I felt on realizing my ambition of an en-gagement at the Marie Theatre. Now, ran my thoughts, I shall be able to develop and strengthen the powers with which I have been gifted, I shall find liberty and peace and a true concept of art. Thenceforward my dreams were radiant with the starry glitter of the twinkling footlights.

CHAPTER XII

*I find more serpents than apples in my paradise: Red tape:
Despotism of the bureaucrats: A director who objects to bortsch
and the reek of vodka: Peasants dressed like Spanish hidalgos:
Distrust of the new Russian music, Moussorgski in particular:
Drawn in two directions, I am tortured by my own uncertainty*

❧ ❧

THERE WERE NO vacancies for basses in the Marie Theatre.
I believe there were as many as ten in the company. The
only justification for my engagement, therefore, was that
the possibilities of my voice had been recognized. I believe that the management was on the alert for potential
talent. It was not a bass that the company needed, but
a new singer whose gift was to be nurtured for the sake
of music in general, and the Marie Theatre in particular.
This being so, I had grounds for hoping that I should
attract serious notice when I appeared on the famous stage,
that the management would prove itself sympathetic, and
that I should have scope for intelligent work. To my utter
dismay, I was very soon convinced that there were more
serpents than apples in this so-called Eden. . . .

I found that I was faced with something that killed
originality and spontaneity — the tyranny of red tape.
The complete failure of my first appearance in the Imperial Theatre was due, not to any ill will, but to the
predominance of officialdom.

What struck me most after my engagement at the Marie
Theatre was the fact that the management of the company, instead of being entrusted to the most accomplished

[47]

artistes, as I had naïvely supposed, was, on the contrary, in the hands of certain extraordinary individuals, bearded or beardless, but all dressed in gold-buttoned uniforms with velvet collars. These individuals were the *tchinovniks*.

I discovered that the actors whom I had venerated as gods were merely ordinary human beings who intoned on an endless scale of notes the one and only phrase: " As you will, gentlemen! " It took me a long time to grasp the state of affairs. I did not know what to do. Ought I to protest against it, or accept it with resignation, like all the rest? Perhaps such a régime was essential to the upkeep of the Eden I had entered, I told myself. After all, actors are bound by contracts, and so they've got to obey their masters. Surely their masters must be the superior beings who cultivate the Tree of Knowledge, with its fruits of good and evil. . . .

But a strange incident soon convinced me that the management was only active in upholding the *principle of power* in the theatre, a principle to which all considerations, artistic and otherwise, were secondary. . . .

We were in the middle of rehearsing Rimski-Korsakov's *Christmas Eve,* taken from Gogol's story. I had been given the small part of Panas. This was when I first met Rimski-Korsakov. The magical composer impressed me by his extreme shyness and modesty. He was very unfashionably dressed; his black beard, which grew unchecked, flowed over a narrow, carelessly knotted black stock, he wore a black frock-coat that was hopelessly out of date, and his trouser-pockets were inset horizontally in the manner of bygone days. He had two pairs of spectacles on his nose, one in front of the other. A deep crease between his brows gave him a melancholy look. He was profoundly silent. He was in the auditorium with the rest of us; sometimes he would withdraw himself to a seat in the aisle, from which point of vantage he would follow the rehearsal in intense silence.

CHALIAPIN

WITH RUSSIAN ARTISTES OF THE OLD SCHOOL IN THE

MAISON DE RETRAITE

At practically every rehearsal Napravnik, the conductor, would make some remark to the composer. For instance, he would say:

"In my opinion, Nicolas Andreievitch, this act drags — I suggest that you cut it."

Rimski-Korsakov would get up, looking disturbed, lean over the conductor's stand, and say, in a somewhat tremulous and deprecatory voice:

"Frankly, I can't see that the act drags. . . ." Then hesitatingly he would explain: "The construction of my work necessitates in this act a musical interpretation of the theme which is the foundation on which the rest of the opera rests."

Whereupon the cold, methodical voice of Napravnik would reply, in a Czech accent and with pedantic emphasis:

"You may be right, but you are influenced by love of your own work. You must consider your public. . . . Years of experience have convinced me that when a composer rigidly refuses to alter a note of his music, the result is often very long drawn out and wearisome to an audience. I am saying all this because I really feel for you. You'll have to condense it."

Perhaps he was right, but what finally brought the discussion to a close was the fact that Vsevolojski, the director, was inveterately hostile to the diffuseness of Russian composers.

However much sympathy Napravnik may have had for Rimski-Korsakov, however excellent the latter's reasoning might be from an artistic standpoint, it was neither sympathy nor reasoning that won the day — the field was carried by the personal tastes of the director, briefly, by the authority in charge, who could not stomach "the long-windedness of Russian composers."

It was not only the "long-windedness," it was Russian music in general that Vsevolojski could not stomach. This I learnt from an infallible source when I was playing

Sousanin in *The Life of the Tzar*. The costume I was to wear in the part of the sturdy moujik from northern Russia was like a fancy dress. Instead of the *laptis,* I was presented with a pair of dainty red morocco boots. When I remarked to the dresser that it was striking a false note to play Sousanin in this kind of gear, he stared at me as though I had come from the moon, and said:

" The director can't stand all this Russian display. Get those *laptis* out of your head. The director says that every time he produces a Russian opera, the whole theatre stinks of cabbage soup and gruel. The moment the overture strikes up, it literally reeks of vodka. . . ."

Cabbage soup, gruel, and vodka — that was all the management was capable of sensing in the new Russian music which was to conquer the whole world. This limitation narrowed down the repertory and delayed the success of those remarkable Russian composers to whom my future destiny was bound with invisible chains.

Although my mind was not altogether made up, and my allegiance wavered between *La Donna e mobile* and Moussorgski, I was being drawn instinctively closer to the latter. I was astounded by the realization that he was no more understood by Petersburg than by Tiflis. I can clearly recall that after a concert, when I had sung *Raiechnik,* a musical satire by Moussorgski, a well-known musician who was a professor at the Moscow Conservatoire said to me at supper with light irony:

" Tell me, Chaliapin, why do you amuse yourself by singing such third-rate stuff as this *Moskovski Listok?* " [1]

This opinion was shared by all the influential critics. I used to think of all the technique I had been taught, "control your breathing," "keep your voice even," and so on, and I would ask myself: "Is that really all that matters in singing?"

[1] A Moscow paper of the yellow-press type.

CHAPTER XIII

Officialdom, and my lot in the Marie Theatre: Two important repulses: A useful lesson

༄ ༄

THE CONDITIONS OF my life in the Marie Theatre were also affected by officialdom.

Having placed great hopes in me, the management was naturally desirous of giving me some chance to prove myself. But the artistic side of the matter was never in question. It was simply a case of finding an important part for Chaliapin to sing — that is, a part that should head the bill. Whether it suited him, whether it was within his scope, whether it was likely to prove disastrous to him — these aspects of the case were never considered. The result was as follows:

In the Marie Theatre, Melnikov was considered the finest exponent of Rouslan in Glinka's famous opera *Rouslan and Ludmilla*. His death, shortly after I had joined the company, left this part more or less available. None of the other basses could take his place. All had tried, but none had succeeded. In comparison with Melnikov, their rendering was empty and insignificant.

When the time of my first appearance drew near, Kondratiev, the stage-manager, sent for me.

" Dost thou know Rouslan's part? " he asked me (he " thee'd " and " thou'd " everyone) .

[51]

I had a vague idea of it, but said: " No, I don't know it."

Kondratiev thought for a moment, and added: " If you would like to play Rouslan for your first performance, I'll give you a couple of weeks to learn it. Can you do it in a fortnight? "

In provincial Russian opera companies it sometimes happens that a singer is obliged to be word-perfect in his part in literally no more than two hours. One gets into the habit of rushing into the breach to save a situation. This lightning memorization had fallen to my lot at Tiflis. I had learnt my part mechanically, for better or worse, had sketched out the way I should play it, and had not stumbled across any insurmountable difficulties. Remembering Tiflis, therefore, I answered:

" Can I do it in a fortnight? Of course I can! "

So I applied myself to my new rôle to save the situation, as at Tiflis. But at the first rehearsal I realized that a couple of weeks was not nearly long enough if I were to play Rouslan in any way adequately. It was too late to back out, it would have been awkward — more forcibly still, disgraceful. All I could do was to make sure of the music and get the outlines of the character into my head.

The evening of the production arrived. I dressed and made myself up, according to time-worn custom. My knees shaking with nervousness, I made my appearance in the scene which had once echoed with Melnikov's voice. Whenever I am on the stage, I am always extremely moved, even though I have played the part a hundred times; on this occasion I experienced an added emotion. " If only I can stick the course! " I said to myself, and, obsessed with this idea of "sticking the course," I sang and acted exactly as though I were being forced to assume at a Christmas party a complicated sort of disguise that I had never worn before.

I kept it up to the end, but I made a very bad impression on the audience. For several days afterwards I was ashamed to be seen in the streets or to show myself at the theatre.

But misfortune is an excellent master. A budding artist, no matter in what province his art may lie, has very dangerous enemies to contend with, and these enemies are his admiring friends who congratulate him on his extraordinary talent. The deceptive glitter of premature success, compliments, bouquets, and the praises of pretty girls — these things soon cause the true fire to burn down to lifeless ember and ash. . . . The youthful artist can no longer see himself as he is, but begins to think he is something quite out of the rut. Perhaps at night, face to face with his own conscience, he has qualms as to his exceptional gifts. But the next morning let some well-meaning friend pour another cup of flattery into his mind, and in his fresh intoxication the doubts of the previous night are quickly forgotten.

The management, according to its lights, drew its own conclusions from my failure. As I had not made a success in the exceedingly difficult part of Rouslan, I was in future to be classed among the mediocre members of the company, and accordingly the pitiless toils of officialdom began to tighten automatically round me. The venerably bearded gentlemen in their beautiful uniforms were in the habit of classifying the singers employed at the theatre according to their respective ages and the period of their engagement. Thus, such and such an actor had been with the company fifteen years, therefore he was entitled to so much; another had had his contract for twenty-five years, therefore he was entitled to so much. The golden rule was seniority, and I was only twenty-one, a fact that was never forgotten when parts were being allotted. It was quite clear that a singer of forty had more " right " to no matter what rôle than a smooth-faced stripling. My hard work in the theatre brought me the characters of the Judge in *Werther*, Prince Vereiski in *Doubrovski*, Panas

in *Christmas Eve,* and Lieutenant Zuniga in *Carmen.* Of
course a singer should not despise small parts, provided
that they have artistic merit, but my youthful ardour rebelled against this quasi-inaction. Gradually the management became convinced that I was intended for these
minute rôles. Perhaps this would not have been so preju-
dicial to me had they not also remembered the hopes they
had placed in me and thus felt it incumbent on them to
give Chaliapin a chance of success, come what might. This
display of interest on my behalf resulted in my losing as
much esteem in the public eye as I lost in my own. I was
allotted another leading part, but, far from giving me a
chance of showing my capacities and distinguishing myself, it set me decisively back amongst a group of young
singers fated to the rôle of Lieutenant Zuniga.

I was given Count Robinson in Cimarosa's *Secret Marriage.* I realize now that this is a charming opera. Cimarosa's music completely expresses the elegant niceness and
affected grace of the late eighteenth century. It was quite
inappropriate to stage *The Secret Marriage* as a gorgeous
spectacle with the lavishness of which the Imperial Theatre was capable. It needed an intimate setting and a
stylized production in keeping with it. The part of Count
Robinson did not suit me in the least. It was not in accordance with my musical culture, then hardly developed, nor
with my natural tendencies. The opera was a dismal failure, and so was I. I am deeply thankful for these first
failures. They were a lasting lesson to me and cured me
of the self-conceit that would have been fostered in me
by the praises of my friends. I came to the conclusion that
the mere mechanical study of this or that part was insufficient; and just as the bird which is pursued mistrusts
the thicket where dangers lurk, so I learnt to mistrust reckless and impatient haste in tackling my work.

Later in my career I have frequently experienced a
strong desire to sing Rouslan. I have often tried to master

the part when I have been alone, but whenever I have had to decide whether I would sing it or not, I have always found a thousand reasons against it. I have felt that there was something in this part that I should never be able to express — but what was it?

Even now I cannot explain it to myself, although I understand that to give a perfect interpretation of a character, one must carry it in one's mind and in one's heart until, after a long space of time, it begins to live of itself.

CHAPTER XIV

The management puts me under a ban: "Nothing can be made of Chaliapin": My disgust of the commonplace in opera: I try to find my line: I am accused of affectation: An unexpected success in Dargomyjski's Rousalka, *the last production of the season*

§ §

AFTER *The Secret Marriage* my chances of success were at a discount in the Marie Theatre. The management seemed disposed to put a ban on me: "Nothing can be made of Chaliapin" was implied. "He's got a good voice, an extraordinarily good voice, but when he is given important parts, either he makes a failure of them, as he did in *The Secret Marriage* and *Rouslan*, or he cultivates appalling affectations." The management was in no doubt of the fact that "Chaliapin cultivated affectations." . . .

I must in fairness admit that there was a particle of truth in the latter opinion. I was not, of course, putting on affectations. Had I done so, I should never have come to anything. For the remainder of my life I should have been a grimacing humbug, an insincere actor, a completely useless, sick intelligence that only death could cure. The real facts of the case were probably these:

At that time I had an instinctive dislike of the commonplace in opera. As I only had occasional parts, I had plenty of spare evenings, and would sit amongst the audience, watching and listening to our productions. With increas-

ing frequency I realized that sham predominated. The
settings were lavish to a degree, there were quantities of
silk and satin and gold, and yet, curious to relate, all this
splendour seemed to be only a cloak for naked poverty.
Singers moved majestically through the operas, uttering
exquisite notes with technical perfection, but the whole
effect was as lifeless and mechanical as a marionette-show.

Thus, when I occasionally appeared — two or three
times during the entire season — in parts which I was afterwards to make famous — Mephistopheles and Prince Galitski, for instance — I made the mistake of gross exaggera-
tion in an ineffectual attempt to avoid the commonplace.
I was trying to find my particular " line," and it was far
from easy. In trying to avoid the conventional gesture, I
was no doubt bizarre and uncouth.

This applied more or less to my renderings of Moussorgski, to whom I was obstinately loyal, and whose music
I sang at all my concerts. I sang his romances according
to all the canons of singing, but in spite of this my renderings were lifeless. I was particularly dismayed by the
realization of my inadequacy in his *Song of the Flea;* my
version of it was so mediocre that for a long time I refrained from singing it in public.

My season at the Marie Theatre was drawing to a close,
and so far I had achieved nothing. I was depressed by the
ending of this, to me, completely unproductive season,
and my belief in my own powers was at a low ebb. Unexpectedly on the last night of the season a friend — a *true*
friend, whose like is unfortunately not often met with in a
lifetime — gave me the opportunity of my first real success.
It chanced that *Rousalka* was then fairly frequently produced. The management was aware that I had often sung
the Miller's part with unvarying success in Tiflis, but I
had never been offered the part in the Marie Theatre.
Koriakin was to have played the Miller in the final performance, but this wonderful friend, aware of how much

[57]

I longed to appear in the character, feigned illness at the eleventh hour. As he had no understudy, the management had no alternative but to fall back on me: " It's the last night of the season, so it doesn't matter one way or the other if Chaliapin *does* sing! "

I have no idea how it happened, but the opera, in spite of its third-rate production and the premonitory groans of the management, swept the audience off its feet, and the evening resembled a gala night organized for my benefit. . . .

It seemed as though the applause and the encores would never come to an end.

Of this performance a music critic wrote that Dargo-myjski's magnificent opera, so full of subtlety and tragic depths, had brought a new and arresting singer to light in the rôle of the Miller. The critic then went on to prophesy that this singer would contribute an element of originality and significance to Russian opera.

Naturally, the management cast a slightly more favourable eye on me after this unexpected success.

A providential conversation with Dalski, the famous actor: His mention of the word "intonation" formulates my confused desires for expressionist singing: I turn to the dramatic theatre for enlightenment: A glittering galaxy of talent: Olga Sadovskaia: My choice is made

✌ ✌

SUCCESS HAD NOT blinded me to the knowledge that at the beginning of *Rousalka* my Miller had lacked light and shade, and that the audience had only superficially reacted to me. In the third act my rendering had, in my opinion, been much more adequate. A prey to doubt, I told myself that the part of the Miller was not altogether suited to me, and that this was not my real line. I confided my doubts to a celebrated actor, Mamont-Dalski, whose sheer talent and debauchery made him the Russian counterpart of Kean. Dalski heard me out and said:

" You opera-singers are all alike. As soon as you have a part given you, you immediately feel it is the wrong one. 'The Miller's rôle is not suited to you' — I believe you are not suited to it. Read it to me. . . ."

" What shall I read? Poushkin's *Rousalka?* "

" Read it as you usually do — by singing it, I mean. Begin with the opening aria, in which the Miller is pitying himself."

I " read " the aria to him, not forgetting the full stops,

[59]

the commas and pauses which occurred according to grammar and context.

When he had heard me, Dalski said:

"The intonations by which you interpret your character are false. That explains the whole thing. You utter the Miller's reproaches and complaints to his daughter in the accents of a petty tradesman, although the Miller is a steady-going peasant, the owner of a windmill and other property."

I was cut to the quick by Dalski's criticism. I immediately grasped the truth of what he said, and while I was ashamed of my unsuitable renderings, I was nevertheless glad that Dalski had given a form to my confused ideas. Intonations — that was the essential. I was justified in my dissatisfaction with *The Song of the Flea;* the entire value of a song lay in the correctness of the intonations.

Now I understood why *bel canto* nearly always gives rise to boredom. I thought of singers I knew, with magnificent voices, so perfectly trained that at any moment they could sing *piano* or *forte,* but who nearly all sang notes to which the words were merely of secondary importance. In fact, so little stress was laid on the words that more often than not the audience could not make out a syllable of what they were supposed to be saying. Singers in this category sing in an agreeable manner; their voices never sound strained, and are produced effortlessly; but, should they have to sing several times in an evening, no one song would sound very different from any other. Love or hate — there is really nothing to distinguish them! I don't know what impression this makes on the average listener, but I do know that I am bored after the second song on the program. Only exceptional singers, such as Mazzini, Gailhard, and Caruso, can hold the attention of the public and rouse it to enthusiasm by the mere beauty of their voices. . . .

Olga Sadovskaia

Intonation! Does not this explain why there are so many excellent *singers* and so few good *actors* in opera? How many opera-singers can express the sorrow of a mother whose son has been killed in battle, the grief of a young girl for her beloved, in simple, natural, convincing language? . . . On the other hand, Russian drama has no lack of excellent exponents.

After my conversation with Dalski, I set myself more ardently than ever to the study of my much-loved *Song of the Flea* and decided to learn the true art of acting in the school of Russian dramatic actors.

My free evenings were no longer spent at the opera, but at the theatre. I began my lesson in Petersburg and continued it in Moscow. With passionate interest, I watched our great actors and actresses — Savina, Ermolova, Fedotova, Strielskaia, Lechkovskaia, Juleva, Strepetova, Varlamov, Davydov, Lenski, Rybakov, and, above all, Olga Sadovskaia, the great comedienne. Eleanora Duse is said to have lost all sense of acting when on the stage and to have become the character she was creating; the same may be said even more truly of Olga Sadovskaia.

The actors of the Imperial Theatres vied keenly with each other, but no one could hold a candle to Olga Sadovskaia, whose art made an indelible impression on my mind. You should have seen her as a matchmaker, a parsimonious housewife, an officer's widow!

" How did you learn to act like that, Olga Osipovna? " I asked her timidly one day.

" My dear Feodor, I don't act."

" What do you mean? "

" Exactly what I say. I appear on the stage, and talk. I talk just as I do at home. What acting is there in that? I talk to everybody in the same way."

" But in this play you're supposed to be a matchmaker."

" Well? "

" Well, nowadays matchmakers like that don't exist. You're re-creating the good old days — how do you do it? "

" My dear Feodor, life doesn't change. You say that matchmakers like that don't exist. Even if they don't, others do. Our Russian vocabulary is inexhaustible — any matchmaker can make use of it to express herself. It is the author's business to decide what type of matchmaker she shall be. The author's wishes must be respected, and the particular character he has in mind brought to life on the stage."

Sadovskaia did not parade her technique, but she could give every word its exact intonation. As soon as she appeared on the stage, the audience was instantly aware that she was expressing the quintessence of a matchmaker, the matchmaker *par excellence,* and that her characterization could not be surpassed in its clear-cut, delicate verisimilitude.

Russian drama made such a strong impression on me that I *thought* of giving up opera and trying my luck in the theatre. I say " I *thought* " because my feelings evidently deceived me. I was bound to opera by my very heart-strings, for my heart bore for ever the " divine stigmata " of music, as Poushkin expresses it.

Meanwhile the management of the Marie Theatre was planning next season's repertory, and Kondratiev, the stage-manager, sent for me.

" Chaliapin, here is the score of *Judith,*" he said. " Try to learn the part of Holophernes during the summer."

The character of Holophernes in Sierov's opera *Judith* has extraordinary power. It is both interesting and difficult to play, facts which make it doubly tempting!

My spirits rose and the resentment I had felt against the Imperial Theatres suddenly seemed baseless.

I carried away the score of *Judith* with elation, and, filled with happiness, I went back to my " Palais Royal," a bohemian hotel in the rue Poushkin, firmly resolved to devote my whole summer to the study of Holophernes.

But fate had planned otherwise.

I was about to move to the country near Petersburg when I received an unexpected offer to go to Nijni-Novgorod and sing in opera at the famous fair. Every actor has a weakness for travel, and I was no exception. Quite forgetting the Assyrian general and *Judith,* I set out, overjoyed, for Nijni-Novgorod, that delightful Russian town, where the old Kremlin is built on the hill-top over-looking the confluence of two lovely rivers, the Volga and the Oka.

CHAPTER XVI

A summer season at Nijni-Novgorod: Mamontov, a rich Mœ-
cenas: I am called a sword-swallower by some of my associates:
Mamontov undertakes to mould my taste for modern painting: I
like landscapes that resemble photographs: Mamontov gives me a
lesson

ᴄᴏ ᴄᴏ

COUNTLESS BOATS AND barges blocked up the port, and
the fair re-echoed with sounds more varied than could
have been conceived prior to the discovery of tonic sol-fa.

In the fair itself the brilliant colours of Russia mingled
with the variegated hues of the East. The heart of this
vast market-place throbbed to a wild bacchanalian measure. It pleased me enormously.

The municipal theatre was newly built and most attractive. The opera was ostensibly controlled by Madame
Winter, but, as I soon learnt, the real power behind
her was Savva Mamontov, the Muscovite railway king.
I was only twenty-three and had no great experience of
life, so that when, on being presented to Mamontov, I was
told that he was a famous Mæcenas, I did not immediately
grasp what it meant.

I was informed that the millionaire was greatly interested in music and painting, actors and artists. In his few
leisure moments he was an artist himself, and, in a spirit of
true appreciation, he devoted large sums of money to the
furthering of art.

[64]

At Nijni-Novgorod

As has been said, Madame Winter was the official genius of the opera, but the actual controller was Mamontov, who had vested his capital and energy in the enterprise.

I did not then suspect the important part this remarkable man was to play in my life.

But, from the first rehearsals, I felt the difference between the luxurious necropolis of the Marie Theatre with its magnificent sarcophagi, and this green field with its sweet-smelling wild flowers. Here we all worked happily together behind the scenes, untrammelled by red tape. Here there were no *tchinovniks* with angry frowns and shouted orders. I was struck by the friendly relations that existed between the actors. Everyone helped everyone else as much as he could, and the question of how to make a scene as effective as possible was discussed by all of us. We worked with a will.

The season at Nijni-Novgorod was a complete success for me, but, in spite of this, I was disturbed by a frequent comment made by older, more experienced members of the company.

"You act well, Feodor, but in opera you must be able to sing, too; that's essential."

"Am I not able to sing?" I wondered, not clearly understanding what they meant. Others of the company said about me: "Chaliapin is an interesting young man, but his acting has rather a sword-swallowing tendency." I suppose by "sword-swallowing" they meant the affectations I had been accused of in Petersburg. Incidentally, I had by this time lost faith in the power of spangles. I no longer believed that properties could work wonders, but with growing restlessness was tirelessly seeking the sincerest forms through which to express emotion. Truth in art was now definitely my goal, and it was because of this pursuit of an ideal that I was ironically termed a "sword-swallower."

The first person who seemed to understand my attempts

[65]

to attain this end was our fascinating Mæcenas. It must
be emphasized that Mamontov himself had wanted to be
a singer; he had studied in Italy, and had been on the
point of signing a contract when a telegram from Moscow
entirely altered the course of his life. Thereafter he was
obliged to engross himself in family business. He was also
a moderately good sculptor. Altogether, he was a man of
extremely cultured tastes. Sympathy from such a man was
a pearl of great price.

I had merely guessed at the state of Mamontov's sympathy with my work. He never openly showed me approval
or disapproval, but he often honoured me with his company, invited me to dine with him, and took me to the
Exhibition of Art. During our visits to the Exhibition, he
took endless pains to develop my taste, and this more than
anything confirmed my feeling that Mamontov was interested in me, in the same way that an artist is interested in
a good model.

I must confess that my tastes were then very primitive.

"Don't stop in front of those pictures, Fedia," Mamontov would say; "they're none of them worth looking at."

I would be staring at one with admiring eyes.

"What's wrong with it, Savva Ivanovitch? It's as good
as a photograph."

"That's exactly what's wrong with it, Fedia," he would
reply with a good-natured smile. "Who wants a photograph? The camera's a dull invention."

And he led me to a gallery which he had had erected
for Vroubel's pictures. There he pointed out the "*Princesse Lointaine*," and said: "That's a remarkable picture,
Fedia. That *is* art."

I looked at it and thought:

"Our Mæcenas has extraordinary ideas. What's good
about that picture? It's a hideous daub. That little landscape I saw in the main hall was quite different. The
apples looked so real I wanted to bite them, and the tree

CHALIAPIN
AS SALIERI IN *Mozart and Salieri*

itself was lovely. Then there was a bench on which sat a young girl and her sweetheart—how wonderfully he was dressed (I must buy myself some trousers like those he had on)!"

To tell the truth, I had not much faith in Mamontov's judgment. And one day, in a moment of sincerity, I said:

"Tell me, Savva Ivanovitch, why do you say that the '*Princesse Lointaine*' is a good picture, and the landscape I like a bad one? I think it should be the other way round."

"You are still young," responded my teacher, "you haven't seen much yet. *There is great feeling in Vroubel's picture.*"

His explanation did not seem particularly satisfactory to me, but it disturbed me. I kept on saying to myself:

"How does it come about that I think one thing when Mamontov, who has endless knowledge, and is an art connoisseur, thinks entirely the reverse?"

I was unable to solve this problem at Nijni-Novgorod, but fate favoured me. It took me shortly afterwards to Moscow, where I succeeded in answering not only that particular question, but others of equal importance in my life.

CHAPTER XVII

Mamontov invites me to leave the Marie Theatre and join his opera company in Moscow: Hesitation: The prevailing atmosphere of the Marie Theatre: I leave St. Petersburg

ᴍ *ᴍ*

MAMONTOV HAD AN opera company in Moscow, and he now invited me to join it.

But I had signed a contract with the Marie Theatre for the coming season, and I should incur a heavy penalty if I broke it. Also I had been offered the important part of Holophernes, and my success at the end of last season had been marked. It was difficult to make a break, yet, on the other hand, personal as well as artistic reasons urged me to fall in with Mamontov's proposal. I hesitated.

I cannot altogether determine which consideration most strongly influenced me in my decision to forfeit my money and sever my connexion with the Marie Theatre, but I must make some mention of that consideration which, among others, greatly assisted me in making up my mind.

This was the atmosphere which then prevailed in the Marie Theatre.

"The director!" calls the commissionaire at the stage-door.

Instantly we are all glued to our places, as Vsevolojski enters. A worthy gentleman with numerous decorations, he comes in with an air of embarrassment similar to that of a *pomiechtchik* in the midst of his peasants, utters various " good mornings," and offers us in turn, myself included, two fingers to shake. Other uniformed individuals appear between the acts; they stand in the centre of the stage, hold weighty discussions with much gesticulation, and often prevent us from working. After which, the stage-manager shouts as though he were deaf:

" Grigori! Throw the limes more to the left! Switch on the footlights in the fourth act! "

" Stepan! Put that angel's wing straight! "

The stage hands run about helter-skelter, carrying out orders and straightening the angels.

Standing in the wings, I overhear the comments of Grigori, Stepan, and the rest, on the uniformed gentlemen:

" Lazy louts, time-servers, lousy swine! "

In such terms the workmen comfortably give vent to their feelings, while we singers voice amongst ourselves loud praises of this or that " time-server." These praises ring false. Sometimes I would be asked if I knew a certain official.

" Yes, I know him slightly, I occasionally see him in the theatre," I would say.

" Don't you think he's a delightful and congenial kind of man? "

" He's a good sort," I would concede warily.

But the tone of voice in which I said " good sort " must have left a reverse impression on my interlocutor.

The smug acceptance of everything the *tchinovniks* said on questions that essentially concerned none but the actors themselves was repulsive to me. Thanks to a merciful Providence, they did not quite go to the length of showing us *how* to sing and act, but they uttered sententious pronouncements, coloured at times by obvious partiality, dismissing the good as bad, and vice versa. I had occasion to note that in the Imperial Theatres, as well as in the Imperial Opera, those in charge were equally officious.

One day I said to one of my associates:

"Can you tell me why Russian operas are so rarely produced?"

"Rarely produced? Surely we produce enough of them. We produce *Rousalka, The Life of the Tzar, Rouslan and Ludmilla,* and *Rognieda.*"

"But there are other Russian operas besides these."

"Their turn will come. For the time being, we produce quite enough of them."

And Rimski-Korsakov's *Pskovitaine* was rejected. Did Ivan the Terrible also reek of cabbage soup and vodka?

As I did not want to make use of spangles in the part of Mephistopheles, I asked the stage-manager and the wardrobe-master to let me have a costume which would enable me to give a somewhat different interpretation of the character. As soon as I expressed this desire, the two men looked at me with lack-lustre eyes, and with no show of anger said:

"Don't be so exacting, my boy, don't excite yourself. When Stravinski plays Mephistopheles, he makes no complaints about the costume we give him. Whom do you take yourself for? Don't put on airs. Do your job unassumingly. The more unassuming you are, the further you will get. . . ."

Such episodes as these oppressed me like so much poison gas. My headstrong temperament rebelled.

I said farewell to my Assyrian general, gathered together all my possessions, and started off to join Mamontov's company in Moscow.

Was I only setting out to find Mamontov? I had reached that period in a man's life when he must inevitably fall in love. And my love was to be found — in Moscow.

CHAPTER XVIII

*Moscow: The masters of painting: The influence of Russian
painting on my art: A lesson from the famous landscape-painter,
Isaac Levitan: Mephistopheles—the bitterest disappointment of
my whole career: My appearance as Mephistopheles in Mamontov's company: A great triumph*

༄ ༄

IT WAS IN Moscow that I was to solve the problem of the
delectable apple-tree that had so enchanted me, and the
unpalatable "*Princesse Lointaine*" so dear to Mamontov.
I should like to elucidate this matter before proceeding
any further.

This period of my life in Moscow (during which I finally
found my true bent, and when my subconscious desires
took definite shape) came under the happy influence of
several remarkable Russian painters. I should never have
been able to create characters that really mattered had I
not outgrown the naïf and primitive tastes that had so
much amused Mamontov at Nijni-Novgorod. It was essential for me to feel and understand the beauty and poetry
in the masterpieces of painting if I were ever to attain the
goal I had in sight.

In Mamontov's circle I met those talented artists who
were bringing a new era of life to Russian painting. I was
fortunate enough to learn a great deal from association
with them.

Isaac Levitan

These artists were Sierov, Levitan, the brothers Vasnetsov, Korovin, Polienov, Ostrooukov, Nesterev, and that very Vroubel whose "*Princesse Lointaine*" had struck me so unfavourably. All these artists were, in the future, to give me their co-operation in the productions I was to stage in Moscow.

Levitan, the famous landscape-painter, did not actively participate in my theatrical activities, but it was he who made me realize the insignificance of my apple-tree and the banality of the young man's magnificent trousers. . . .

The more I saw of the friendly, unaffected, simple Levitan, and the more I looked at his pictures, so fraught with deep poetic meaning, the more I understood and appreciated that great *feeling* in art which Mamontov had explained to me.

" Mere accuracy conveys nothing," Levitan said to me one day. " What is important is the fact that it is *your* song, and *you* that are singing of forest-paths or garden-alleys."

I remembered Mamontov's allusion to the camera as a wearisome invention, and realized what he had meant by it. The camera cannot make the forest-path or the garden-alley eloquent, it can only accurately represent them. Now I understood that care must be taken not simply to copy and colour objects in order to make the maximum effect; now I understood that in *all* art it is the underlying expression of thought and emotion that signifies Logos, the Word with which the Prophet was ordained to kindle the hearts of men. The Word might be found in colour, line, gesture, speech, and from this new-found knowledge I drew conclusions relevant to my own art as an opera-singer.

My first appearance with Mamontov's opera company was in Gounod's *Faust*.

Mephistopheles is considered one of my best parts. In the course of forty years I have sung it in every opera-house in the world. My interpretation has thus in a sense become

CHALIAPIN
AS MEPHISTOPHELES IN *Faust*

a classic. I must admit, however, that Mephistopheles has been one of the bitterest disappointments of my career. I carry about in my heart a Mephistopheles I have never been able to incarnate, and when I compare this dream-figure with the figure I have made of it, it literally sets my teeth on edge.

So remote from life, so undefinable, so abstract and geometrical is the character of Mephistopheles that I believe sculpture to be the only medium through which it could be expressed. Gaudy raiment and tricks of make-up cannot take the place of the clean-cut, chiselled line, icily mysterious in its starkness. A sculptural element is usually inherent in the theatre (one finds it in every gesture) , but the part of Mephistopheles demands sculpture, pure and simple, as its first principle. I visualize Mephistopheles as a bare framework stripped of all unessentials and carved into everlasting sculptural vitality.

I have tried hard to realize this concept of Mephistopheles on the stage, but have never been satisfied; I have only been able to approach my idea, but have never entirely arrived. Art, as we all know, cannot brook half measures. I wanted to create a stark sculptural figure, but as starkness (even conventional starkness, from the point of view of the stage) approximates to nudity, I had to content myself with stripping as far as custom would allow. . . . In addition, I encountered difficulties of technique. However that may be, in my playing of Mephistopheles, I drew inspiration from the rendering that so many poets and singers have already traditionalized. As this rendering unquestionably makes a big impression on the minds of the audience, this is its justification.

My first Mephistopheles in Moscow departed a good deal from precedent. I wore a new costume which had nothing in common with the usual German-soldier apparel. Mephistopheles always boasted two feathers in his cap, and waxed and pointed mustachios. I gave him only one feather and no mustachios, and it seemed to me that his face gained in expression in consequence of these deprivations. A single feather was better suited to his whiskerless face; the absence of mustachios only served to show up the structure of his bones. Thus I succeeded in making him more *sculptural,* more outwardly in keeping with his inner self.

My Mephistopheles received an ovation. I was young, lithe, and plastic; my singing, like myself, was full of vitality. The audience rose at me. My innovations were subsequently pointed out and underlined by various critics, who kindly allowed me some credit for them. But, more than all this, I received what I had essentially needed: Mamontov's appreciation, and that of my new friends and inspirers, the artists and painters. After the production Mamontov generously gave me *carte blanche* to order whatever costumes I chose for my parts, besides authorizing me to alter the settings as I wished in any scene in which I was playing.

From an artistic standpoint, this was a very considerable advantage. As a rule, the costumes of all but the Imperial Theatres were deplorable. In the wardrobes, crammed full of rubbish, there was a mass of ready-to-wear apparel for the simulation of Spanish grandees, peasants, and so on. When Mephistopheles was to be clothed, the stage-manager would yell:

" Hi, Grigori! Fetch out No. 16, the German rig-out! "

But where a Mæcenas, such as Mamontov, was concerned, things were different. Nevertheless, his permission to order what costumes I required was a large gesture, even in such a company as his. In addition, Mamontov himself advised and helped me in the choice of the colours of my materials, so that my dresses should be in keeping with the settings which were so eagerly designed for him by the best artists in Moscow.

[74]

CHAPTER XIX

*Mamontov's repertory: The triumph of the new Russian music:
My first venturesome attempt in Sierov's* Judith: *Valentin Sierov,
the painter and son of the composer, collaborates: I give Holophernes the stern aspect of a stone bas-relief*

ᔕ ᔕ

Nowadays I still recall with delight those wonderful
days in Moscow. I felt my latent powers waxing tenfold in
an atmosphere of trust and friendship. I worked with enthusiasm and soaked up like a sponge the best tendencies
of that era, which was struggling to renew spirit and form
in every province of art. Mamontov had opened the doors
of his opera-house to the great Russian composers who had
been rejected by the Imperial Opera. In a brief space he
produced four of Rimski-Korsakov's operas, and had done
honour to Moussorgski with new settings of *Boris Godounov* and *Khovantchina.*

In Mamontov's opera company I found a repertory that
enabled me to develop particular aspects of my nature and
artistic temperament. I need say no more than that out of
the nineteen parts I sang in Moscow, fifteen were from
Russian repertory, towards which I was drawn by every
fibre. But the greatest privilege I enjoyed in Moscow was
certainly that of being able to venture on attempts which
would have come to nothing among the uniformed *tchinovniks* of Petersburg.

During one of the seasons I was rehearsing the part of Holophernes in Sierov's *Judith*. Valentin Alexandrovitch Sierov, the son of the composer, the celebrated artist and my good friend, undertook the scenery and the décor. We often mutually discussed our work. Sierov spoke with enthusiasm of the life and spirit of ancient Assyria.

I wondered uneasily how Holophernes should be represented on the stage. As a rule, he was made up as a shaggy, unchained monster. The Assyrian accessories were powerless to conceal the impersonal emptiness of this figure which, moreover, had no trace of authentic antiquity. In fact, it was no more than a crazy marionette.

My wish was to present a living as well as a characteristic picture of the Assyrian general. But easier said than done. How was I to understand a civilization dead and buried beneath the weight of years? How was I to seize hold of its intangible heart-beat? One day, when I was at Sierov's house, turning over photographs of ancient Egyptian and Assyrian monuments, I stumbled across an album containing reproductions of bas-reliefs on which, carved in stone, were warriors and kings, enthroned, galloping in chariots, alone or in groups of two or three. I was struck by the attitudes of arms and legs in this multitude seen in profile — they were all alike. Always the same broken line of the arms, elbow, and wrist forming two acute angles that jutted out in front. There were no projections of arm and leg sideways.

These hieratic poses gave me an impression of profound calm, solemn slowness, and at the same time of a terrific dynamic force. It would not be a bad idea, I thought, to represent a Holophernes with these typical petrified and arresting gestures. In real life the kings and warriors could not have used exactly these gestures; obviously they could not have walked with such rigid lines through palace and stronghold — but all their attitudes had been conventionalized. Yet, as I told myself, conventionalization is not pure invention, since it borrows from reality. Obsessed by the fantastic idea of playing the Assyrian general according to the bas-reliefs, I asked Sierov for his opinion.

Sierov literally bubbled over with enthusiasm, and, after a moment's thought, said:

"It's a marvellous scheme — magnificent! But listen to me — take care not to make the whole thing ridiculous by overdoing it!"

My new-found idea would give me no rest. Day and night my mind was full of it. When I walked along the streets, I would turn my head sideways, put my arms into Assyrian postures, and persuade myself that I was on the right road. But would such an attitudinizing Holophernes find it easy to clasp Judith in his arms? I would see if it were possible.

A girl walked into me on the pavement.

"How dare you?" she cried angrily.

I came to myself, burst out laughing, and said to myself joyfully:

"It *is* possible. . . ."

And so, in 1897, in the Solodovnikov Theatre on the Moskva, I gave my Holophernes the stern aspect of a bas-relief, but of a bas-relief charged with power and passion and tremendous majesty. The ovation I received was far beyond my wildest hopes. I fully believe that I was the first actor who had dared to carry out so startling an innovation.

After my success I had the satisfaction of finding that famous Russian dancers frequently had recourse to this new form of movement and perfected it in their ballets.

The significant episode of Holophernes proved to me that pose and gesture, however archaic, however conventional and however strange they may be, may appear natural and lifelike on the stage if the artist feels them deeply in his own heart.

CHAPTER XX

The unforgettable lesson of Rimski-Korsakov's Pskovitaine:
*Victor Vasnetsov, the famous painter: I return to Petersburg
with Mamontov's opera company: My triumph, and the triumph
of the new Russian music: I again appear at the Marie Theatre
with my Russian repertoire: A revolution*

～∽ ∽

Dᴜʀɪɴɢ ᴛʜɪs ꜰʀᴜɪᴛꜰᴜʟ period the study of each part
showed me unexpected possibilities, taught me new lessons, and confirmed my previous convictions, all of which
benefited my art. I had long been conscious of the value
and importance of intonation, ever since my training with
Ousatov, in fact, and particularly after my conversation
with Dalski on the subject of the Miller.

But on the production of Rimski-Korsakov's *Pskovitaine* I suffered for my convictions in a quite dramatic
fashion.

I was to play the part of Ivan the Terrible in *Pskovitaine,* and the thought of it filled me with great emotion.
I had to represent the tragic figure of Ivan the Terrible —
one of the most complex and awe-inspiring in the history
of Russia.

I could not sleep at night. I feverishly read the books
that had been written about the Tzar, and visited museums and private collections to look at portraits of him,
as well as the paintings that depicted the events of his life
and reign. I learnt my part by heart and began to re-

[78]

hearse it. I rehearsed it with accuracy and care, but, alas, the whole thing was meaningless. Whichever way I attacked it, the result was the same.

I grew nervous; I flew into rages, answered rudely when the stage-manager and my friends spoke to me about the part, and one fine day tore up my script, rushed back to my dressing-room, and literally burst out crying. There Mamontov found me and, when he saw my swollen red eyes, asked me what was the matter; I stammered out my tale of woe — from first to last, my part had refused to go right.

"Pull yourself together and try again," he said.

I went back to the stage, and Mamontov sat in the orchestra to listen to me.

In the opera, Ivan the Terrible, having reduced the independent town of Novgorod to ashes, descends on Pskov with the like intention of smothering the spirit of liberty. The first scene shows the Tzar standing on the threshold of the boyar Tokmakov, the Governor of Pskov.

"To enter or not to enter?" These are the opening words of the Tzar.

On the lips of Ivan this question is as pregnant as Hamlet's "To be or not to be? . . ." It must give an instant impression of the Tzar's character and bring the inherent cruelty of his nature to the surface. It must make the spectator who has not read Ivan's history, and in a greater degree the spectator who has read it, understand why the boyar Tokmakov shudders at the bare sight of the Tzar.

I say: "To enter or not to enter?" but the sentence falls flat and has no effect whatever. The act drags itself, wearisome and colourless, to an end.

Mamontov comes up to me and remarks casually:

"There is cunning and hypocrisy in your Ivan, but one does not feel that he is Terrible."

This slight observation was the lightning-flash that illumined my darkness. "My intonation is wrong," I instantly said to myself. "I utter the question in a malicious, hypocritical, ironic voice, and this creates a weak, characterless picture of the Tzar. The lines and shadows of his face appear, but not the face itself." Now I realized that this opening sentence must express the whole essence of Ivan's nature, and I started again from: "To enter or not to enter?"

This time, as though I were striking with a metal rod, I uttered the question in a resounding voice that was charged with menace and cruel cunning, meanwhile casting a fierce gaze over the scene.

Immediately the act became vivid, woke to life, and became deeply impressive. The correct intonation of a single phrase had transformed the sly serpent (the suggested image of my first intonation) into a raging tiger. . . .

From the conventional point of view, I had sung the part with perfect accuracy. With mathematical precision I had followed the score, but even had I had the most magnificent voice in the world, it would not have been sufficient to produce the artistic effect that the part needed. This meant, and I understood it once and for all, that mere mathematical accuracy, even though combined with the most perfect voice, is lifeless unless it is transfigured by feeling and creative imagination. There was something more in the art of singing than the brilliance of *bel canto*. . . .

I have already mentioned that each new production brought me in contact with some famous Russian artist. Through *Pskovitaine* I met Victor Vasnetsov, who proved very friendly to me.

This remarkable artist was born in the province of Viatka. From those forests, whose trees are rooted in sand, men come forth and make their way to the effeminate cities, men who seem shaped in the clay of ancient Scythia.

The brothers Vasnetsov were cast in this mould and,

like the *bogatyrs,* had dauntless spirits and strong bodies. It is not for me to say which of them was the more distinguished — Victor or Apollinari. But it was Victor towards whom I was most drawn. When I gazed at his "Virgin and Child," surrounded by transparently lucid angels and cherubim, I felt the clarity and spirituality of the man behind the power of his work. The cavaliers and knights through whom he re-created heroic Russia gave me a sensation of tremendous power, both physical and moral. Victor Vasnetsov's work brings to mind the *Saga of Prince Igor.* His stern, dark-browed warriors on their huge horses, their eyes gazing through their visors towards the far-off cross-roads, are unforgettable. . . . The souls of the two artist-brothers were filled with the icy strength of warriors dead and gone. . . .

Victor lived in an extraordinary house which he had built himself in one of the Miechtchanski roads of Moscow. It was a cross between the modern peasant *izba* and the *terem* of Russian princes of bygone days. It was made entirely of wood. Inside, there were no cushioned sofas, divans, or arm-chairs. Along the walls stood rows of uncompromising oak benches; in the centre was a massive oak table without a cloth, and here and there on the floor squat wooden stools were distributed.

The room was but dimly lit, for the windows were very small, but upstairs in the studio, which was reached by a narrow wooden staircase, there was plenty of light and sun. In these surroundings, from which all unessentials had been banished, I was happy, listening to the warm praises that Victor bestowed on my Ivan the Terrible. I said that I could not take all the laurels, since I had borrowed many of the characteristics of my picture from him.

Incidentally, I had seen a canvas in a friend's house which had struck me enormously; it was a study of Ivan the Terrible, his black eyes looking sternly sideways. This picture was one of Victor's. I was tremendously flattered

when I learnt that my creation of Ivan had inspired Vasnetsov with the idea for another picture of the Tzar. In
this he was shown descending a flight of stairs, his gloved
hands clasped on his staff. Praise from a man like Victor
was very precious to me. I remembered his words when a
critic, writing in the *Novoie Vremia,* said about my Ivan:
" Here is no Tzar of Russia, but a Louis XI. . . ."

It is curious how different tastes and opinions can be.

My success in Mamontov's opera company had nothing
factitious in it, nor was it due to a caprice of Moscow
audiences, who sometimes allowed themselves to score over
their eternal rivals, the St. Petersburg public.

Thus it came about that when I returned to Petersburg
with Mamontov's company, more than two years after my
one outstanding success in *Rousalka,* I had an enthusiastic
reception. " How Chaliapin has changed! " said audience
and critic. " How he has refined his art during the last
year or so! "

The word " refined " pleased me particularly; in it I
saw the recognition of my work and struggles. . . .

To sum up, St. Petersburg, following in Moscow's foot-
steps, accepted my stage innovations as the expression of
truth in the theatre. Now I was really triumphant. But
I was not alone in my triumph — I shared it with my beloved *Song of the Flea,* which I sang at concerts. . . .

I had overcome all the difficulties of Moussorgski; my
renderings of his songs and romances no longer lacked
colour, for I had discovered the exact intonations to give
them. To be sure, the enemies of the new Russian music
had not yet laid aside their weapons; the incomparable
Stasov had still to thunder on his drum for many years to
defend Moussorgski and myself against the " blockheads,"
as he termed the obstinately reactionary critics. The " fashionable " public still clung to *La Donna e mobile,* but the
front line of defence was broken by the impetuous offensive
of the brilliant modern Russian composers.

A Revolution

When I was engaged for the second time by the Imperial Opera, then under the management of Teliakovski, who was prepared to acknowledge the spirit of the times, Russian music was solemnly ushered, through the medium of my repertoire, on to the Imperial stage. The reeking spectre of cabbage soup, gruel, and vodka had somehow vanished. . . .

The change that had come about in the general atmosphere of the Imperial Opera and in my own circumstances finds symbolic expression in the following story, which is not lacking in piquancy:

The reader may remember that in 1895 I had timidly criticized the peasant costume of Sousanin in *The Life of the Tzar*. During my second engagement at the Marie Theatre I was almost immediately given the afore-mentioned part. The same wardrobe-master brought me the very same costume, I do believe, the fancy-dress affair with the dainty red leather boots. I flung this beautiful raiment on the floor and began to trample on it, shouting:

" Bring me a moujik's *armiak* and a pair of *laptis* immediately! "

The wardrobe-master was evidently startled by my fierce tones, for he jumped violently. This must have been the first time in the annals of the Imperial Theatres that a *tchinovnik* had trembled before an actor — until then the actors had trembled before the *tchinovniks*. . . .

The wardrobe-master, one may assume, carried his tale to headquarters, and the management, no doubt, discussed the matter; it was a case of grave insubordination — worse, of doing material damage to Imperial property. . . . I waited long and patiently for my costume, but I did not wait in vain: a dark yellow *armiak, laptis,* and linen swathing-bands for my feet were brought to me.

The revolution had triumphed! Sousanin, the moujik of Kostroma, stood on the summit of the barricade, his feet shod in indisputable and authentic *laptis*!

[83]

CHAPTER XXI

*Talent and work: Baubles and Paul Veronese: Beauty is truth,
truth beauty*

⨭ ⨭

IT GOES WITHOUT saying that I could not consider the
success I had achieved in Moscow and Petersburg as lasting,
in spite of the *ne plus ultra* praises that my countrymen,
and, later, critics of other nations, showered on me. My
triumph had certainly been greatly exaggerated. It is true
that at Moscow I had set my feet on the strait and narrow
path, and that I was now going in the right direction, but
I was still far from perfection. All my life I have sought
this goal, but I sincerely believe that I am as far from
attaining it now as I was then. The roads that lead to perfection, like those that lead to the stars, stretch endless
distances beyond human reach. Though man ascend, not
sixteen, but a hundred and sixty leagues in space, Sirius
remains immeasurably high above him. . . .

If I have a certain merit, if I credit myself with so much,
it is only because I have achieved it by tireless, incessant
struggle. Not once, not even after my most brilliant successes, did I say to myself: " Now, my friend, you can rest
on your laurels — the wreath that is intertwined with decoration ribbons and innumerable inscriptions." Instead, I
remembered that my troika with its chiming bells was
waiting at the gate, that there was no time to lose in rest,
that I must go ever onward.

Talent and Work

I was young and heedless, I loved pleasure and the delights of *dolce far niente* after evenings of gaiety with friends, when we drank, not too sparingly, of vodka and champagne. But when work was in question, I devoted myself, heart and soul, to the study of my part. I had resolutely excluded the fatal *avos*[1] from my time-table and put all my trust in conscious and creative effort.

The development of talent, I believe, almost invariably means endless effort. Without this the greatest gift dries up like a desert stream that has not been able to cleave its way through the sands.

I don't remember who said that "genius is an infinite capacity for taking pains," but this saying can obviously be stretched to false premises, for it was not Salieri, in spite of the "infinite pains" he took (did he not dissect music like a corpse?), but Mozart who composed the *Requiem*. Yet the definition contains a great deal of truth. I am certain that Mozart, whom Salieri contemptuously called an idler, in reality put his whole mind into music and made endless efforts to develop his genius.

Incidentally, what is work? In Moscow today it is said and believed that work is the zeal for erecting new steel-mills, and according to this it follows that Glinka, to quote an instance, was nothing but a *pomiechtchik* and a parasite. . . . Mozart's work was obviously in another category. It was a continual search for the right note, the true harmony, it was the incessant control of his mental diapason. . . .

Salieri, the pedant, was indignant because Mozart appeared to gain amusement from listening to a blind fiddler in a tavern playing one of his compositions. To Salieri, the fiddler's scraping was equivalent to a "wretched dauber desecrating Raphael's Madonna by copying it," or to "a scribbler dishonouring Dante by unconscious parody." . . . To Mozart's genius, it was "amusing" because he

[1] *Avos* = Russian fatalism—the *ça ira* of life.

[85]

found food for thought in the fiddler's execrable playing. He would equally have found food for thought in the "wretched dauber desecrating Raphael's Madonna by copying it" and the "scribbler dishonouring Dante by unconscious parody."

By dint of moulding myself on the best models, I continued to learn when opportunity occurred; I kept on working even after a success sufficient to turn the head of the most level-headed young man.

One day Mamontov invited me to go to Paris with him, and took me through the Louvre. As I stared, absorbed, at the Crown Diamonds, he said with his usual smiling good nature:

"Those are mere baubles, Fedia. Don't waste time on them, come and look instead at the grandeur and simplicity and luminosity of Paul Veronese."

No labour can prove fruitful unless it is based on an ideal. My work had as its leit-motif the struggle against the sham glitter which eclipses the inner light, the complexities which kill simplicity, the vulgar externals which diminish true grandeur. There may exist different conceptions of beauty; everyone has his own personal opinion, but there can be no question about the truth of the feeling of beauty. That is real and palpable. There can be no two truths, and from this I recognized that there is only one road that leads to the attainment of beauty. That road is truth — *nel vero e il bello. . . .*

The conscious and unconscious element in art: My method of work: My increasing study of characters: Fictitious and historical characters: V. Klioutchevski, the historian, my wonderful teacher

༞ ༞

THERE ARE ELEMENTS in art which cannot be expressed in words. Religion, I believe, also contains such elements. This explains why, although much can be said about art and religion, the whole meaning of both cannot be formulated. We come to a certain point, or, rather, we find ourselves up against a certain barrier, and although we know there are immeasurable distances beyond, we cannot define what is to be found there. Human speech is utterly inadequate. We are encroaching on the world of incorporeal emotion. The alphabet has its letters, music its symbols; you can spell out everything with these letters, set down all music with these symbols, but . . . the cadence of a sigh — how to put its intonation on paper? It cannot be compassed by the letters of any alphabet.

The creation of a character in an actor's mind can only be partially explained. Only half of the complex mental travail can be revealed — the half which lies on this side of the barrier. I must stress, however, that the conscious side of an actor's work is of extreme, possibly decisive, importance, for it brings out the intuitive idea, it nurtures and fructifies it.

[87]

The pilot of an aeroplane must have a suitable, intelligently chosen aerodrome if he is to take off successfully for unknown heights. The actor will discover what inspiration will come to him after the final study of his part. He cannot realize it at the time, and he must not think of it — it springs from his subconsciousness. Nor can he determine it in advance by an effort of will. But he must be absolutely certain of his aerodrome, of the exact stage from which he will start on his creative flight. I use the word "certain" advisedly; by a conscious effort of mind and will he must form an opinion on the work he is undertaking. The paragraphs that follow on my method of study concern exclusively the *conscious* side of creative work. I say nothing about the mystic element, which, if I feel in my most sublime moments of inspiration, I feel confusedly; it would be impossible for me to analyse it.

I am given score and script of an opera in which I am to sing. It is obvious that I must begin by studying the character I am to represent on the stage. I read the script, and ask myself: What sort of a man is this supposed to be — is he good or bad, handsome or hideous, intelligent or stupid, honest or cunning? Is he a mixture of all these things? If the character has been conceived in a spirit of genius, all the attributes will be understandable. I have the script and score in front of me; if the language is descriptive, if the score is expressive, the character in whom I am interested will take shape of itself. It appears in its entirety in the opera, and all I have to do is to give an exact rendering.

To do this, I must learn, not only my own part, but all the parts without exception — not only the principal part, but even the most trifling parts, including the cue of the chorus. This cue would hardly appear to concern me . . . but it *does.* I must feel at home in a part — I must make it even more familiar than my home. It does not matter if I am uncertain of the position of a chair in my own room —

I must be sure of it on the stage in order that nothing untoward can occur, in order that I may feel perfectly at ease.

If I do not know an opera from the opening to the closing bar, I cannot feel the style in which it has been conceived and composed; it follows, therefore, that I cannot feel the character I am to present. Consequently, I can have no definite idea of him until I have thoroughly studied the environment in which he moves and the atmosphere which surrounds him. It sometimes happens that an apparently insignificant phrase sung by a supernumerary — the second guard of the palace, for instance — throws an unexpected light on an important incident which is taking place in the hall of state or in a bedroom of the palace. No detail can be meaningless to me, provided that it has not been superfluously introduced by the author without rhyme or reason.

When I have mastered every word and every note, when I have pondered over the acts of all the characters, great and small, and noted their reactions to one another; when I have realized time, place, and atmosphere — then I have an adequate understanding of the part I am to play. The character has a bass voice, is intelligent and passionate; I am aware of impatience and rashness in his emotions and contacts, or, on the other hand, of his caution and reflection. He is impulsive and artless, or he is subtle and on the alert. Has he a definite individuality? Obviously, for otherwise he would talk and think entirely differently. To sum up, I know him as well as if he were an old school-friend, or a bridge-partner of many years' standing.

If the character is a fictitious creation of the author's mind, I know all that it is possible and essential to know about him from the script — he is to be found there in his entirety, I need no other light on his personality and do not look for it. If the character is historical, the foregoing does not apply. In this case I must unquestionably consult history. I must know the actual events that concerned him,

or others through him; I must know in what way he differed from other men of his times, I must learn how his
contemporaries saw him and how historians pictured him.
Why must I acquire this knowledge? I am not writing a
history-book, but representing a character in a work of art,
and so much the worse if the work of art does not conform
to historical truth. Yet such knowledge *is* essential, and
the reason is this:

If the actor adheres strictly to historical truth, history
will help me to a fuller and deeper comprehension of his
intentions; if he is deliberately doing the reverse and devi-
ating from actual fact, it is even more essential for me to
know the true historical events. It is exactly in the actor's
refusal to conform to historical truth that the audience is
able to grasp the most intimate essence of his thought. History hesitates, for instance, to state whether the Tzar Boris
is guilty or innocent of the murder of the Tzarewitch
Dmitri at Ouglitch. Poushkin holds him responsible; ac-
cepting Poushkin's judgment, Moussorgski gives Boris a
conscience in which his crime rages like a wild beast in a
cage. I can understand Poushkin's work and Moussorgski's
conception of Boris far better if I realize that it is not an
incontestable historical fact that is in question, but a subjective interpretation of history. I remain faithful, I cannot be other than faithful, to Poushkin's judgment and
Moussorgski's conception. I always create a criminal Boris,
but my knowledge of history enables me to put light and
shade into my creation that would otherwise be lacking.
Although I cannot absolutely confirm it, I think it is very
likely that because of my historical knowledge my interpretation of the Tzar gains in sympathy and tragedy.

This explains why I went to our eminent historian
Klioutchevski while I was studying the part of Boris. I
recall with grateful pleasure the marvellous pictures he
painted of Boris, his times and environment. An artist in
words, and gifted with a most powerful historical imagina-

CHALIAPIN
AS BORIS GODOUNOV

tion, Klioutchevski was, in addition to being a historian, a most remarkable actor.

It was during the course of a walk in the forest in the province of Vladimir that he expounded the character of Prince Vasili Chouiski to me. How marvellously he did it! He stopped dead, took two steps sideways, held out his hand to me in a wheedling manner, and said in a timid and ingratiating voice:

> " *Thou know'st it well, the idiot populace*
> *Is savage, superstitious, and inconstant,*
> *And follows eagerly the wildest hope;*
> *It readily obeys a new command;*
> *To truth indifferent, and dull of heart,*
> *It battens on most falsely fabulous tales*
> *And dearly loves audacious cynicism;*
> *Thus, when a nameless libertine appeared*
> *Across the Lithuanian border . . ."*

As he recited Poushkin's lines, he kept his eyes fixed on me with a cunning look, as if to discover the impression made on me — Boris — by his words: am I frightened, disturbed? It is essential that he should know for his political ends.

Thus incarnated by Klioutchevski, Chouiski rose before me as though he were living. And I realized that when so subtle and crafty a statesman speaks to me, I must listen as though he were a schemer and not a mere courtier making a straightforward report.

To be brief, it is the careful study of my part and its origin, a purely intellectual study, that enables me to get at the core of the character. Like the schoolboy and his text-book, I simply learn a lesson. But that, obviously, is only the beginning.

Visualization of a character: The part played by imagination: The mentality of a character and its outward appearance: Boris Godounov's beard: Don Quixote: Don Basilio in The Barber of Seville

✍ ✍

However perfect the written description of a character may be, a certain measure of doubt must exist in its visualization. No book or script gives the exact proportions of a character, there are no details as to the actual length to an inch of his nose.

The finest artist in words cannot draw a *plastic* picture of a face, cannot convey the tones of a voice or describe the gait of a character. Tolstoi was a superlative artist, but if ten celebrated painters were asked to outline the portrait of Anna Karenina in accordance with Tolstoi's description, the result would be ten entirely different portraits, even though each contained the salient features of the heroine. Obviously, here is no question of objective truth, and, moreover, a written description is only of very slight interest. Nevertheless, if an actress is playing the part of Anna Karenina — for which may God forgive her! — the dramatic incarnation of Anna must in no way do violence to the Anna of Tolstoi's story. A close approximation to the original is the most rudimentary lesson that the actress must learn. Let us extend this and say that a mere out-

[92]

ward resemblance to Tolstoi's Anna is not enough; over and above this, the physical characteristics must be in sympathy with the mental attributes of the heroine, so as to give these attributes more light and shade and convey more meaning to the audience. The closer the external picture of Anna corresponds with the inner conception of her character, the nearer the representation will approach to perfection. It goes without saying that by " external picture " I mean, not simply " make-up," colour of hair, etc., but personal touches such as the way in which the character walks, sits down, listens, talks, laughs, and weeps. . . .

How is this to be achieved? Here, plainly, intellectual effort is not enough, and it is now that imagination enters the lists — imagination, one of the essential elements in artistic creation.

To imagine is to visualize. A swift, clear-cut, exact picture appears on the mental retina; at first the picture as a whole, later the typical details of the picture — facial expression, bearing, gesture. We must know the character intimately if we are to get a convincing picture. If we are aware of a man's inner nature, we can almost accurately guess his physical aspect. The audience will grasp the hero's personality the moment he steps on the boards if the actor has faithfully imagined and realized the character. The actor's imagination must be in complete sympathy with the author's imagination; it must strike the essential note of the character's personality. How lifelike and true to type an impersonation is may be gauged by the measure of the audience's conviction. Thus, we must assure ourselves that the character we are to create will carry conviction to an audience.

Let us take Boris Godounov. There are coins on which his head is engraved, and on these he is shown without a beard; he has a moustache only. His hair, I believe, has been cropped. This picture is probably historically correct,

but, having thought the matter out, I became convinced
that documentary evidence would be of no interest whatever. Let us admit that Boris was beardless. Does it necessarily follow that I must appear on the stage with a shorn
face? Must I represent Boris with blond locks? Obviously
not, for were I to do so, I should present an emasculated
picture of Boris. He is of Mongol descent — the audience
expect a black beard, and therefore I always give him a
black beard. Those who have seen me in the part can
judge how greatly this exterior detail has helped to produce an impression of power and strength.

Now let us turn to Don Quixote. I don't know what he
was really like, but having carefully read Cervantes, I can
shut my eyes and make a picture of Don Quixote as much
like him as the ten portraits were like Anna Karenina.
I may say to myself, for instance, that this dreamer, sunk
in his own dreams, must be slow in his movements, and
that his eyes must not be cold and hard. I see plenty of
varying characteristics and details, but this is not enough.
What was his appearance as a whole? How can I make
the audience, when they first catch sight of Don Quixote,
say with sympathetic recognition: "Yes, that's you all
right, old friend and comrade . . ."? Clearly, the external
picture must express imagination, candour, bravado, child-
ish weakness, the pride of an ancient knight of Castile,
and the simplicity of a saint. There must be a mingling of
comedy and pathos.

It was Don Quixote's inner nature that showed me his
external appearance. I pictured it, detail by detail, and
gradually evolved an image that was imposing when seen
from afar, but both ludicrous and touching when seen
from near. I have given him a pointed tuft on his chin,
and a drooping lock over his forehead; I have made him
long and lean and have set his frame on spindling, bony,
tottering legs. I have also given him a moustache, laugh-
able no doubt, but which is actually supposed to have

CHALIAPIN
AS DON BASILIO IN *The Barber of Seville*

adorned the countenance of the Spanish knight. . . .
Swearing fidelity on shield and visor, he has an artless,
innocent face on which smiles and tears and contortions of
anguish have a particularly moving effect.

In the same way Don Basilio's mentality has helped me
to a conception of the part in *The Barber of Seville*. Don
Basilio says: "Give me money and I'll do anything you
like for it." And his whole nature comes out in this single
phrase. From his first appearance the audience must realize
what sort of a rascal he is, to what depths he can sink, and
this from his mere attitude, before he has uttered a word.
My imagination told me that Don Basilio would be doubly
effective if he were not realistically represented, and therefore I deviated from strict reality and turned to the grotesque. My Don Basilio is to some extent as pliable and
elastic as his conscience. When he appears in the doorway,
he is of dwarfish bearing, but suddenly, before the very
eyes of the audience, he springs up to giant proportions.
When occasion calls, the giant can become the dwarf again.
He can assume any stature so long as money is laid in his
itching palm.

For that reason Don Basilio is both ludicrous and terrifying. In company with him, the audience may expect
anything to happen. His encomiums on slander are entirely
in keeping with his character.

It must be understood that imagination must feed on
observation of real life. If one is to delineate a Spanish
organist, one must go to Spain.

At the time when I was creating the part of Don Basilio,
I had not yet been to Spain. But I sometimes went to the
French side of the Spanish frontier, and there I saw all
types of clerics and priests, both fat and thin. . . . Organist and abbé — they were as like as two peas.

One day I started off from Dijon to go to a château,
Corman, as far as I remember. You know the French
trains — on the main lines the train de luxe, the wonderful

Blue Train, thunders past, but on the branch lines the engines puff along so sluggishly that you begin to wonder where you are going, why you are making such protracted halts, and when you are likely to reach your destination.

On this particular occasion my sluggard train was no exception. During the usual long wait at a station, whose name I have forgotten, a priest entered my compartment. He gazed at the other passengers, myself included, in an indifferent silence, huddled himself in a seat by the window, hunched his shoulders, pressed his hands together, and stared motionless through the pane.

I gave him a sidelong glance; he had a scarf round his throat and wore a hat. What sort of a man was he? Probably he was an excellent fellow, but I thought to myself: " There sits Don Basilio! " and I modelled myself in his image.

CHAPTER XXIV

Make-up: Its use and the part it plays: Composite effect, make-up and facial expression: I play Boris Godounov minus make-up at the Paris Opera House

∽ ∽

IT HAS OFTEN been said that I have made innovations in the matter of make-up, but I do not believe this to be so. I learnt how to make up from the best Russian actors, and I have simply tried to follow their directions accurately.

In our opera-house, actors were frequently to be found whose make-up was confined to their faces. Seen from the front, such an actor was well enough, but when he turned round, the audience could perceive his own hair beneath the wig; his countenance was that of a Hindu, while his smooth white neck was that of a youthful lead.

The same thing applied to their hands An actor is made up as an old man; he wears a white wig and a false white beard, but his smooth, ringed hands betray his years. . . . I myself have always taken pains not to give Sousanin Chaliapin's neck and hands — they would be of no use to him! Sousanin is a peasant who toils all day with bent back in the blazing sun: I give him a deeply tanned neck and the clumsy hands of a labourer.

Make-up is important, but I have always been guided by the wise principle of not adding any unnecessary details in make-up, as in acting. A superabundance of detail is disastrous — it underscores the picture far too heavily

Make-up

The art of make-up must be as simple as possible. One needs to get to the core of one's subject and then attempt a composite effect. Sometimes a single striking detail will isolate a figure from the crowd. Amongst a thousand men, one may be recognized simply by his upright carriage or his way of wearing his hat at the back of his head. " There goes Ivan Grigorievichi," you say, absolutely certain of his identity. A single detail has singled him out from the mass. . . .

I have never for a moment forgotten that make-up is only an auxiliary to the actor, that even though it helps him in his portrayal of a type, the part it plays is of secondary importance; clothing must not hinder an actor's gestures, and, in the same way, make-up must not prevent the freedom of his facial expressions. Its chief value lies in the fact that it hides the actor's own features. My face is as much unsuited to the part of Boris Godounov as my waistcoat would be out of place on him; and as Boris's costume is designed for the purpose of concealing my waistcoat, so my make-up as Boris must primarily mask my face. Incidentally, I may say that a person whose features are too marked is at a disadvantage as an actor. Picture a man gifted by Heaven with beetling brows, so thick and tufted that a dozen pairs could be made of them, or favoured with a nose like Cyrano de Bergerac's. It would be difficult to hide such characteristics beneath a layer of make-up, and so there are few parts he could play. I can create and play the part of Sancho Panza, but my physical characteristics stand in the way of a complete illusion.

Individuality is a very precious possession, but in spirit only, not in flesh. I will go so far as to say that no make-up will help an actor to create a lifelike personality unless he can combine with it the inspirations that spring from his own mind — in other words, with *psychological* make-up. Psychological make-up is not inherent in hare's-foot and

[98]

grease-paint, it exists independently of them. An actor may not be made-up, but his mental impersonation will persist if he is an artist, and not a mere machine. . . . I will not enlarge further on the subject, but will content myself with quoting the following incident as proof:

When Diaghilev organized the first season of Russian opera and ballet in Paris (in 1908, I believe), *Boris Godounov* was given for the first time. From every point of view, it was a lavish production. The décor was by two of our most outstanding artists — Golovin and Korovin — the costumes came from the Imperial Theatres, and the chorus was chosen from the pick of the Moscow and Petersburg companies. As this was a quite exceptional theatrical event for the Paris of those days, all the celebrities of the capital and the members of the press were invited to the dress rehearsal. But the world of the theatre has always a surprise in store. On the day of the dress rehearsal, some of the scenery could not be erected; most likely it was not ready. Similarly, some of the costumes could not be produced — most likely they were not yet unpacked. It was impossible to put off the rehearsal. . . .

As usual, I was keyed up.

" As the scenery and costumes aren't ready, I'm not ready either. I won't make myself up, I won't get dressed, I'll go through the rehearsal in my everyday clothes! " I exclaimed.

Which threats I carried out. I appeared on the stage as though it were an ordinary performance and sang:

> " *My child and my darling, I bid you depart*
> *And rest in your* terem, *oh sorrowful heart. . . .*"

And later, still as though it were an ordinary performance, I sang to my son:

> " *One day, not long hereafter,*
> *The whole of this, my kingdom, shall be thine . . .*
> *School yourself well, my son. . . .*"

[99]

Perhaps I should never have realized how natural my words and monologue sounded had I not heard, at the moment when I rose up, glancing fearfully towards a corner of the stage, to declaim:

"*What's that? There's something in the ingle-nook,*
  Something that stirs . . ."

had I not heard, I say, a strange sound in the auditorium that disturbed me. I looked askance to see what was happening, and this is what I saw: the spectators had risen to their feet, some of them were even standing on their seats, and all were gazing towards that corner of the stage towards which I myself was peering. They actually believed that I *had* seen something. . . . I was singing in Russian; my words were incomprehensible to them, but from the expression in my eyes they were aware that I was afraid of something.

Could make-up and costume have driven home this impression more vividly? It is very unlikely. They might have added to it, but only from the point of view of mere decorative effect.

CHAPTER XXV

Dramatic gesture: Can words be illustrated by gestures?: Gesture not a physical but a mental movement: A young actor's doubts: Gorbounov, the famous "diseur": An Iago who points out his Othello to the audience

୶ ୶

GESTURE IS OBVIOUSLY the very soul of dramatic creation, and to stress it further would be very like opening an already open door. The slightest movement of the face, of eyes and eyebrows — which is known as mime — all these are comprised in the word "gesture." Fitness of gesture, and the impression that gesture can convey, are the first principle of dramatic art. Unfortunately, to so many dramatic students and actors, gesture conveys nothing more than movements of arms and legs. So they move their arms; they lay their hands on their hearts, snatch them away, and let them sink downward; or, alternatively, they raise the right arm and the left, like oars cleaving the air. They are persuaded that they are acting well because their gestures are "theatre." In their minds the word "theatre" stands for the accompaniment of words with actions that are intended to add more significance to them.

Yet, in all truth, pupils in Russian dramatic academies are taught that a word must not be underlined by a gesture, that to do so is entirely false and incorrect. But the

[101]

coming generation of actors refuses to accept this statement. "What do you mean? Why mustn't we illustrate our words with actions when all the famous actors do it? You must prove that it is wrong. . . ."

One day, while I was in Moscow, a young man came to see me for the purpose of verifying his teacher's statements. He told me of his doubts and asked for my opinion.

"Your teacher's perfectly right," I said. "You must take his advice."

He was only waiting for this to pounce on me. He sat bolt upright on the sofa, and said with an air of triumph:

"But the last time you recited to the Literary Society, M. Chaliapin, when you came to the line: 'Silks, ruffs, and embroideries are reflected in the vast mirrors that cover the wall from floor to frieze,' your hand traced a line in space."

"Did it? It's quite likely," I said, "but when I traced this line with my hand, my eyes measured the distance so carefully that my gesture did not in the least describe the height of the mirrors. It was subordinated to an entirely different principle. Most probably I did not know that I was making this gesture, any more than I notice the gestures I make when I am talking to you. . . . But to come back to the point, tell me what you mean by gesture?"

The youth in some confusion informed me that gesture meant the movement of arms, legs, shoulder, and so on. . . .

"And to me," I said, "gesture means, not a physical, but a mental manifestation. If I allow my lips to smile without the slightest suggestion of another movement, that is in itself a gesture. Has your academy forbidden you to accompany a word with a smile if that smile comes from the soul of your character? No. What have been forbidden are the mechanical gestures with which you interlard your words. The gesture that comes into being independent of the word and which expresses an emotion *parallel* to that of the word is quite another matter. In that case the gesture serves a purpose — it describes something living that has sprung from the imagination."

I hope my interrogator understood me, and that when he became a full-fledged actor, he refrained from the *illustration* of his words by automatic movements of hand, shoulder, etc. . . .

One of those great artists who can call up the most vivid pictures by the mere expression of their face and eyes is I. F. Gorbounov, our celebrated "diseur." His sketches sound colourless enough when read, but when you hear him recite them, when you see how much *gesture* he puts into them by mere facial expression and the flicker of his lashes, you realize their profound truth. Had you seen Gorbounov as a preceptor, a bard, or a peasant humming a snatch of song — had you seen this peasant start at the lash laid unexpectedly across his shoulders by the coachman driving his lady, you would have understood the meaning of artistic gesture independent of words. It is impossible to live or create without such actions, for neither words nor letters of the alphabet can take their place. There are certain doors that open by means of a brick attached to a string — a kind of primitive pulley. You probably all know and have seen these doors. But the way such a door creaks, the noise it makes when it is slammed, the clouds of warm steam that issue from it — all this can only be conveyed by the carefully planned, picturesque gestures of that art in which Gorbounov excelled. Gesture cannot illustrate speech, or it would be such gesture as caused Hamlet to say:

"Do not saw the air too much with your hand, thus. . . ."

On the other hand, complete pictures can be painted by gestures that accompany words.

The subject of dramatic gesture, true dramatic gesture, strikes me as so important that I am anxious for every

would-be actor to understand all I have said in regard to
it. At the risk of being called too insistent, I will cite two
examples (one fictitious, the other true) of the inadmis-
sible illustration of words by gesture.

A duet is being sung; that is to say, a conversation is
taking place. The first singer says: "I advise you not to
marry Lisette; marry Caroline instead." The second singer
finds this unacceptable and, before the sentence has come
to an end, begins to register his objections by actions. He
twiddles his finger in the air — no! . . . He loves Lisette
— he lays his hand on his heart! When the name " Caroline" is pronounced, he dashes to the footlights, faces the
audience; maliciously points over his shoulder at his
mentor, as though he were saying: "You and that everlasting Caroline of yours!" . . .

Sad to relate, the above description is not a pure fabric
of my imagination.

On another occasion I was present at a performance of
Othello. Tamagno was singing the name-rôle, and I have
never seen a more remarkable Othello on the stage. The
part of Iago was played by a singer who, not without
reason, was supposed to be one of the finest in Italy. When
he had repeated the story of the handkerchief with much
eloquence, and as the Moor in his fury chewed the table-
cloth with his finger, Iago, enraptured, stepped back a
few paces and pointed out Othello to the audience with
a sly finger, while his other hand performed an action
familiar to Italians (he passed it across his stomach) as
though he were saying confidentially to the listeners:

" He-he-he! Haven't I made a fool of him, eh?"

God preserve us from seeing such actors and such
gestures on the stage!

CHAPTER XXVI

*Sympathy in singing: The hidden meaning of a song: Marfa in
Moussorgski's* Khovantchina: *Ivan the Terrible, lover and despot*

∽ ∽

THE SYMPATHETIC UNDERSTANDING that must be present
in gesture to give it life and artistic value must also be
present in every spoken word and musical phrase. Otherwise, word and phrase will be inanimate. Here again, as
in the plastic presentation of a character, the actor must
resort to *imagination.* He must imagine the state of mind
of the character during every event. Nothing can save a
singer who lacks imagination from creative sterility; a
beautiful voice, a sense of the theatre, an imposing presence are all equally powerless to help him. Only imagination can give a character vitality and meaning.

Take the story of the peasant who, all her life long, re-
members with unvarying emotion the handsome Uhlan
who passed through the village in her youth and kissed
her hand. Grown old, she meets him again, time-changed
like herself, and tears gush hotly from her sunken eyes.
I am speaking of the song: *Quand j'étais une fillette, toute
jeunette.* I cannot sing this song as it should be sung unless
I imagine that the village is not only *my* village, but
Russia personified; I must picture life in this village and
feel the heart-beat in this song. I must realize the young
girl's existence if I am to understand how the memory of

an officer's chance kiss could fill her old age with ecstasy. The singer must imagine all this, I say, if he is to be moved by the song. Moved he certainly will be if he can evoke the life of the village — how its peasants toiled, how they rose before dawn, and how, in the crude, harsh surroundings, a girl's heart awoke to love.

Similarly, I must imagine, feel, live, and sympathize with the grief of the mad Miller in *Rousalka* when reason returns to him and he sings:

" I am old, and witless. . . ."

Thereupon he begins to sob. He has surely sinned, but he is suffering torments, and I must feel and imagine these torments with sympathy. . . . In the same way I must love and pity Don Quixote if I am to give a moving picture of the old hidalgo on the stage.

Sometimes the singer must utter words beneath which the character conceals his true state of mind. Words at this juncture are like a cloak covering an emotion which, though present in the character's inner being, does not betray its existence externally. How can I explain this more clearly?

Picture a man clasping the rosary given him by his beloved; although he appears to be completely absorbed in the mechanical action of slipping the beads through his fingers, he is in reality thinking of the dead girl whose gift it was. In Moussorgski's *Khovantchina* Marfa sits on a fallen tree-trunk beneath the window of her false lover, Prince Khovanski. She sings an artless strain in which she recalls her love for him:

> " Once I wandered as a maid
> Over marsh and over wold,
> Through the cornfields, yellow-gold;
> Now my feet are scarred and sore
> In the search for my beloved —
> I shall find him nevermore."

Marfa sings these words in a tone of dreary indifference, and yet she has not come as a spiritless victim of betrayal. Seated on the tree-trunk, she counts out her memories like beads on a rosary, and all the time she is thinking, not of the past, but of the future. Her soul is filled with the agony and terror of the martyrdom to which she is self-destined. With him, with Khovanski, her beloved, she will soon ascend the pyre — and they will burn together for their faith:

> *"Like holy tapers burning bright,*
> *We shall be kindled and alight,*
> *Baptized together in the fire,*
> *Through smoke and flame our souls shall spire."*

This fulfilment, passionate and fanatic, filled with frenzy, and yet holding a deep serenity, is what she has in her mind as she finishes her song.

Marfa's song must be sung, therefore, so that the audience can realize her secret soul; they must be aware, not of the rosary of her memories, but of the underlying emotion which her surface thoughts disguise. If the singer can achieve this, then the double image of Marfa will be created, and this achievement is no light thing. Marfa is one of those deep and complex characters that seem to exist only in Russia, and that need the rugged genius of a Moussorgski to interpret them. Marfa's soul seethes with carnal love, passion, repentance, torments of jealousy, religious fanaticism, ecstasy, and the luminous rapture of mysticism — and all these contrasting elements commingle in the instant where she utters amidst the mounting flames: "Alleluia, Alleluia. . . ."

If Marfa's secret thoughts are not visible in her songs, then there will be no Marfa on the stage, but a lady of more or less stout proportions who sings more or less adequately words devoid of all meaning.

I have already said that to succeed in a part the actor

must imagine the character's state of mind during the entire action. Sometimes, however, a fault in the score or a slip in the orchestra's playing is enough to prevent the character from appearing lifelike. In such a case the actor finds himself in difficulties. Here is an instance:

In *Pskovitaine* I sing the part of Ivan the Terrible. At the beginning of the last act I am aware of something untoward, and cannot proceed as I should. Why? For the following reason: Ivan is supposed to be deep in thought. He recalls his lost youth, and how, on the day he met Vera, Olga's mother, in the forest, his heart leapt up, and he yielded to a sudden burst of passion: " My heart leapt up, I sowed the seed of desire, and now we are reaping the harvest." Up to this point everything has gone well with me, but immediately afterwards his thoughts take a very different form:

> *" I am alone in power — the populace*
> *Of this my mighty kingdom are assured*
> *They have but one great leader over them,*
> *A flock beneath this single shepherd's care."*

The amorous dreamer plunged in memories of his youth becomes a despot in a single stroke, a schooled thinker who proclaims the power of concentrated strength and who lauds the benefits of autocracy. He changes abruptly from one state of mind to another — there should have been a pause, but the composer has omitted it.

Thereupon I ask the conductor to draw out the final bar, so as to give me time and the chance to compose my countenance and alter my expression. I suggested this pause to Rimski-Korsakov himself. I have a boundless admiration for him, but I must be truthful and admit that he hated criticism. He listened to me grudgingly, and said in a sulky voice:

" Very well, I'll do as you suggest. . . ."

A short time afterwards he brought me a new recitative

for this scene in *Pskovitaine*. It was dedicated to me — I still possess the manuscript — but I sang it only once, on the day of the rehearsal. The original recitative was magnificent in spite of its one error, while the second, which had been composed to take its place, was thoroughly unsuitable. I had no wish to hear a pretty tune on the lips of Ivan the Terrible. I felt that it would impede the straightforward development of my part.

Had I not been in the habit of controlling myself at every moment, I should probably not have noticed that a pause was required in the score, and my interpretation of Ivan would undeniably have suffered.

CHAPTER XXVII

Freedom and discipline of emotion on the stage: The art of convincing an audience: Balance: Sympathetic tears that distort a character: A too sensitive tenor: Mode of expression, and artistic purpose

   ᔆ᳁ ᔆ᳁

IN THE PRECEDING chapter I have done my best to define the part played by imagination in creating characters that will carry conviction to the audience. I have said that imagination's chief function is the elimination of everything mechanical. By these remarks I have, to a certain extent, confirmed the principle of *liberty* in dramatic art. But liberty in art, as in life, is only good so long as it is controlled and reinforced by innate discipline.

It is on the subject of discipline on the stage that I now wish to say a few words.

I have told you that a Hindu with a white neck, and an old man with unwrinkled hands, cannot possibly convince an audience. I have proved that a fair-haired Boris would outrage all sense of fitness, and have stated that a song sung without sympathy for its inner meaning could move nobody. If an audience is to be convinced, it must be suitably duped, or, better still, put into a state of mind in which it is willing to be duped into the belief that fiction is fact. The audience knows perfectly well, for instance, that the actor now lying dead on the stage will probably be seated in a café drinking beer a few minutes later, yet it sheds tears of real pity for him.

An audience can only be convinced, duped, by the actor's preserving a sense of balance. Obviously an actor must primarily be convinced himself of the fact that he is trying to persuade others to accept. He must believe that the character he is representing really lived and died. If he does not feel this inward conviction, he will fail in convincing an audience, but he will fail equally, whether his art lies in the world of music, painting, or drama, if he cannot blend all the elements of his character into a harmonious whole. He must express the emotions, use the intonations, and make those gestures in the exact proportion to which they correspond with the nature of the character and the situation. If the hero weeps, for example, the singer must control his own emotion and keep back his tears lest they should distort the character. Emotion, instead of being personal, must be inherent in the character, and in that case they will ring true.

I will give a concrete illustration of my meaning. During a tour in South Russia, I found myself at Kichinev and took advantage of a free evening to go and hear Leoncavallo's *Pagliacci* at the opera-house. The opera proceeded with mediocre merit in an atmosphere of boredom, but when the tenor embarked on Pagliacci's famous recitative, the house came back to life. The singer acted with dramatic intensity, but laughter began to sputter in the audience. The more dramatic he became, the more he wept as he sang: "Laugh then, Pagliacci, laugh though your own heart's breaking," the more the audience roared. I fell a victim to the general contagion. I bit my lip and controlled myself as far as I could, but my whole being was inwardly convulsed with merriment. I might possibly have left with the conviction that this singer had no talent, and that his acting was ridiculous, had I not gone behind the scenes at the end of the act while the audience streamed out to finish their laugh in the foyer. I hardly knew the tenor, but I had met him before; as I strolled past his dressing-room, I decided to go in and say good evening to him. Entering, I saw a man still under the stress of the scene he had just finished playing. Tears were rolling down his cheeks.

" Good . . . good evening," he said, with an effort.

" What's the matter? Are you ill? "

" N-no, I — I'm n-not . . . ill."

" Why are you crying? "

" It's because I can't control myself. The same thing happens every time I play a very dramatic part. . . . I feel so intensely sorry for poor Pagliacci! "

I understood in a moment. This singer, who undoubtedly had talent, was ruining his part simply because he was not shedding Pagliacci's tears, but tears of sympathy for him. . . . It became ludicrous for the excellent reason that the tenor's tears were of no interest to anyone.

The above is an extreme instance, but it is significant. The excessive lack of balance had provoked an excessive reaction in the audience — general hilarity. Had the lack been less excessive, the reaction would no doubt have been less excessive also — smiles instead of laughter. If the singer had tipped the scales in the reverse direction, the reaction would likewise have been reversed. Supposing that the tenor had been of an unemotional nature and that, feeling no pity for Pagliacci, he had betrayed this indifference in his singing of the famous recitative . . . the audience would probably have pelted him with rotten apples.

The ideal adaptation of means of an expression to an artistic end is the only condition under which a harmonious and balanced character can be created, infused with its own life — through the medium of the actor, of course, but independent of him. Through the medium of the actor creator, not of the actor individual.

CHAPTER XXVIII

Self-control: Two Chaliapins on the stage: The actor and the observer, the singer and the critic: "Subconscious" creation: An actor in the "divine frenzy"

ॐ ॐ

THE DISCIPLINE OF emotion brings us back into the sphere of conscious and purely intellectual effort. A sense of balance presupposes self-control. I would never willingly advise an actor to depend on the audience's reaction. " The audience reacts favourably, therefore the performance must be good " — this is a very dangerous formula. The audience's appreciation of a character created by an actor must not be considered by him as proof absolute of its truth and harmony. An audience is sometimes mistaken. There are, of course, connoisseurs amongst them who are rarely at fault, but the mass of the public is only able to judge by comparison. You sometimes hear it said of an actor: " How well he acts! " when actually he is acting very badly, but the public does not realize this until they see the part played far better, more naturally and more intelligently. " That's how it ought to be played! " is then the cry. Somebody shows you a piece of furniture in the Louis XV style. The workmanship is perfect — shape, mouldings, and gildings are in the manner of the period, but the illusion dies as soon as you see genuine Louis XV furniture with its indescribable authenticity and its inimitable

[113]

beauty. Only rigid self-control will allow an actor to act authentically and win the lasting favour of his audience.

Here the actor is confronted with an extremely difficult problem: he is faced with the necessity of being two people at the same time on the stage. When I am singing, the character that I am creating is always present in my mind. It never for an instant leaves me. I sing and listen, I act and take notice. I am never alone on the stage. Two Chaliapins are always there. One of them plays his part, the other watches him play it.

"Far too many tears, old man," says the critic to the actor. "Remember that the character, not you, is crying. Keep back a tear." Or, on the other hand: "Put a little more substance into your grief, don't make it quite so arid, shed an extra tear."

It sometimes happens, be it understood, that one's emotions are not under control. I remember that in *The Life of the Tzar*, when Sousanin says: "I have been ordered to go, I must obey," and when he holds his daughter Antoinette in his arms and sings:

> *"Do not grieve, my dearest child,*
> *Do not weep, my dearest daughter,"*

I remember that at those moments I felt tears trickle down my cheeks. At first I paid no attention to them, thinking that it was Sousanin who wept, but suddenly I was aware that, instead of the agreeable tones of my voice, a kind of plaintive bleating sound was issuing from my throat. I was horrified and immediately realized that it was I, Chaliapin, who was weeping for pity, that, too poignantly moved by Sousanin's grief, I was shedding futile tears. I pulled myself together in an instant and recovered my self-control. "Not too much sensibility, old man," said the critic in me; "leave your Sousanin to his own sorrows, and sing and act as well as you can. . . ."

I am always conscious of myself on the stage. I never

for a second relax my guard on the harmony of my action.
Is my leg in the correct position? Is my attitude in keeping
with the sentiments I have to express? I notice the slightest movement, the least noise; a member of the chorus
is wearing boots that creak. . . . "The slacker!" I think,
"He might have oiled them!" And while I think this,
I sing: "I am dying. . . ."

I have not overmuch admiration for "unconscious"
creation, so dear to some actors. A certain actor, in the
throes of the divine afflatus, so far lost himself in his part
that he actually wounded his stage adversary with a
dagger-stroke. In my opinion, the perpetrator of such an
"unconscious" thrust deserved to be locked up in a
police-cell. . . . When a stage-blow is struck, the audience
must naturally feel the shock of it, but it is not really
necessary to bruise your opponent black and blue. If you
actually fell him to the ground, the management will be
obliged to lower the curtain for fifteen minutes and offer
the audience some such apology as this:

"Ladies and gentlemen, we crave your indulgence for
the delay in proceeding with the play. There has been a
slight mishap — one of the actors was so inspired that . . ."

CHAPTER XXIX

*Imagination and practice: Mother and foster-mother: Nuances:
The perfect image: The arrow that hits the mark: The* consciousness *of the audience*

༄ ༄

THE ACTOR HAS made a searching study of his part; his
fertile imagination has had free rein; he is fully conscious
of the gamut of his character's emotions; at rehearsals
he has carefully worked out his actions and intonations;
by exercising strict control over his means of expression,
he has attained a harmonious whole. The picture that he
had in mind before the rehearsals started is now finished
and complete.

At the first performance of the opera he surpasses himself and makes a conquest of the audience. Has the part,
then, reached its zenith?

No, not yet. It has still to be mellowed by performance
after performance, during many years. Agreed that there
is work and knowledge and talent in the picture, there
still lacks one thing to perfect it, and that is — practice.

If imagination is the mother from whom a part is born,
practice is the foster-mother who encourages its normal
development.

No shoemaker — and here I speak with authority, having
had the honour of being a shoemaker in my youth — no
shoemaker, however skilled, can stitch shoes to perfection

without practice, not even after a five years' apprenticeship. If he is a good shoemaker, he will certainly stitch
them very well, but it is only after long practice that he
will be able to tell at a glance the type of shoe that will
fit your foot.

Even if you carry conviction to the audience, there are
many small details that never reach it. There is something
intangible. . . . Up to the present I have not grasped what
it is, but I feel that it is this that prevents the audience
from understanding and believing me — why, I cannot tell.
If the lighting in the theatre does not correspond absolutely with the lighting on the stage, it prevents the secret
emotions of the audience from showing themselves, it
smothers and disperses these hidden feelings.

Or perhaps there is something in the dresses, the décor,
or the setting, for the actor, in the creation of a part,
depends a great deal on the atmosphere that surrounds
him and on certain details that assist or fail him.

Only practice can teach the actor to discern the detail,
the almost imperceptible detail, that has detracted from
the impression he is making. This detail was correct, that
incorrect, that other false. Flowing currents of emotion
stream from the auditorium on to the stage and continually polish and repolish the created image. You can only
act freely and vividly when you feel you are holding your
audience; mere talent is not enough, the experience and
practice acquired after long years of work must be super-
added.

A day comes when you know that your part is perfected. How has it come about? In the foregoing chapters
I have discussed this fairly exhaustively, and it is impossible to say much more. The final attainment of perfection
cannot be achieved by study, nor can it be explained in
words — it lies on the other side of the barrier. The actor
has so identified himself with the character that everything — actions, intonations, shades of expression — is

absolutely exact and true to type. I can think of no better comparison than to liken such an actor to a sped arrow which so accurately hits the mark that the bell rings. The arrow may as well go wide by a mile as by the hundredth part of an inch — in neither case will the bell tinkle.

This simile holds good for every part. It is not so easy to ring the bell. Often enough one is almost on the mark, within an inch of it, perhaps, but never directly on it. It is a curious sensation.

At one moment I hear the ringing of the bell, but at a hundred other moments I hear nothing. What really matters is to be capable of knowing whether the bell is ringing or not. . . . And so, if one of my audience feels that he has " pins and needles," I feel the pricking on *his* skin. I know he has " pins and needles." How do I know? I cannot explain. The explanation lies on the other side of the barrier.

CHAPTER XXX

The plastic qualities of the body: Freedom and ease of movement:
Philip II of Spain does not know how to walk correctly: Ivan
Platonovitch Kiselevski and his salad: Perfection of gesture

๛ ๛

It is not mere idle talk to say that there can be beauty
even in the representation of ugliness. It is as simple and
incontestable a truth as this: a beggar's rags may be picturesque. For every reason, the representation of beauty
on the stage must be more beautiful, and nobility more
noble, than in reality. If he is really to attain this beauty,
the actor must do his best to develop the suppleness of
his body. Harmonious creation depends on the freedom,
ease, and naturalness of his movements — all this is as
indispensable as the timbre, resonance, and naturalness
of his voice. Sometimes the actor fails to realize this, and
the results are comic or tragic.

A youth leaves the conservatoire or a private school of
singing and dramatic art; he knows how to use his voice,
has learnt his part to the last note, and is convinced in all
good faith of his ability to play the part of Raoul in *The*
Huguenots, or that of Ivan the Terrible. But he soon finds
himself ill at ease in the costume the dresser has given
him — the charming and intelligent young man who has
an intimate knowledge of the Huguenots and Raoul de
Nangis looks more than anything like a hairdresser's

assistant in carnival array when he appears before the footlights. He has no idea how to walk on the stage, his limbs are not under control. There is a discord between himself and the cavalier he is supposed to be.

One day, a young man, who brought an introduction from a writer-friend, came to see me in Moscow. In the letter of introduction my friend informed me that the boy was gifted, was even a poet, but that he had no means, and wanted to learn to sing. He asked me to hear him and help him.

The young man wore a black blouse caught in round his hips with a leather belt. I noticed that he walked in an ungainly manner, reminiscent of the intellectuals risen from the people who dream of relieving the " oppressed."

I also noticed that he possessed physical strength far above the average — his handshake had proved painful.

I listened to him. In a moderately agreeable bass voice he sang an operatic air. His singing was monotonous, and I told him so frankly. He admitted it and told me that so far he had had no lessons. He needed forty roubles a month for his studies, which I promised to pay, and I gave him some money in advance; I told him to come to me from time to time and let me hear his voice. He went to a school of singing. I hardly ever saw him except on the days when he had to pay for his lessons. Six months later he came to tell me of his progress, wearing the same black blouse caught in round the hips with the same leather belt. . . . He gripped my hand too heartily, as before, trailed slowly over to the piano, and began to sing.

His singing was not strikingly different from what it had been the first time I heard him. The only change I re-marked was in the sustaining of his notes, a doubtful improvement; he explained why these sustained notes were logically indispensable. I made a few comments on his singing and then asked him a question about his blouse; was he so used to it that he never left it off, or hadn't he enough money to buy himself some other garment? He was obviously taken aback, but smiled and said that his voice was the same no matter whether he wore a blouse or a coat. I made no reply to this truism. Incidentally, I thought, it *is* the same voice. . . .

At this time I was singing the part of King Philip II in *Don Carlos.* The young man often asked me for tickets for this opera; he wanted to study my playing, for he felt drawn towards Philip II and hoped that it would be his best part when he started on his career. I willingly gave him the passes; immediately after the first performance he came to thank me, and told me that my acting had fired him with enthusiasm.

" That's splendid," I said. " I'm delighted that you are having some lessons in acting."

A year slipped by, and he came once again to see me, still in the eternal black blouse and leather belt, still with the excruciating handshake.

This time I spoke to him severely, and said:

"You've been studying for two years, young man. You've been to see me in different parts, and you are very much attracted to the character of King Philip II of Spain, but you still slouch, you still wear a blouse, and you will shake hands so heartily that I feel it for hours afterwards! Hasn't your singing-master explained to you that, apart from the notes that must be logically sustained, as you informed me the last time we met, you must learn to walk, not only on the stage, but in the streets? I'm surprised this hasn't occurred to you. Whatever changes of costume you make, your voice is always the same, and you will never be able to play the part of Philip II, as you intend. I believe your two years' experience is sufficient to prove it. . . ."

The young man no doubt complained to his friends that great actors brush new-comers out of their path and bar the way to them. He would not have said this had he understood that an actor only becomes a great actor by cultivating his talent and his plastic expressionism with equal vigour.

The outstanding type of actor who is completely master of plastic expressionism was, in my opinion, Ivan Platono-vitch Kiselevski. This remarkable actor at the end of the last century had devoted himself to such parts as " noble fathers" and "gentlemen" in general. I saw him act at Kazan when I was quite young. Much later I made his acquaintance at Tiflis in the house of a lady, a friend of mine who was giving a party in honour of the company from the capital which was then playing in the town.

As I was too shy to address Kiselevski, I remained in a corner and gazed at him. He had snow-white hair, was clean-shaven, and, although not handsome, his face was expressive to the last degree. He wore a black frock-coat and an impeccably knotted cravat. He had a marvellous voice, smooth and rich as velvet. He spoke quietly, but very distinctly. I could not take my eyes off this magnificent apparition. Somebody offered him refreshments. He went up to a table on which were the *zakouskis* and, before drinking a glass of vodka, took a plate, sprinkled it with salt and pepper, poured out oil and vinegar, mixed it all up with his fork, and poured the compound over some salad on another plate. No doubt the reader wonders what I am getting at. The man had simply made a dressing and had eaten some salad with his vodka. Quite so — but I still recall the manner in which Kiselevski helped him-self, as one of the most marvellous motion-pictures that could ever be witnessed.

I remember how his beautifully shaped hand took up each object, how, fork in hand, he stirred the simple salad dressing, and I still remember the tones of his voice as he cried out:

" Friends and fellow-actors, let us drink to our hostess, who has given us such a wonderful entertainment."

Kiselevski

Everything in Kiselevski savoured of greatness. " I am sure English lords must be exactly like him," I thought artlessly. In the time to come, I saw plenty of aristocrats, lords, and even kings, but always I remember with an actor's pride — Ivan Platonovitch Kiselevski.

CHAPTER XXXI

The bygone generation of Russian actors: The varnish of Stradi-
varius violins: The peasant origin of Russian actors: Once
slaves, now kings: Their life of hardship: His Excellency's two
fingers: The Director of the Imperial Theatres: The old bass
singer: Crime and punishment

৵ ৵

THE BELOVED RUSSIAN actors of bygone days!

I still see many of them on the stage — all the galaxy
that glittered so brightly at the end of the nineteenth
century — but I saw the celebrities of a still earlier time
ending their days in a home in St. Petersburg.

Although they were a pathetic sight, these old actors
and actresses crippled with illness, I felt a particular
pleasure in going to see them. They reminded me of
pictures by old masters. Their faces were so luminous
that they seemed to have been brushed over with a kind
of varnish — the varnish of Stradivarius violins, which
never loses its lustre. The wonderful luminosity on the old
actors' faces is a secret that our generation has lost for
all time. It mirrored lives that art had filled with a mystic
thrill. They acted in the theatres with the sacred emotion
of those who go to Holy Communion, although they were
not always strictly temperate. . . .

The actors of old were like one big family; they knew
nothing of the display and self-advertisement, grandilo-

quence and false flatteries which later became fashionable. They gathered together in friendly and intimate little clubs, sought one another out, gave each other advice, did one another a good turn, and, when necessary, were outspoken in criticism:

"Zaraiski, old man, you're not acting that well."

And Zaraiski, in spite of his personal pride, would take his friend's advice to heart. Thus the art of the Russian actor flourished and grew apace.

We know that the guild of Russian actors dates from the reign of Catherine II. The actors were slaves; they left the plough and the farmyards of feudal lords to appear in the theatre. They were obliged to unite together, for they were treated with scant leniency by the masters before whom they acted. I myself remember the time when His Excellency the Director of the Imperial Theatres offered only two fingers to the most famous actors. To these two fingers, His Excellency would deign to add an amiable smile, but I learnt from the old actors who had finished their careers in the Imperial Theatres that in their time the directors did not even condescend to proffer two fingers; they would appear behind the scenes and shout:

"The next time you dare to stutter and stammer on the stage as you did today, you'll find yourself in jail. . . ."

This sounds like fiction. . . . Nevertheless it is the truth. This was the way in which actors were treated in the good old days.

When I was young, I saw a very old singer on the stage; I don't know why, but he took a fancy to me. He was a talented artiste with an excellent bass voice. Also he was a gardener and grew radishes, cucumbers, and other green stuff for making *zakouskis* to accompany vodka.

One fine day, before appearing at an important concert at which the Tzar was to be present, this remarkable old man, singer and gardener, had copiously wetted his whistle; he stood on the stage and began to sing a song that was not down on the program. The manager, who had probably drawn the Tzar's attention to this particular singer, rushed furiously behind the scenes and hurled every possible insult that can wound an inferior at the old man. At the end of his tirade, interlarded with the grossest remarks, he brought both his fists violently down on the music the singer was holding in his hands. The leaves scattered to the ground. The old man, who until then had said nothing, lost patience, and as he stooped to gather up his music, said calmly and suavely:

"Your Excellency, I beg of you, do not force me, Your Excellency, to say ' S—! ' to you! " . . .

The manager, majestic in his rage and his uniform starred with decorations, was so taken aback that he stopped short, looked utterly crestfallen, and abruptly withdrew. The event was suppressed. . . .

You can understand how the actors of bygone days, deprived of human decency, drew together for comfort.

Not only in the capitals where the Imperial Theatres stood, but in the provinces — particularly in the provinces — they led a life amongst themselves. Envy and hatred must, no doubt, have existed among them at times — as everywhere and always — but they were alien to the atmosphere where pure and sincere friendship ruled supreme.

The actor of those days did not travel first-class, as we do today, fortunate mortals that we are — often he went on foot from town to town, covering many miles. But the further he turned his face from the world of fashion, the more deeply and lastingly it was engraved on that glorious medal which we call the theatre.

CHAPTER XXXII

Decadence of contemporary Russian drama: The causes: Tradi-
tion, dead and living: Brutal rupture of a glorious tradition: At
all costs let there be change: Fatal "properties": Ostrovski under
a bridge: Molière on the Eiffel Tower: A peculiar production of
Glinka's Rouslan and Ludmilla

૭ ૭

I SOMETIMES ASK MYSELF: "What has happened to the Russian actor? Why has he masked the beauty and purity of his face? Why has Russian drama lost its one-time strength and vitality? Why have audiences ceased to laugh and weep whole-heartedly? Have we become so barren in actors and genius? No, thank God, we can draw on a great reserve of talent."

Among the numerous causes that have contributed to the decadence of the Russian theatre — a decadence that cannot be disguised by idle babblings of a so-called renaissance in drama, or by shameless self-advertisement — the brutal breaking-away from our dramatic traditions must come first.

Conflicting opinions may exist as to tradition in art. There is the canon of beauty, traditional and static, which suggests comparison with a senile and decrepit ancient, a prey to every form of illness, with one foot in the grave. The gouty old misery should have been under the sod years ago, but he hangs on to life, useless to everybody, exhaling the odour of decay. I do not take it upon myself to defend this conventional and sinister tradition — my defence is on behalf of the tradition of living elements in art, which is still bearing fruit. I cannot believe in the parthenogenesis of new art-forms — if they have life, spirit, and flesh, this life must necessarily have a link, a tie, with the past. The past cannot be severed from the future by the stroke of an axe. The dead and done-with must be distinguished from the living and worthy to live. I cannot imagine that in poetry, for instance, Poushkin's tradition has lost all vitality; nor that, in painting and music, the traditions of the Italian Renaissance and Rembrandt, of Bach, Mozart, and Beethoven, are dead. . . . Nor can I in any way understand, or believe it possible, that the immortal tradition which sets the living personality of the actor, the soul of man, and the divine word on the stage can ever disappear from the drama.

Notwithstanding, to the great misfortune of the theatre and the new generation of actors, this hallowed tradition of the stage has been partially uprooted. This has been done by those who clamour for change at all costs, even at the cost of violating the natural laws of the theatre. These people call themselves innovators; for the most part, their innovations consist in violating the canons of art. True art creates itself without violence, for violence leads to nothing. Moussorgski was a great innovator, but he never had recourse to violence. Stanislavski, who renewed the art of décor, never went contrary to natural feelings, and never thought of using violence simply for the sake of appearing to be an innovator.

If I may be allowed to say so, I myself was in some respects responsible for innovations, but I never forced them. I only felt instinctively that it was necessary to penetrate more deeply into the heart and soul of the audience, touch the strings of its emotions, and constrain it to laughter and tears without having recourse to tricks and inventions, but, on the contrary, by keeping in mind the lessons of my predecessors, the old-time Russian actors. . . . None but sham innovators rack their brains to originate new *tours-de-force* that will astound their associates.

What is the meaning of the words "always onward" and "cost what may" in the region of dramatic art? The meaning is that the author's text, the actor's individuality, are of secondary interest, and that what really matters is that the settings should be in the style of Picasso (note that they should only be in the *style* of, not by Picasso himself . . .). Others say: "No, it is not that. There is no need of settings. Back cloths and draperies are enough." Still others maintain that the actor must pitch his voice as softly as possible — the more softly he speaks, the more atmosphere he will create. . . . Those in disagreement on this point are all for thunders and lightnings, while the most daring innovators have gone as far as to state that the audience itself must take part in the action and constitute itself a kind of collective actor. . . .

These extraordinary innovations are chiefly the work of our managers and producers. Most of them can neither sing nor act. They have only the most elementary knowledge of music, but, on the other hand, they are past masters in the art of inventing "new forms." They can turn a classical four-act comedy into a revue in thirty-eight scenes. Above all, they excel in the matter of stage effects. If the action of the play takes place in a country town at midday on a Sunday morning, the hour of the carillon, the audience is treated to a hearty peal of bells. The dialogue is submerged, but what does it matter? The author's implication has been brought out. The curious thing is that, while these gentlemen respect his implications, they treat his script and his definite stage-directions with scant courtesy. Why does the action of Ostrovski's *The Forest* take place under a bridge? Ostrovski had no need of a bridge. He himself described the scene of the action and the settings. It would not surprise me in the least if tomorrow plays from Shakspere or Molière had the Eiffel Tower for setting. . . . The producer's ideal is not to carry out what the author imagined and realized in his work, but what he himself, as " interpreter " of the author's secret thoughts, thinks fit to add from his own brain.

This being so, it is quite natural that, on the play-bills of *Revizor,* for instance, the name of Gogol is printed in diminutive letters, while that of the famous producer X or Y appears in enormous block capitals.

Glinka composed *Rouslan and Ludmilla.* I recently had the doubtful pleasure of seeing this old Russian opera in a very modern setting. Ye gods! The highly ingenious producer had scorned to express himself in honest fustian — he must at all costs invent something new and original. Poushkin's story is as clear as daylight, but the producer had thought it necessary to turn it into a most dazzling affair.

In this production Svietozar and Rouslan were symbolic of Day and the Sun, while Tchernomor personified Night. Possibly this might not have been without interest to an academic assembly, but I am at a loss to understand what the idea was of imposing these " scientific " subtleties on an audience who had come to hear Glinka's opera. The sole result of this conception, undreamed-of by either Poushkin or Glinka, was a cabalistic setting and décor. Take, for instance, the banquet-scene in the great hall of Svietozar's palace at Kiev. Although no astronomer, Glinka had pictured this scene very well. The producer, however, thinks it insufficient, and instead of the great hall, he erects a " Ladder of Life," according to popular legend; Youth ascending and Age descending, as the guests continue their feast on the symbolic stairway, for no apparent reason. Stars of varying size appear in the heavens, and *on the earth* the crescent moon is set askew; it is the custom probably. . . . In place of the moon, Venetian lights dazzle the eyes of the audience and prevent them from taking in the other innovations.

Tchernomor's beard is carried in on a special cushion, which is no doubt intended to symbolize the shadow of night or something of the sort. But, most inexplicable of all, in the perfectly ordinary scene where Naina and Farlaf appear, weird creatures issue from the wings without rhyme or reason, looking like the twisted and tortuous branches of trees, or the demons that attend on delirium tremens. There are twelve of these monsters, who have no existence either in Poushkin's libretto or in Glinka's music.

There is another such case in Dargomyjski's *Rousalka*. There is a windmill, as everyone knows, in the first act, but the producer is not content simply with the artist's representation of a windmill. Handsome youths go to and from the mill with *sacks of flour*. . . . Do you remember that at that moment a profound drama is taking place? Natacha is on the scene, her body lax, half-fainting; she is on the point of throwing herself into the water.

"What is the idea of those sacks of flour?" I ask the producer.

"My dear Feodor Ivanovitch, there must be a little *life* in the scene. . . ."

What answer can I make? I feel he would get his deserts if I said:

"Get a rope and hang yourself! Perhaps when you've done it, I may fetch someone to bring *you* back to life. . . ."

But he'd fly in a rage if I said it. He'd complain that "Chaliapin insulted me. . . ."

CHAPTER XXXIII

Essential and accessory: The spirit of a great work, and distract-ing "props": The producer who kills art: Dargomyjski's L'Invité de pierre, given at the Imperial Theatre, Moscow, in the style of Rodrigo del Stupidos

ᔕᑎ ᔕᑎ

IT IS NOT in the name of strict realism that I attack the "innovations" of which I have just spoken. I am not a pedant, or an enemy of innovations and new conceptions. Was not my Holophernes a daring innovation? Was not my Don Basilio an original? No, what shocks and grieves me profoundly is the fact that the essential is sacrificed to the accessory, the inward to the outward, the soul of a work to meaningless "props." I object to the Ladder of Life and the sacks of flour because they divert attention to themselves; they impede the singers from singing and acting freely, they prevent the audience from listening quietly to the music and the singers. A banqueting-hall is a simpler setting than a Ladder of Life — the former concentrates attention, the latter disperses it. As to the sacks of flour and the delirium tremens monstrosities, they are nothing short of scandalous.

I personally require settings to be beautiful, effective, and unusual. To me, the particular value of an opera lies in the fact that it is a combination of all the arts — music, poetry, painting, sculpture, and architecture. I cannot hold myself guilty of a lack of interest in the importance of settings. I recognize and appreciate the effect of *décor*, but when it has made its first impression on the audience, it must sink into the general harmony of the scene. Unfortunately, innovators, obsessed by a mass of decorative schemes that are harmful and often absurd, end up by totally neglecting the one essential — the spirit and character of the work itself. The actors, the protagonists of the action, are entirely overshadowed.

I have always admired and respected the skill of a producer, but if, by learned researches, he kills the very soul of art, away with him and his plans from theatre and stage.

A producer stages *Boris Godounov*. He has learnt from historians that the impostor, Grichka Otrepiev, fled from the monastery in September. Consequently, in the tavern scene with Grichka and Varlaam, the window is left wide open to display an autumn landscape complete with withered leaves. The result is a chronological triumph at the expense of the scene. Moussorgski composed a wintry music for it, filled with concentrated sadness — and the open window destroys the whole atmosphere.

I have seen equally devastating consequences on the Imperial stage.

One day Vladimir Stasov said to me:

" Feodor Ivanovitch, you are in my debt; you promised to sing the part of Leporello in Dargomyjski's *L'Invité de pierre (Don Juan)* ."

Where I was concerned, Stasov's wish was a command. I told Teliakovski, the director of the Imperial Theatre, that I wanted to sing in *L'Invité de pierre,* to which he agreed. I set to work — that is to say, I began to study my part and all the parts in the opera, in accordance with my usual custom. I was at home, in my dressing-gown, going through the script, when I was told that there was a gentleman to see me.

L'Invité de Pierre

"Tell him to come in."

Whereupon the stranger appeared, with a whole library under his arm, and introduced himself. He informed me that he had been entrusted with the settings for *L'Invité de pierre*.

"I'm delighted to meet you. Is there anything I can do for you?"

It appeared that there was.

The legend of Don Juan, he explained, is of very ancient origin. The Abbé Etienne, on page 37 of Volume III of his classic book on the subject, ascribes it to the twelfth century. Did I think the settings for the opera could be done in the style of the twelfth century?

"Why not? The twelfth century, by all means," I said.

"Yes, but on page 72 of Volume II of his no less classic work, Rodrigo del Stupidos has ascribed the legend of Don Juan to the fourteenth century," pointed out my learned colleague.

"Well, then, stick to the fourteenth century. The fourteenth century's as good as any other."

And in full expectation of the fourteenth century I attend the first rehearsal. The first thing I learn is that Dargomyjski's opera after Poushkin is mounted in twelfth-century style. This is how I learn it:

The scene represents a merry banquet in Laura's house. There must naturally be candelabra on the festive board. Suddenly my learned colleague perceives that the candelabra are not of twelfth-century design and is seized by indescribable emotion:

"Are you mad, Grigori? What is the meaning of these candlesticks? Bring some twelfth-century candlesticks at once . . . Grigori. . . ."

The property-man appears. In all probability the unhappy wretch has never even heard of the twelfth century. A finger against his nose, he remarks lymphatically:

"Please, sir, we've only got the candlesticks that

CHALIAPIN
MODELLING HIS OWN HEAD (PETROGRAD, 1915)

are used in *The Huguenots* . . . we haven't got no others. . . ."

"Oh well," I think, "let them go on amusing themselves with this tomfoolery. . . ."

The rehearsals proceed. The festive board is so spread that it is impossible to sit down to it, much less relax in comfort.

Enter Don Carlos. In the opera he is a coarse-grained mercenary. To Laura, a charming girl of eighteen, he finds nothing better to say than the following:

> " *Time shall dim and fade your eyes,*
> *Wrinkle lids and forehead sleek,*
> *Sprinkle silver in the gold*
> *Of your hair — a sere disguise.*
> *Then, when they shall call you old,*
> *What the answer you will speak?* "

The part of this rough boor should be taken by a bass with harsh accents, but in this case it was sung by a lyrical baritone with melting notes. Of course the whole meaning of the character was lost; but the producer was so hypnotized by the candlesticks that he found no fault with the die-away singing, which he passed without comment. Neither the Abbé Etienne nor Rodrigo del Stupidos had been able to enlighten him.

I listened and listened, and then, unable to bear any more, shouted:

"I'm off to have a bath, gentlemen. I'll have nothing more to do with the opera."

Whereupon I departed. *L'Invité de pierre* was produced without me, and a most deplorable affair it was, too!

CHAPTER XXXIV

The spirit of our time, and its influence on the theatre: Diplomas:
Cheap praise: Capital letters on play-bills: Contemplation and
perseverance in art: Hurry!: "Men of the moment": Vanity Fair:
Boredom and melancholy

ᔕᔐ ᔕᔐ

I SOMETIMES FEEL THAT the spirit of the times has had
a deleterious effect on the theatre. During many years
I have observed theatrical life in our capitals, and am
regretfully forced to admit that the actor no longer has the
same attitude towards the theatre as formerly. Sceptics
often ridicule such superannuated expressions as " the
sacred art," " the divine sense of the theatre," " the temple
of art," and so on. . . . Perhaps they are ridiculous, but
they were no mere idle phrases to our elders. They held a
profound meaning. Today, on the contrary, it seems that
our young actors only study their art in order to win a
diploma, and play Ruy Blas then and there. They do not
appear to question the adequacy of their training. They
are in a hurry to get on, and their minds are occupied with
other schemes.

They concentrate on getting favourable notices. Instead
of putting their whole soul into the play and into the interpretation of the character, they are taken up with unimportant theatrical reviews, and their one desire is to see
their names in large print among the contents. I agree that

it is flattering to see your photograph on the first page of a magazine, and beneath it a caption which reads: "Ousikov, one of the most promising of our younger actors." This is very pleasant, and the actor is in ecstasies, but these very ecstasies prevent him from realizing that he has already exchanged "the sacred art" for Vanity Fair. He has rubbed shoulders with the dramatic critic. . . .

He panders to his self-conceit by enthusiastically frequenting green-room clubs, mutual admiration and publicity societies, where he meets theatrical pressmen. Serious criticism strikes him as irritating, troublesome, and unbearable, and, worst of all, he has lost the desire and ability to criticize himself.

In all fairness it must be said that contemporary youth is in a difficult position — it commands my sympathy. Art exacts not only perseverance, but contemplation. Present-day civilization has broken the back of perseverance — life is a scramble and a rush. It is the age of aviation. We fly above the clouds, and on earth we shoulder each other out of the way. Although I am not very old, when we, the older generation, went to the baths, we soaked, rubbed, and made ourselves tingle by beating our bodies slowly and deliberately with willow twigs. This leisure was good for art. Today you are seated in an arm-chair with a well-sprung seat, and in a moment you are washed and dried, and your hair is brilliantined. Brilliantine and comfortable chairs are harmful to art. . . . Art exacts calm and contemplation, a lovely landscape drowned in moonlight. But now there are racing cars and the Eiffel Tower — we are all rushing headlong onwards, trying to exceed our own speed-limits.

Actor, musician, singer — one and all attempt to snatch the flying moment. If they succeed, they are happy. If anything goes wrong, they say: "We are out of luck. We're being cold-shouldered, there is a conspiracy against us."

These men of the moment never accuse themselves — it is always someone else who is responsible.

From year to year I have seen Vanity Fair taking on more and more sinister proportions. The number of professionals ignorant of their professions to be met with in every corner of the globe fills me with horror. The actor is ignorant of the drama, the musician knows very little about music, the conductor has no respect for rhythm or punctuation. He is not only incapable of expressing the soul of a great work; he cannot even follow accurately the events which are taking place on the stage; and yet it is he who should command the production, as Napoleon commanded in battle. But we see him wave his baton with an air of conviction, we see his intensely frowning brows and the exquisite ring on his little finger. . . .

Loving the theatre, as I do, more than anything in the world, it grieves me to say these things, but it grieves me still more to witness them. I am like a fly that haunts the theatre — chase it through the window, it will return by the door. I am bound to the stage by an indissoluble tie. I have done everything that could be done. I have cleaned footlights, scrambled up in the flies, nailed up scenery, lit flares in the transformation scenes; I have danced with a company from Little Russia, acted in vaudeville, and sung *Boris Godounov*. The most wretched provincial actor, the clumsiest circus-juggler, are dear to my heart, so great is my love of the theatre. How, then, can I confess without pain that in most of the theatres today, I feel bored and melancholy?

But I hope — I am certain — that not all young actors have renounced the good and honest traditions of the theatre. And it is in all confidence that I say to them:

"Don't give in. Be true to yourself, and you will succeed."

CHAPTER XXXV

*Life in Moscow: The Russian merchant: His origin and the part
he plays: A purchaser of Gauguins, Picassos, and Matisses:
Jeunesse dorée—"waifs and strays"*

WHEN I JOINED the company of the Imperial Theatre
for the second time, my activities were not confined to the
one capital. I sang alternately at the Marie Theatre in
Petersburg and the Grand Theatre in Moscow.

A singer who takes his work seriously has very little
leisure; his time is taken up with rehearsals and productions. My free hours were spent in the quiet of my own
home or amongst friends — musicians, artists, writers. I
had very little to do with what is called "society," but
I took a keen interest in the merchant guilds and industrial
circles which set the tone to Moscow and the other towns.
I believe that during the fifty years that preceded the
Revolution, the guild of Russian merchants played a leading part in the life and customs of the country.

What sort of man is this merchant, the Russian *koupiets*?
At bottom he is a simple Russian peasant who, after the
liberation of the serfs, came to find work in the town.
He is very like the ridged cucumber which has sucked
up all the sap of the country-side in spring, has ripened
in the sun, and has been taken to town from its native
orchard to be put in brine for the winter. A fresh

cucumber in an orchard is perhaps more attractive and appetizing than one of the pickled variety — it all depends on tastes — but in spite of its condition, a pickled cucumber conserves within itself the heat and lustiness of the sun in the country. On cold winter days, after an appetizing glass of vodka, a cucumber warms the belly of the bourgeois, as well as that of the proletarian and the humble workman. . . . In fact it was not for himself that the Russian merchant toiled — he created life, he organized labour. . . .

I see him in his village days, this future leading light of commerce and industry in Moscow. He puffs and sweats as he learns his A B C by most extraordinary methods in the country school. He spells out each letter in the time-honoured manner from *The Key to Thinking*, a primer of legends written round Bova Koralievitch and Rouslan Lazarievitch. . . . But although he can scarcely read or write, he demonstrates the fact that he has an enviable brain. One day, in spite of his lack of mechanical and technical knowledge, he invents a potato-mashing machine, or he finds some substance in the soil that can be used for axle-grease — he is always making the most surprising discoveries. He endeavours to hit on the means whereby a plot of land can be cultivated with the least labour and the greatest return. He does not frequent the one vodka-bar, nor does he waste precious time on holidays in useless walks. Every minute is spent in stable, orchard, field, and forest. He never reads the papers, but all the same he knows — goodness knows how — that manure is at a low price, and that if he buys it now, he will be able to sell at a profit in a month's time.

According to ideas of morality current in Russia, he is a " *koulak*," a criminal. He has bought low, therefore he has cheated someone; he has sold higher, therefore he has cheated someone else to a greater extent. . . . But I frankly admit that in my opinion he has proved himself possessed of intelligence, *savoir-faire*, smartness and energy. The Naples beggars may be "poetic" enough, as they bask idly in the sunshine, but they amount to very little in life.

Another moujik leaves his native village at an early age and begins his career of potential merchant by hawking his stock in the streets of Moscow. He sells *sbitene* (a popular Russian drink made of honey and boiling water) in the Khitrovo market (the green-market) ; he vends little cakes, drenches his pancakes in oil, vigorously extols his wares, and keeps a weather eye on life and its vicissitudes. Life does not treat him kindly. More often than not, he spends the night in the Khitrovo market or in the Priesnia quarter; he gorges himself on tripe in a crowded eating-house, and swallows a few mouthfuls of tea from a saucer [1] with a bite or so of black bread. He is paralysed with cold, but is always light-hearted; he never grumbles, but builds all his hopes on the future. It is no odds to him what wares he peddles — today they are ikons, tomorrow stockings; the day after, yellow amber or pamphlets of some kind or other. Gradually he accumulates a few roubles and becomes a "capitalist." Next, he installs himself as proprietor of a small shop or store. Then he establishes himself as a merchant of the first guild. Wait a little. . . . Behold, his eldest son purchases the first Picasso and the first Gauguin and brings the first Matisse to Moscow. . . . We intelligentsia regard Matisse, Renoir, and Manet with dire dislike, their value has not yet dawned on us, and we exclaim with a superior air:

"What an extravagant fellow! "

But these same extravagant fellows were meanwhile quietly collecting priceless treasures, erecting galleries and museums, and building theatres and hospitals for the benefit of all Moscow.

[1] The Russian peasant pours his tea into a saucer, puts a lump of sugar in his mouth, and takes a few sips.

The Russian Merchant

I remember a typical sentence spoken by Savva Timo-
feievitch Morozov, one of the chief members of the guild
of Russian merchants. He had built a new house in the
Arbat district, and on its completion gave a magnificent
house-warming, to which I was invited. In the hall, at the
foot of the dignified oak staircase which led to the reception
rooms on the first floor, I saw a kind of fountain, and behind it huge windows of coloured glass lighted from within.
A design on these windows showed young girls offering
garlands to a cavalier astride a splendidly caparisoned
horse.

" I see you like battle-pictures," I remarked to my host.

" I like victory," answered Morozov with a smile.

Yes, the Russian merchants liked victory, and they *vanquished.* They vanquished poverty, obscurity, the insults of
uniformed *tchinovniks,* and the blank disdain of aristocratic snobs and dandies. I hardly ever paid visits to the
merchants, but whenever I was their guest, I was struck
by the munificence of their hospitality.

I have been practically all over the world, and have
been invited to the houses of the wealthiest Americans and
Europeans, but I must say that I have never encountered
anything to equal the lavishness of the Russian merchant.
I do not believe Europeans could have any idea of its
scale.

When I have to talk to people that I do not care for,
I always feel a certain constraint, and this constraint comes
from the fact that at the bottom of my heart I am persuaded that there ought not to exist people incapable of
arousing sympathy. But they do exist — truth compels me
to admit the fact.

The sympathy I felt for the Russian merchants who had
achieved such remarkable things by dint of earnestness
and stability was equal to the detestation I had for the so-
called *jeunesse dorée* of the same class. Taken out of their
natural country environment, they had not adapted them-

selves to the life of a town. When they had finished a super-ficial course at the university, these gilded youths, who were fully aware that their "governors" would pay for their most costly pranks, had but one aim in life — the pursuit of pleasure and those joys that were to be found in the haunts of the underworld. They spent their days and nights in a continual orgy, and amused themselves by smearing mustard on the waiters' "traps," as they expressed it in their bestial language, devoid of human decency. Not in America nor in Europe, nor, I believe, in Asia, could any idea be formed of the extent of their debauchery. . . .

It would be unfair to class these rakes as merchants — they can only be called civilization's waifs and strays.

CHAPTER XXXVI

Fyodor Grigoriev, my hairdresser, one of the people, and a re-markable artist: A friend and dear companion of bygone days

ᔥ ᔥ

I HAVE ALREADY SAID that many great actors came from the peasants before the liberation of the serfs.

From the same class, as I have just pointed out, came the famous corporation of Russian merchants. The Russian country-side, indeed, is rich in talent. Whenever I think of this, the name that comes into my head is not the name of any celebrated writer, artist, or scholar who has sprung from the people, but that of a humble Russian artisan, Fyodor Grigoriev. This man, who was only a theatrical hairdresser, was not merely, when he chose, an artist (which is not so unusual); he was also an expert, scrupulous and attentive to his work — attributes which nowadays have unfortunately become excessively rare. . . .

I have one or two " bourgeois " weaknesses; I like well-cut suits, good linen, and elegant hand-sewn footwear. I spend a great deal of money in the gratification of these weaknesses.

I order a suit. The fitters ascertain my height and breadth, and note down all my measurements. When the suit is fitted, it is too tight across the chest, one sleeve is too short, the other too long. . . .

" Your right shoulder slopes much more than your left, sir."

"But you took my exact measurements."

"I beg your pardon, sir, I did not notice it at the time."

The same thing occurs with my shirts and boots. So much so that when I have a suit, shirt, or shoes made, I look the cutters straight in the eye, and say:

"You see that I'm slightly deformed, don't you?"

Great astonishment.

"For instance, my right shoulder slopes more than my left."

The cutter proceeds to verify my statement. "Perhaps it *does* slope a little more, sir."

"Do you notice that bunion on my left foot near the big toe?"

"Yes, sir."

"And do you see that my neck's abnormally long?"

"Is that so, sir?"

"Make a note of all my peculiarities, and see that my things are made accordingly."

"Very good, sir."

But when they are made, the right shoulder of my coat is still five inches lower than the left, my shoes are still too tight and hurt me, and my shirt-collar hugs my ears. . . .

I have the same trouble with my hairdressers. Since I left Russia, I have been unable to get wigs, beards, moustaches, or eyebrows to suit my rôles. The theatrical wig-maker — strange though it may seem — is the actor's chief friend and confederate. A great deal depends on him. Fyodor Grigoriev performed miracles. He had the talent and the manual skill of the Russian who has risen from the people. He was an excellent fellow, always full of fun; he stammered, and was bald — what an advertisement for his profession! He was a foundling, brought up in an orphan-age, and had been apprenticed to a barber, one of the brothers who "trim and shave and draw blood." Even while serving with this barber, he had found opportunity to display his talent. At Christmas he made wigs, beards, and moustaches for fancy-dress dances, and in this way he soon became an accomplished artist in make-up. He had taught himself how to apply grease-paint and knew exactly where to shade in the dark and the light.

When I had described my part and the character I was to represent, he would say:

" I th-think, F-f-feodor Ivanovitch, you ought to h-h-have a w-wig with a t-t-touch of r-red in it."

And he would send me up a marvellously realistic coiffure. It was a pleasure to behold it in my dressing-room mirror, to see dear Fyodor Grigoriev's face over my shoulder, to smile at him, and wink with no necessity for words. . . .

He accepted this silent compliment in equal silence, clearing his throat a little.

When it was my benefit-night, he would curl up my wig afresh, and say:

" D-d-dear Feodor Ivanovitch, I must take extra p-p-pains tonight — it's a g-g-gala night for Ch-chaliapin."

And, needless to say, he *did* take extra pains.

There is only one way for a man to reach my heart where the stage is concerned, and that is for him to do his work thoroughly, whatever it may be: conducting an orchestra, singing a part, or making a wig. I loved Fyodor Grigoriev whole-heartedly. I took him abroad with me, even though I had no use for his services, as everything had been prepared in advance. But it gave me pleasure just to have his company and to witness his delight at finding roses and acacias in full bloom in January. How Fyodor revelled in Monte Carlo! He spent the day in exploring the vicinity, and at night he would come to my dressing-room and talk to me.

" Oysters are v-very cheap here, F-f-feodor Ivanovitch. In R-r-russia they're luxuries. I've d-discovered a r-r-remarkable cheese here, F-f-feodor Ivanovitch, it's c-called

Roquefort — I eat a quarter of a p-p-pound of it every m-morning w-with my coffee. . . ."

I felt deeply grieved when I learnt he had died of apoplexy in St. Petersburg. Peace to your ashes, old comrade-in-arms!

CHAPTER XXXVII

Serge Rachmaninov: A visit to Leo Tolstoi

༶

Destiny threw me in the way of a great many remarkable men. My meeting with Serge Rachmaninov dates back to the first stirring memories of my life in Moscow. It occurred during my season with Mamontov. Rachmaninov was very young when he came to the theatre and I was introduced to him. I learnt that he was a musician who had just completed his studies at the Conservatoire. His first composition — *Aleko*, an opera founded on a story of Poushkin's — had won him a gold medal. He was going to conduct *Samson and Delilah* in Mamontov's opera-house.

All this awed me considerably. But warm feelings of friendship soon brought us together, and we often went *chez* Tiestov to eat *rastiegai*[1] and exchange ideas on the subject of music and the theatre.

It came about that during a certain period I very rarely saw him. A man with an intense spiritual life, he was then going through a moral crisis. He fled the society of men. He composed music which he destroyed, but happily his will-power was strong enough to see him safely through this crisis of youth; he outlived the Hamlet phase and with new-found energy composed many beautiful works. Our friendship was renewed. A remarkable pianist, Rachmani-

[1] Small pies.

[148]

nov is, with Toscanini, one of the best conductors I have
ever heard. When Rachmaninov holds the baton, he in-
spires complete confidence in a singer. When he is at the
piano, I am not singing alone — we are *both* singing. He
interprets the very soul of a composition with the utmost
delicacy, and if a pause or a suspended note is required, the
singer may be sure that he will indicate them perfectly.
As a composer, he is the personification of simplicity,
clarity, and sincerity. When he is composing, he sits bolt
upright, his eyes fixed straight ahead, and if his right ear
itches, he puts up his right hand to scratch it, instead of
bringing his left hand behind his back. This has proved
displeasing to certain " innovators."

Rachmaninov has a cold, gloomy, even stern aspect, yet
he is of a childlike candour, and loves to laugh. When
I go to see him, I am always ready with a joke or a story
of some sort, because I adore hearing this old friend of
mine laugh.

The memory of those early days with Rachmaninov is
linked with the cherished memory of my first visit to Leo
Tolstoi.

It took place in Moscow on January 9, 1900. Tolstoi was
then living with his family at Khamovniki, a district of
Moscow. Rachmaninov and I received an invitation to
visit him. We climbed an unpretentious wooden staircase
to the second floor of a charming house, modest and intimate in character, built partially of wood, if I remember
rightly. We were cordially welcomed by Sofia Andrievna
(Countess Tolstoi) and by her sons, Michael, André, and,
I think, Serge. Tea was offered to us, but I was in such a
state of excitement that I was in no fit state to drink it.
Just think — for the first time in my life I was going to see
in the flesh the man whose words had stirred the world. Up
till then I had only seen portraits of Tolstoi, and now he
himself appeared.

He stood by a small chess-table, and talked to young

Goldenweiser. (The Goldenweisers, father and son, were invariably Tolstoi's associates in the family games of chess.)

He seemed to me to be below average height, which surprised me extremely, for his photographs had always given me the idea that he was a giant, not only morally but physically, a very tall, massive man with broad shoulders. . . . My wretched acuteness of hearing (a professional habit!) informed me at this moment, significant as it was, that he spoke in a slightly bleating voice, and that a certain letter — no doubt because several of his teeth were missing — issued with a lisping, whistling sound. I noticed this, moved as I was by his nearness; and when he unostentatiously shook hands with me, my emotion increased. He asked me, as far as I can remember, how long I had been acting, as I looked so young, and I answered in that same tremulous voice in which I had said, at the Kazan municipal theatre: " A piece of string."

Serge Rachmaninov was not so shy as I was, but he was deeply moved, and his hands were cold. " If I'm asked to play," he whispered to me, " I don't know what I shall do — my fingers are numb." The next moment Tolstoi begged him to play. I can't remember what he played. I was too agitated by the thought that it would be my turn next. My agitation was doubled when Tolstoi said point-blank to Rachmaninov:

" Tell me, has that type of music any interest whatever? "

I was asked to sing. I remember that I sang *Le Destin,* a song that Rachmaninov had just composed round the leit-motif of Beethoven's *Fifth Symphony,* with words by Apoukhtine. Rachmaninov accompanied me. We both did our utmost to give the song its full value, but we could not tell if it had pleased Tolstoi. He said nothing. Then, as before, he asked:

" What kind of music is most necessary to men — classical or popular music? "

I was asked to sing again. I sang several songs, amongst others a melody by Dargomyjski, *Le Vieux Caporal,* to Bérenger's words.

Tolstoi was seated face to face with me, his hands thrust through the belt of his blouse. Watching him from time to time, I noticed that he was following with interest the expressions of my eyes and mouth. When, with tears in my voice, I uttered the last words of the old soldier who is about to be shot:

> *"Don't shoot too low — I pray God sends*
> *You safely to your homes, my friends,"*

Tolstoi withdrew one hand from his belt and brushed away the tears that had sprung to his eyes. I rather hesitate to tell you this, for it sounds as though I were hinting that it was my singing that so moved Tolstoi . . . it is possible that I did justice to Bérenger's touching words and Dargomyjski's music, but I attributed Tolstoi's emotion to the picture I had called up of an old soldier face to face with a firing squad.

When I had finished, there was a burst of applause, and I received many compliments. Leo Tolstoi, however, neither applauded nor spoke.

Taking me aside, Sofia Andrievna said:

"For heaven's sake, don't comment on Leo Nikolaie-vitch's tears. He has strange moods at times. He says one thing, but at bottom, in spite of his cold reasoning, his soul is full of passionate feeling."

"Did my song about the old corporal really please him?" I asked.

Sofia Andrievna squeezed my hand.

"I'm sure it pleased him very much," she said.

I myself had felt that there was a wealth of tenderness and goodness in the stern apostle, and the realization made me very happy. But Tolstoi's sons, who were my friends and of the same age as myself, dragged me into the next room.

" I say, Chaliapin, you'll be bored if you stay here any longer. Let's go to the Yar [1] and listen to the Zingari. They do know how to sing! "

I don't know whether I should have been bored in Tolstoi's house, but I did feel embarrassed and almost paralysed. I was terrified lest he should suddenly ask me a question to which I had no suitable answer. . . . Whereas I had a reply to anything a Zingaro might ask me. . . . And so, an hour later, we were listening to *The Little Golden Ring* sung by a gypsy chorus. . . .

[1] A celebrated restaurant

Ilia Riepin, the famous painter, and his yearning for a tchoubouk: *Valentin Sierov, the great portrait-painter: Midnight
Mass in the Church of St. Saviour at Moscow*

၈ၣ ၈ၣ

I AM RATHER ASHAMED to admit that I let many things
slip by unnoticed to which I ought to have paid great
attention. Mine is the story of the man born in Moscow
who goes indifferently past the Kremlin, or the Parisian
who takes no interest in the Louvre. . . . My youth and
heedlessness made me press onward in many cases with
the same carelessness. Ought I not to have sought a closer
acquaintance with Leo Tolstoi? Ought I not to have looked
more often and with more warmth at the bespectacled
eyes of Nicolas Rimski-Korsakov? Ought I not to have
experienced more sympathy when I saw dear Anton
Tchekov expectorate into paper funnels as he listened to
Moskvin reading his stories? I saw him do so, but I was not
as much moved as I might have been, and it is a matter for
regret. . . .

I remember, as though it were all a dream, my meetings
in the past with the famous Russians of that day. I see
myself as I sat with my bulldog on a divan in Ilia Riepin's
studio at Kuokalla.

"I want to paint you as a *barin,* Feodor Ivanovitch,"
said Riepin.

[153]

Ilia Riepin

" But why? "

" Because that is how I see you. You are stretched out on a sofa in your dressing-gown. . . . It's a pity you haven't one of those old pipes they used to smoke " (a *tchoubouk*).

At the mention of the *tchoubouk,* now fallen into disuse, the great painter fell into a reverie of the past. I looked at his face and gathered a confused impression of his thoughts, but I did not understand them then. I understand them now. I, too, look backwards, and I, too, like Riepin, remember the old *tchoubouk;* I know now what it was that stirred the incomparable Ilia Efimovitch to the depths — it was not the wooden-stemmed *tchoubouk,* but the memory of the peace and serenity and fulfilment that we felt as we smoked it. . . .

Riepin spoke of art so simply that, although I was no painter, I learnt, as I listened, how to distinguish the beautiful from the ugly, the pretty from the lovely, the noble from the common.

Many of the artists who were my teachers are dead, but the nature of Russia interpreted by their genius is a vital force that will never die.

The outward appearance of many gifted men is often in strong contradiction to the infinite resources of their true nature.

Valentin Sierov appeared stern, sullen, and taciturn. At first sight, he gave the impression of a recluse, but this was only an impression. You ought to have seen this apparently cold man when he was going fishing with Constantin Korovin and me. He bubbled over with light-heartedness; everything he said was witty and full of meaning. We spent whole days on the water, and at night we retired to our primitive fishing-shack.

Korovin stretched himself out on a rough sort of bed, whose springs invariably pressed into the back of the unfortunate sleeper. At the head of the bed a candle-end, stuck in a bottle-neck, burned on a stone slab, and at the foot Vassili Kniazev, a most delightful tramp, leaned against the wall and chatted to Korovin about fish, their stupidity in letting themselves be caught, and their cunning in escaping. . . . Sierov listened to the talk, laughed heartily, and hastened to immortalize the little scene, so full of truth and humour, on canvas.

Sierov has bequeathed to the nation a large number of contemporary portraits, and his brush has spoken more eloquently of his times than many a book. Each one of his portraits is almost a biography in itself. I wonder if mine, which used to hang in the Cercle Artistique in Moscow, is still there, or whether it has been removed. I do not know.

What happy moments I passed in Sierov's company! Often, after our work was done, we spent hours strolling through Moscow and observing all its features. This reminds me of a little incident. . . . He made a small sketch of me in charcoal, and when it was completed, suggested a walk. It was Easter Eve. At midnight we went into the Church of St. Saviour, which has recently been pulled down. During Midnight Mass we felt like hardened atheists, in spite of the spiritual grandeur of the service. "Poisoned" by the atmosphere of the theatre, we were left cold by the strange "setting" for the Mass. In the centre of the cathedral, a kind of quadrangular platform had been erected; at the four corners stood deacons in rich chasubles, holding long tapers in their hands, and alternately intoning the prayers in hollow-sounding, resonant voices. The Bishop, a little old man whose minute white head emerged comically from his sumptuous sacerdotal vestments, climbed painfully on to the platform upheld by the deacons. It appeared to us as though the smoke of the incense was wafted upward from the neighbourhood of his minute white head. We looked at each other in silence. The next moment we caught sight of a workman in his

Sunday best, his hair sleekly combed and oiled, who held a lighted taper close to the forage-cap of a soldier in front of him; with lively interest he watched the shaggy material singeing in the candle-flame. . . . Again we interchanged glances and perceived that we were decidedly in no state of grace on this holy night. . . . When we had elbowed our way through the crowd of worshippers, we went to Sierov's house in the Vagankovski Impasse — to celebrate the end of Lent.

CHAPTER XXXIX

*Isaac Levitan, the landscape-painter: The curious dæmon,
Vroubel: The remarkable painter Polienov divides his interests
between the Russian lakes and the hills of the Holy Land: Kon-
stantin Korovin*

✍ ✍

Isaac Levitan is one of those who linger in my memory.
You should have seen his eyes! I think I never saw deeper,
dreamier, more shadowed eyes than his. Every time I sing
Rubinstein's setting of Poushkin's verses:

> *Hast thou heard within the forest-grove*
> *The midnight voice that sings its grief and love?*

> .   .   .   .

> *Hast thou heard*
> *The reed pipe's plaintive notes that rose and died*
> *When dawn hushed all the fields and nothing stirred,*
> *And hast thou sighed? . . .*

Whenever I sing these words, I nearly always think of
Levitan. He it is who wanders in the forest and hearkens
to the plaintive notes of the reed pipe. He is the singer of
love and grief. He sees a little church, a twisting path in
the forest, a lonely tree, the bend of the river, the convent
walls; but Levitan's shadowed eyes do not starkly register
these things. No, he stands sighing on the path near the
church-tower, at the foot of the lonely tree, his gaze intent
upon the clouds. . . .

Vroubel, that curious individual, also remains in my mind. He was a dæmon who gave the impression of being a pedant. In the dreary years of hardship he had painted archangels in cathedrals, and it was those very archangels who begot his dæmons. And what dæmons! Powerful, terrible, soul-shaking, irresistible. I am no art-critic, but it seems to me that Vroubel's genius was so great that he must have been fretted by the confines of his feeble body. He died in the conflict of spirit and flesh. One felt that there was a tragic element in his dreams. My " Dæmon " is by Vroubel, and so too was my " Salieri," a sketch which was lost through the carelessness of some wig-maker or costumier.

I think, too, of Polienov, another remarkable painter. One of his pictures, a yellow water-lily on a lake, exhales a perfume of which one could never weary. This extremely talented Russian had in a way divided his interests between the water-lilied lakes of Russia and the harsh hill-sides of the Holy Land, the burning sands of the Asiatic desert. His Biblical scene, his Evangelists, his Christ — how could he have reconciled these magnificently coloured visions with the tranquillity of a Russian lake teeming with carp? Is it because he was able to reconcile them that a divine spirit breathes upon the placid waters of his lakes? . . .

All these painters are dead; of the illustrious group of Moscow artists in Paris none remain save Constantin Korovin, a gifted painter, who has done the most original theatrical décor, and who gave proof of his talent in Mamontov's opera at the end of last century.

CHAPTER XL

The coterie of great composers at St. Petersburg: Meetings at Stasov's and Rimski-Korsakov's: Moussorgski, the great "rag-picker" of music: Russian "classics" and Moussorgski's "realism": Moussorgski's power: Spring in Russia *or* The Strait of Gibraltar: *Music minus atmosphere: Moussorgski and his scents*

ৎ৯ ৎ৯

THE YOUNG COMPOSERS of my generation lived in a kind of retirement. They had the music of the past for inspiration.

With this rich heritage of music, each of my young contemporaries was able to work in his own niche. But the lot of their elders had been far otherwise. Their heritage of music had been far less abundant. There had been Glinka with his genius, then Dargomyjski and Sierov. But it fell to their immediate successors to create Russian national music from its very root. Bound together in the common cause, each had to help the other, and so they lived together in friendship. In St. Petersburg all these famous composers formed a wonderful coterie. I have always considered, and shall always consider, that I was extraordinarily fortunate in meeting this group at the beginning of my career.

The composers usually assembled at the house of V. Stasov, their inspirer and bard, or else at Rimski-Korsakov's apartment in the Zagoredni Prospect.

Rimski-Korsakov's quarters were very modest in character. The truth is that the great writers and musicians led a far less prosperous life than — forgive me for saying so — opera-singers. . . . A small drawing-room, one or two chairs, a grand piano. A small table in the dining-room . . .

Sometimes we were a little pressed for room, we were jammed against one another shoulder to shoulder, like so many diced morsels of *chachlik*.[1] . . . The *zakouskis* were of the simplest, but we talked of the latest composition by this or that musician, of the success of a certain production, agreed that a certain ballet had been beautifully mounted, and that a certain opera had been very badly done, the blame for which we laid on Napravnik who had cut out half the score — the excellent conductor sometimes committed frightful blunders. . . . Or else we got up part-songs — Rimski-Korsakov, Cesar, Cui, Felix Blumenfeld, and I.

One of my greatest regrets is that I never met Moussorgski. He died before my arrival in Petersburg. It was an overwhelming loss to me. It was as though I had failed to catch a momentous train — reaching the station as it steamed away before my eyes — for ever. . . .

Happily, our coterie of composers had preserved the memory of Moussorgski with loving pride. Moussorgski had at last been recognized as the genius he was. It was that recognition that urged Rimski-Korsakov with truly religious fervour to perfect *Boris Godounov,* the greatest work that Moussorgski has left us. Today a number of people inveigh against Rimski-Korsakov for having "disfigured" Moussorgski, as they term it. I am not a composer, but in my humble opinion such a reproach seems to be profoundly unjust. Even the *material* work that Rimski-Korsakov accomplished is astounding and unforgettable. Without this work, the world would still be ignorant of

[1] A Caucasian dish consisting of small pieces of grilled mutton.

CHALIAPIN

WITH A RUSSIAN GROUP, INCLUDING RIMSKI-KORSAKOV (ON THE
EXTREME LEFT), GLAZOUNOV, CUI, STASOV, AND THE
CELEBRATED ACTRESS SAVINA

Boris Godounov. Moussorgski laid no claims to recognition, and that Europe might be interested in his work never so much as entered his head. He was possessed by the dæmon of music. He composed because he could not do otherwise than compose. Wherever he might be, he was always composing.

Picture him in Mali Yaroslavets, the little tavern in Morskaia Street, St. Petersburg. Alone in a private room, he drinks vodka and scrawls down music. He scrawls it on napkins, menu-cards, and ends of grease-proof paper. . . . He was a rag-picker of great discrimination, and even a cigarette-stub of his finding exhales a perfume. He had written so much for *Boris Godounov* that had it been produced in strict accordance with the original score, the performance would have had to begin at four o'clock in the afternoon if it were to end no later than three in the morning. . . . Rimski-Korsakov condensed it, but his version retains all that is worth while. He made errors in his condensation, no doubt. He was a pure classicist, who disliked and had no feeling for dissonances. Or, rather, he felt them and they hurt him. A consecutive fifth was more than enough to upset him.

I remember the occasion when Rimski-Korsakov and I heard Richard Strauss's *Salome* in Paris. How Strauss's music excruciated him! After the performance we went to the Café de la Paix; and he was literally ill. He spoke rather nasally. " What filth it is! " he burst out. " It's absolutely revolting! Stuff of that sort makes you sick! " . . .

On the whole, although our classical composers bowed to Moussorgski's genius, they were conscious in their heart of hearts of a certain prejudice against his " realism," which was too harsh to be assimilated by them.

Moussorgski is usually described as a great realist. His warmest admirers term him thus. I am not sufficiently versed in music to give an absolute opinion, but as a singer of Moussorgski's music, I modestly put forth the suggestion that this description is too limited and that it in no way embraces the whole of Moussorgski's genius. Some creative art is so great that formal definitions lose their meaning and have only a secondary value. Certainly Moussorgski is a realist, but his power lies, not in the fact that his music is realistic, but in the fact that his *realism is music* in the fullest sense of the word. Behind his realism, as behind a curtain, there is a whole world of meaning and emotion that cannot owe its existence to realism. To me, Varlaam, who appears to be realistic through and through, is something beyond mere realism — he is soul-sickness, and fear in all the power of musical expression.

During my tours in Russia, I used to have an accompanist who was a friend of mine and an accomplished musician. Between the songs he would often play his own compositions on the piano. One of them had a special appeal for me. It called up an April morning when mischievous small boys bore holes in willow branches to suck the sap. . . . "What's the name of that thing you're playing?" I asked him one day, and when he mentioned some such title as *The Strait of Gibraltar,* I was more than surprised. . . . After the concert I invited him to my room, begged him to play the piece again, and stopped him in the middle to ask him what interpretation he put on such and such a passage. He could not answer, and burbled incoherently. . . . There was no trace of Gibraltar in the development of the theme or the variations. . . . I told him that to me his music suggested the month of April, thaw, sparrows, drifting mist in the forest. . . .

He stared at me and asked if he might play the piece again for his own benefit. He concentrated on listening to it note by note, and at the end he said, abashed:

"You're right — it does suggest spring, and, moreover, spring in Russia — there's no Gibraltar spring in it at all. . . ."

I quote this incident to prove that sometimes when a

composer thinks he has expressed a certain character in his
music, there is no trace of this character to be found in it;
or if the character is expressed, it is in an altogether superficial manner. On one side there is the story, on the other
the music. If the scene represents a fight, the orchestra
makes a loud noise, but this loud noise is not a fight, it
does not contain the *atmosphere* of a fight, the music gives
no indication of how the hero has come to such a pass. . . .

Moussorgski is so keenly aware of all the scents of a garden and all the smells of a tavern, he describes them so
vividly in his music, that the audience actually inhales all
the varied perfumes.

That is undeniably realism. But it is a particular kind
of realism; it makes me think of the Russian moujiks, who
arm themselves with clumsy beams and primitive axes
(they have no other tools) with which to build a cathedral.
With their axes they make the most delicately fretted carvings, carvings that can stand comparison with the finest
examples of woodwork.

CHAPTER XLI

Gaucherie: The timidity of Rimski-Korsakov: The aristocratic quality of his work: His lyricism and reserve: Tchaikovski's tears and the tears of Rimski-Korsakov: The sorrow that gives birth to joy: Sniegourotchka *and* The City of Kitège: *A nameless prayer*

<o><o>

Russians OFTEN REVEAL an incurable awkwardness that irritates me immensely, though I find it in some ways pathetic. My irritation is caused by the knowledge that it is really the reflection of our long years of slavery. I look on foreigners with envy — their actions are so free and easy, their speech is so untrammelled. This free-and-easiness is not always displayed in the best of taste, but I always feel that in some way it expresses the personality and inalienable dignity of the European. It is, moreover, a legacy of the great plastic culture of the West.

The soul of the Russian is as free as the wind, his thoughts are as daring as eagles, nightingales trill in his heart; but look at him in a drawing-room — he is sure to overturn a chair, spill his tea, or make a blunder of some sort. Address him at a banquet: he will be ill at ease, stammer out a few words, and stop in confusion.

All this doubt and hesitation is in all probability the result of the long subservience of the Russian boyar to the tzar, the Russian serf to the landed proprietor, the Rus-

sian subject to the law. Too often have they been told:
"Be quiet! Nobody asked you for your opinion!"

This gaucherie was undoubtedly responsible for the fact
that every work conducted by that most famous magician
of music, Rimski-Korsakov, was doomed to failure. He
held himself stiffly, raised his baton with embarrassment,
and waved it as deprecatingly as though he were apolo-
gizing for being alive. . . .

The most striking element in Rimski-Korsakov's music
is its aristocratic quality. His work, though overflowing
with lyricism, has an exquisite reserve in the expression
of emotion, and it is this very reserve that gives his music
such delicate charm. An example will better illustrate my
meaning.

When Tchaikovski, the wonderful composer so dear to
us all, expressed sorrow in music, he always introduced a
personal element into both his songs and his symphonic
poems. (I am not now speaking of his impersonal work,
such as *Eugene Onegin* or his ballet-music.) " Life is melancholy, my friends," he seems to say; " love is dead, the
leaf is withered, old age and sickness are upon us." This
sorrow is quite permissible, because it is human; nevertheless it narrows the scope of the music. Beethoven, too, expressed sorrow, but his sorrow is ineffable and illimitable;
it cannot be defined in words, but we are conscious of its
presence. If you fall through space, you cannot clutch at a
star, and yet the star is there. Now take Tchaikovski's
Sixth Symphony; it is beautiful, but it is permeated by
the personal grief of the composer. And this personal grief,
sincere as it is, weighs heavily on the listener.

There is sadness, too, in Rimski-Korsakov's work, but,
curiously enough, it awakens a feeling of joy. You are conscious of nothing *personal* in his sorrow — its dark wings
plane high above the earth.

His famous setting of Poushkin's *On the Hills of Geor-
gia* in some measure sums up all his work.

Rimski-Korsakov

I feel sorrowful and insubstantial; my grief is transfigured . . .
My desolation is far beyond the reach of torment and terror.

Here we have the same sense of infinite and ineffable
"desolation" to which I referred when speaking of
Beethoven's music.

Ostrovski, the great Russian dramatist, refusing to write
any more society comedies, went one day to the edge of
the forest and played a hymn to the setting sun on a reed
pipe; he wrote *Sniegourotchka*. What luminous and trans-
parent simplicity there is in the sound of Rimski-Korsakov's reed pipe! You hear the music of an Easter holiday,
the orchestra plays *Kyrie Eleison,* and the joy that comes to
you when you hear the glad tidings at Easter matins now
fills your soul as you listen to the music of that same
Rimski-Korsakov, so sombre, taciturn, reserved, and silent
in real life.

Anyone who has heard *The City of Kitège* must have
been struck by the astonishing poetic strength and lim-
pidity of Rimski-Korsakov's music. When I heard this
opera for the first time, I saw a mental picture that thrilled
me with joy. I visualized humanity, living and dead, assembled on a mysterious planet. This planet, with its
knights and warriors, kings, tzars, high priests, and countless mass of mortality, was wrapped in shadow. But in the
darkness all faces were turned towards the horizon; triumph-
phant, serene, radiant with faith, all waited for the dawning of the star. And in a perfect harmony the living and
the dead intoned a nameless and inspired prayer. . . .

This prayer was in the soul of Rimski-Korsakov.

CHAPTER XLII

The tzars and the Imperial Theatres: An anecdote of Nicholas I and Karatyguin: My visits to the box of Nicholas II: Private concerts given by the Grand Dukes in honour of the Tzar: My glass of champagne: A Venetian glass goblet: The Grand Duchess and her comment on my taste for destruction: A bon mot *that was not appreciated: A fancy-dress ball at the Hermitage: Compliments from the Grand Duke Vladimir Alexandrovitch, and my political sally*

ᗌᙣ ᗌᙣ

IN COMPLETE CONTRAST to Moscow, whose tone was set by the merchant class and the intelligentsia, the tone of St. Petersburg was set by the aristocracy and officials of high rank. I frequented " society " in Petersburg as little as I had done in Moscow, but my position as a singer at the Imperial Opera often made it compulsory for me to appear at entertainments given by those belonging to the great world.

The eminent " patrons " generally paid but scant attention to the Imperial Theatres.

Catherine II was interested in the stage, but her attitude towards the theatre in her capital was very similar to that of the feudal lord towards the peasant actors who had been chosen from among his serfs to divert him. There is no indication that Alexander I was interested in theatrical matters. He was too much engrossed in that theatre of war where Napoleon, the greatest actor of his time, was treading the boards. . . .

[167]

Of all the emperors of Russia, it was Nicholas I who showed the greatest interest in the theatre. His attitude was not that of an overlord towards his serfs; it was that of a magnate and potentate. Moreover, when he condescended to talk to the actors, it was in tones that were majestic and at the same time friendly; he often entered at the stage-door, for he liked to chat with the actors — especially dramatic actors — and laugh at the witty speeches of his most gifted subjects.

There is an amusing story in connexion with one of these royal visits behind the scenes.

Appearing on the stage during an interval, Nicholas I addressed Karatyguin, one of the most celebrated actors of the time, and said with a laugh:

" Karatyguin, your impersonations are excellent — you can imitate anyone. It always amuses me."

Karatyguin thanked the Tzar for the compliment, and replied:

" It's true, Your Majesty, I can impersonate both tzars and beggars."

" I'm sure you could not impersonate *me*," laughed the Emperor.

" With Your Majesty's permission, I will give an imitation of you on the spot," said Karatyguin.

The Tzar, who was in good humour at the moment, was intrigued by the idea. Looking at Karatyguin, he said, more seriously this time:

" Very well, then, try. . . ."

Karatyguin immediately assumed Nicholas I's most familiar attitude, and, turning to Guedeonov, the director of the Imperial Theatres, who happened to be present, said in a voice exactly like the Emperor's:

" Listen, Guedeonov. Give orders that from midday tomorrow Karatyguin's salary is to be doubled."

The Tzar could not restrain a smile. " Pretty good, that! "

He took leave of the actors and quitted the stage. Next day, sure enough, Karatyguin found that his salary *had* been doubled!

Alexander II hardly ever visited the theatre except on state occasions. Dramatic art left him cold. Alexander III enjoyed the opera, and was especially fond of Boito's *Mephistopheles*. He had a predilection for the prologue when the trombones re-echo in the mists at the foot of Sabaoth's throne. He loved the summons of the trombones, for he had a passion for this instrument and would play on it himself.

The late Tzar, Nicholas II, loved Tchaikovski's wonderful ballets better than anything, but he also went to the theatre and the opera. I have seen him in his box laughing heartily at Varlamov or Davidov.

Although Nicholas II did not go behind the scenes like Nicholas I, he sometimes condescended to invite actors into his box during the intervals. Amongst others, I was invited into the royal box. The manager would come up to me, and say:

" Follow me, Chaliapin, the Tzar wishes to see you."

I would appear before the Tzar in my make-up as Boris, Mephistopheles, or Holophernes, as the case might be.

The Tzar would congratulate me.

" You sang very well."

But I could not shake off the impression that it was curiosity that was responsible for the summons: the royal party had wanted to see at close quarters how I was made up, and how I had stuck on my false nose and beard. I thought so because there were always Grand Duchesses and ladies-in-waiting in the box, and when I entered, they all stared sedulously at my make-up. Their eyes missed no detail of my false nose and beard, and they asked politely, with many little affectations:

" How do you keep your nose on? With plaster? "

Sometimes I was invited by the Tzar to sing at his

palace, or, to be more accurate, at the palace of the Grand Duke whom he was visiting without ceremony after dinner.

Usually the invitation was issued in this manner:

One of the Grand Duke's couriers would come to my house post-haste.

"The Grand Duke has ordered me to tell you that the Tzar is visiting him tonight and has expressed a wish to hear you sing."

I would dress and go to the Grand Duke's palace. On these occasions other artistes besides myself would be invited. Sometimes it was T. I. Philippov's Russian Choir, or the Precentor of the Holy Synod, or the Archiepiscopal Choir.

I remember a curious incident that took place on one of these occasions. After the concert the Imperial family withdrew into an adjoining drawing-room, probably to drink champagne. A few minutes later the Grand Duke Serge Mikhailovitch brought me some champagne in a marvellous Venetian goblet on a small silver salver. He stopped in front of me, drew himself up to his full height, and said, still holding the tray:

"Chaliapin, the Tzar has asked me to offer you a glass of champagne to thank you for your singing, and so that you may drink His Majesty's health."

I took the goblet, emptied it in silence, and, to dispel a certain embarrassment that had arisen, I looked at the Grand Duke, lowered my eyes to the salver he was still holding, and said:

"I beg that Your Highness will be good enough to tell His Majesty that Chaliapin is keeping the goblet in memory of this never-to-be-forgotten event."

There was nothing for the Grand Duke to do but to smile and bear out the tray.

A little while after this I was again summoned to the royal box. One of the Grand Duchesses showed me her gloves, which she had split by her repeated clapping, and said:

"You see what you've done. You are evidently one of those artistes who have a weakness for destruction. Last time you broke up my set of twelve Venetian goblets."

In my deepest voice I replied:

"Your Highness, it is an easy matter to complete the set by sending the eleven remaining goblets to keep the missing one company."

The Grand Duchess smiled graciously, but she did not take me at my word. So the Venetian glass goblet remained solitary in my possession.

Who has it now, I wonder. . . .

The daily life of the court was not, I imagine, wildly exhilarating, and its pleasures were rare. But at times some extravagant *divertissement* would be planned, such as a costume ball, accompanied by a performance of some kind. This would take place in the little Hermitage Theatre, which belonged to the court.

The invitations issued to the nobles and great families indicated what costumes were to be worn. They were nearly always Russian dresses of the sixteenth or seventeenth centuries. It was somewhat fantastic to hear the Russian aristocrats conversing with a slight foreign accent and to see them sumptuously but tastelessly tricked out as boyars of the seventeenth century. They looked so like puppets that one was conscious of embarrassment while watching the *divertissement,* the more so as it was totally devoid of gaiety. The Tzar took his seat in the centre of the theatre with a solemn and dignified air, whilst we, disguised as seventeenth-century boyars, acted a scene from *Boris Godounov.*

I maltreated Prince Chouiski in good earnest; I took him by the collar of the cloak which I, Godounov, had given him, and forced him to his knees. . . . The boyars in the theatre applauded vigorously. . . .

A Political Sally

At the end of the scene I was making towards the lounge when the old Grand Duke Vladimir Alexandrovitch came up to me, congratulated me, and said:

" In your scene with Chouiski, you acted with great power and sense of character."

To which I replied:

" I did my best, Your Highness, to draw the attention of those whom it may concern to the manner in which boyars should sometimes be treated. . . ."

The Grand Duke had not foreseen this reply. He looked at me with raised brows; for the moment, no doubt, he thought he had heard in my words the motif of the *Doubinouchka,* the workers' song, but he suddenly realized that I was alluding to Peter the Great's cudgel, and burst out laughing.

Had the meaning of my words been understood by the Tzar, most probably the second half of my book would not have been devoted to the description of my life under the Soviet Government.

Part II

IN THE POLITICAL AND
REVOLUTIONARY WHIRLPOOL

MY LIFE UNDER THE
BOLSHEVIKS
ॐ ॐ

IN THE POLITICAL AND REVOLUTIONARY WHIRLPOOL

CHAPTER I

My whole-hearted love of the theatre: My disgust of all politics: A paradox which requires an explanation

ᔥ ᔥ

IF I HAVE been anything in life, I have been an actor and singer; I have given myself entirely to my vocation. Outside the theatre I have had no binding tie, no pronounced inclination. True, I took pleasure in drawing, but must regretfully admit that my ability was doubtful; I ruined many pencils and much paper in a ceaseless attempt to create new artistic make-up and stage pictures that should be more natural and characteristic. Even my great love for the old masters has been no more to me than an echo of my passion for the theatre, where, as in painting, great work can only be achieved by harmonious line, glowing colour, and depths of spiritual meaning.

Politics have interested me less than anything. My whole nature revolts against them. Perhaps this is the outcome of my small knowledge of worldly matters, and of my ever-present desire, at all times, in all circumstances, for peace, understanding, and mutual sympathy. In my clumsy language, I have always declared that a man who can say to another with all his heart: " Hail, friend," possesses the greatest knowledge, the highest wisdom, the most living religion. I am disturbed and made wretched by anything that stirs up division.

It has always seemed to me that every man assumes a social and conventional uniform that does not in reality correspond with his nature or establish his dignity and superiority. It has always seemed to me as though uniform were in constant conflict with uniform, and that to quell these conflicts one more uniform has been thought out — that of the police! Religious disputes, international rivalries, patriotic boasts, intrigues, and party quarrels have always seemed to me to be the negation of that which is most precious in life — concord. I have always believed that a man should be approached straightforwardly, not circuitously, and that he should be judged, not by his breeding, nationality, and party-opinions, but by his actions and ethical codes.

My naïve ideas hardly square with the no doubt inevitable need for party politics, and so these have always bored and disturbed me. To this day, even after the experiences I lived through in my years under the Soviet Government, I am unable to consider the events that took place from a political angle, or to judge them as a politician. Humanity is all that counts in my eyes. Men's actions, good or bad, merciful or cruel, the freedom or enslavement of their souls, discord or harmony — these things, as I see them quite simply, constitute the sum of my interest. If roses bloom on a bush, I know it is a rose-bush. If a régime fetters my liberty and imposes on me fetishes that I am forced to adore even though they sicken me, I disown that régime — not because it is called Bolshevism or anything else, but simply because my whole soul revolts against it.

This attitude of mine towards life and men may appear anarchistic. I do not deny it. Possibly there is a grain of artistic anarchism in my composition. At all events, it does not arise from indifference to good and evil. I have always lived my life to the full. Many people will, no doubt, be surprised to learn that, for nearly twenty years, I sympathized to such an extent with the Socialist movement in Russia that I considered myself almost a perfect Socialist. . . . I remember distinctly the question I launched point-blank at Maxim Gorki, one night, when we were walking on the marvellous island of Capri.

"Don't you think I should be acting more sincerely, Alexis Maximovitch, if I joined the Social-Democratic party?" I asked.

But I never did join it, simply because Gorki looked at me sharply, and said in a friendly voice:

"You're not made in that mould. Listen to what I tell you, and never forget it: never join any party. Be an artist —in other words, be yourself. Nothing more will ever be asked of you."

That a man of artistic temperament, with anarchistic tendencies, loathing politics, could have considered himself a Socialist and have felt so strongly in sympathy with the Socialist movement that he was prepared against all reason to identify himself with a revolutionary party — this is a paradox that can only be explained by the spirit of Russia. In order to understand it, the events which were shaping the course of Russian history from the beginning of the twentieth century, and the attitude of the thinking classes, must be borne in mind. As far as I personally am concerned, it will not be without interest to describe my first experiences of life in Russia.

CHAPTER II

Life in Russia: Childhood memories: An unhappy world: Poverty and arduous toil: The existence of the peasants: The misery of the big cities: Drunkenness, brutality, suffering: Inequality between the rich and the poor: An ill-planned world

✐ ✐

Wᴴᴇɴ I ᴡᴀѕ quite little, I learnt the following couplet in the village school:

> *Field, my field, my golden one,*
> *Your corn-ears ripen in the sun.*

One day, I went for a walk. A meadow stretched endlessly before my eyes. The corn was high, its yellow ears waved on long stalks. I was enchanted with the meadow, and when I got home, I asked my mother:

" What is a field of gold, Mother? "

" A golden field," was all she said.

" A yellow field? "

" No, golden, made of gold. There is money like that, made of shining, precious metal. . . ."

" Who's got money? "

" Rich people."

" Haven't we got any? "

" No. . . ."

Later on, at three o'clock in the morning, I heard the old moujiks groan as they left their rough beds, and sigh

[178]

as they took their scythes and reaping-hooks for the day's toil.

"Why are they getting up so early? Why don't they go on sleeping?" I asked again.

"They're going to work in the fields."

"What work do they do?"

"They're getting in the harvest — the harvest in the golden fields. . . ."

I realized that the golden fields were the source of much trouble and care to the moujiks. From that time onward I was engrossed in the moujiks. On holidays they got drunk. They swore at one another and fought, but they also sang songs. How beautiful they were, the songs of the moujiks! They sang of flowing rivers, and boats gliding along the Volga, they sang of the old man who beat his wife, and of the maiden who weeps because she is betrothed against her will. They sang of brigands, Turks, and Tartars; they sang of tzars, Ivan the Terrible, great lords, and of many, many dignitaries and merchants. . . . All that I saw in the village gathered in my brain in a confused and oppressive mass; I could not understand why life was so unjust. . . .

When, later on, I went to the big town of Kazan, I saw and felt that the dwellers in the Soukonnaia Sloboda shared the same hard lot. I saw that they lived unhappily and shed many tears; I saw suffering, cruel and brutal customs, debauchery. . . .

It was when I lived in a town that I first realized the difference between rich and poor. I noticed that the wealthy merchant had more pull with the police than Sachka, the indigent shoemaker. Even in church the priest offered the Communion bread and wine with more unction to Souslov, the merchant, than to any mere Isaac this or that. It never entered my head that there was any injustice in these things. I was positive that God Himself held the rich in specially high esteem. How could it be otherwise? The merchant had a well-filled belly, a new *poddievka*, and brilliantly varnished boots, while Sachka was thin, ragged, and badly shod and had a perpetual bruise under one eye or the other. . . . The superiority of the rich seemed as it should be. I did not guess that my opinion was also held by the famous German philosopher who said: " All that exists conforms to reason." . . . When a policeman shouted at me that I was not allowed to bathe in the lake, I did not question his right to forbid me; all I did was to plunge deeper in, and fright made me stay in the water until the storm had subsided. . . .

I became a clerk at the law-court. I took for granted the magistrate's disagreeable and unapproachable air and trembled at the mere sight of his wig. . . . At home all I heard was talk about governors, magistrates, and district police-superintendents, and terror seized upon me. By a curious coincidence, every one of these titles contained the letter " r," and this rolling, authoritative " r " vibrated like an echo of menace in my shrinking soul. Strangely enough, the fear of authority that filled my childhood has remained with me all my life. Even today I am still conscious of it, although I am not quite clear what it is I fear. . . .

That life could be reconstructed, that it could be rendered less sordid and unjust, never occurred to me until, when I had reached manhood, I underwent the cruel and bitter hardships of the Volga and Caucasus wanderers — endless toil, nights with no roof for shelter, days of starvation. . . . And yet, truth to tell, physical deprivations did not prevent my being very happy. My youthful voice boomed from my strong chest, there was music in the world, and in the sky I saw the glimmer of a faraway, enthralling dream — the constellated lights of the theatre. . . .

CHAPTER III

*In the capital: I learn that enlightened people are endeavouring
to improve the conditions of Russian life, make the people happier,
and teach them to become masters of their fate: Through Rachmaninov I discover Maxim Gorki: I become his ardent admirer:
I espouse the cause of the revolutionaries: Outside the realm of
politics, I share their aspirations*

꧁ ꧂

IT WAS NOT until much later, when I arrived in the capital as a young singer, that I realized that men were making
ready to reform this world of ours where injustice and
cruelty held sway.

The more I mixed with writers, scholars, and men of
advanced ideas, the more I realized how little I knew,
how little I had learnt. And I longed to assimilate some
part at least of the knowledge of these remarkable men.

I have always felt an instinctive admiration for those
who have studied much, thought deeply, and are in some
way vital. When I had an opportunity of meeting them,
I did my utmost to cultivate their acquaintance. At clubs
and small dinners I listened to their conversation and
gathered that they were attacking the Tzar and the Government; they spoke of the enslavement of the Russian
people, to whom all progress was barred. Some of these
enlightened men, I learnt later, were members of secret
revolutionary societies . . . the logic of all they said persuaded me that they were in the right.

[181]

My sympathy with them gradually grew — especially as I realized that they were genuinely ready to sacrifice themselves for the good of the people. I was sincerely shocked when any of them were arrested and thrown into prison by the authorities. In my eyes, it was a fearful breach of justice, and I tried my utmost to help these visionaries who were fighting in the cause of my countrymen.

One thing only troubled me: I found that differences of opinion on love and hate were rife amongst these men I loved.

Some of them held that force was necessary to obtain right, and they exalted the enormous mass strength of the Russian people; if its scattered units could be welded into one, they said, it would be capable of governing the whole world.

" Like a dæmon, I can control the universe! . . ."

Others, on the contrary, maintained that physical force was useless, that the people would only be truly powerful when its soul was awakened, when it was capable of understanding that resistance to evil is the inspiration of hell, and that the other cheek must be turned. . . . Both sides had ardent followers and enthusiastic disciples who defended their convictions almost to the point of delirium.

From my standpoint as an actor — a limited standpoint, perhaps — it seemed to me that there could not be *two* truths, that truth is a single entity . . . but I did not go very deeply into these niceties. What really affected me was my friends' struggle to attain beauty and justice and truth in life. I was filled with the thought that the darkness of the people would one day be lit with a new light, that men would shed fewer tears, endure less senseless and brutal hardship, and no longer seek to find in drink a gross and morbid pleasure. My whole soul went out to the torch-bearers, and with them I dreamed that the Revolution would make a clean sweep of the vicious system based on injustice, and clear the way for a régime that would achieve the happiness of the Russian people.

One man in particular influenced me greatly. This was Alexis Maximovitch Piechkov — Maxim Gorki. His ardent faith and example tightened my bonds with the Socialists; no one could have inspired me with more confidence than he did with his extraordinary enthusiasm.

I remember when I heard the name of Gorki mentioned for the first time by my friend Serge Rachmaninov. It was in Moscow. Rachmaninov came to my house in the rue Leontiev one day, a book in his hand.

"Read that," he said. "A wonderful new writer has arisen in our midst. I should say he's quite young."

I think the book was Gorki's earliest work: *Malva, Makar, Tchoudra,* and other stories, which he wrote at the beginning of his literary career. These stories impressed me enormously. His words found an echo in my soul, and when I re-read them today, I still feel that the towns and streets and characters he describes are familiar to me. Having seen them all with my own eyes, I never thought I could be so absorbed by reading about them in a book.

I wrote to the author at Nijni-Novgorod to tell him how much his book had interested me. No answer came to my letter. When I sang at the Exhibition of Nijni in 1896, I had still never met Gorki. I visited the town again in 1901 and sang at the theatre of the famous fair. One night, when *The Life of the Tzar* was being given, I was told that Gorki was amongst the audience and wanted to meet me. In the interval, I was confronted by a man who, though not good-looking, had a striking and unusual face. He had long, thick hair, a nose that was more comic than not, very prominent cheek-bones, and ardent, deep-set eyes that were singularly pure and limpid, like the clear waters of a lake. He had a moustache and small beard. With a slight smile, he extended his hand, pressed mine warmly, and said with the accent of the Volga district:

[183]

" I hear we both hail from the same part of the world."
" So I believe," I said.

From that first hand-shake, we felt instinctively drawn to each other (at least, I felt drawn to him). We met frequently. Sometimes he would fetch me from the theatre, even during the day-time, and we would go to Kounavino and eat *pelmens,*[1] our favourite dish. Sometimes I would go to his place, bare of comfort, but invariably crowded. All sorts and conditions of men were to be found there — dreamy, light-hearted, harassed, contemplative — but they were for the most part young men who had come to slake their thirst at the wonder-working spring that was Maxim Gorki.

Gorki's simplicity, goodness, and unaffectedness, his care-free look, his deep love for his small children, the tenderness, characteristic of those who come from the Volga province, for his charming wife — all this completely won my heart. " At last," I thought, " I have found a hearth where the meaning of hatred may be forgotten and where I may learn to live and love in joy and idyllic peace." Here I realized that if there exist on this earth men who are genuinely good and sincere in their love for the people, they are men of Gorki's stamp who, like him, have witnessed the misery and suffering of human existence and have seen the scars they leave. This realization added to my anguish and despair when Gorki was arrested, hurled into prison, and deported to the north.

I began to believe that the men who called themselves Socialists were of the elect, and my soul went out to them.

Later on, I stayed fairly often, in the spring and summer, at Capri, where Gorki was living (in a house which, I may add in passing, was not his own). The atmosphere of this house was revolutionary. I must admit that it was only the humanitarian enthusiasm of all the great idealists that interested and attracted me. When I tried to learn the

[1] Pies filled with chopped meat — a Siberian national dish.

theory of Socialism by reading Socialist pamphlets, I had scarcely read a page before I was overcome with an indescribable feeling of boredom and, yes, distaste.

And, anyhow, was there any need for me to know the exact number of watch-springs that can be made from a ton of steel? Was there any need for me to know the exact profit of the first exploiter and the second and the third, and the exact amount left for the "victimized" workman? It was simple enough to grasp that on one side there was the exploiter, on the other the exploited. To tell the truth, I had no desire to "adjust the scales between the parties."

So I despised the science of Socialism. . . . Which was a pity. For had I had a better understanding of it, had I realized that in the Soviet Revolution I was to lose all I had, down to my last coin, I might perhaps have saved some hundreds of thousands of roubles by sending abroad, at the right moment, Revolutionary Russian roubles to be converted into good bourgeois cash. . . .

CHAPTER IV

*First revolutionary manifestations: General Trepov, head of the
police-force in Moscow, disapproves of my tastes: I disapprove
of his politics: The Russo-Japanese War*

⁓ ⁓

IF I REFER to the past and try to decide when exactly
began the events that finally forced me to leave Russia,
I see how difficult it is to draw a dividing-line between this
or that phase of the Russian revolutionary movement:
there was a first revolution in 1905, a second which burst
out in March 1917, and the third and last, which took place
in October of the same year. People versed in politics
explain how one revolution differs from another; they
docket and pigeon-hole them. I must confess that I see all
these Russian revolutions *en bloc* — or, rather, like a chain,
each link of which is welded closely to the other. A huge
rock breaks loose from the mountain, throws its whole
weight on some obstacle which has too little power of
resistance — and rock and obstacle are precipitated headlong into the abyss. I have already said that caution and
moderation have no place in the Russian character; in
all things, in submission as well as in revolt, my com-
patriots go to the very extreme.

The revolutionary movement made itself felt at the beginning of the present century, but it was, if I may so
express it, a mere hothouse growth. It put out feelers in
universities and factories. But the people were apparently

content, and the Government was sure of its powers. The press was muzzled, and the dissatisfaction of the intelligentsia only manifested itself in timid allusions.

The voice of the Revolution spoke more daringly in literature and verse. Books containing revolutionary sentiments were eagerly snapped up, and any verse that expressed revolt unloosed public enthusiasm, no matter whether it was good or bad.

I recall a highly significant episode that took place at that time. A gala symphony concert was being given on the occasion of the inauguration of the new Conservatoire in Moscow (in V. Safonov's time). All Moscow was present. I was taking part in the concert. In those days the blood ran ardently in my veins, and I was heart and soul for the cause of liberty. The composer Sakhonovski had just set to music some verses by Melchin-Yakoubovitch, the Russian translator of Baudelaire. Yakoubovitch was reputed to be a revolutionary, and his verse bore incontrovertible witness to the truth of this. I put Sakhonovski's song down on the program for the concert and sang the *Invocation to my Country,* the words of which were said to have been translated from the Erse:

> *Why should we love you? Have you been to us*
> *A gentle mother? There was never found*
> *A stepmother who bore herself towards*
> *Her stepchildren so brutally as you,*
> *Who slew us, your own children, without pity. . . .*
> *You have interred us in the dayless night*
> *And scattered us to all the ends of the earth*
> *To freeze to death, deserted by our strength . . .*
> *Our dreams you trampled underneath your feet,*
> *You branded us like thieves with red-hot irons.*
> *Why should we love you? You have been to us*
> *No loving mother. . . . Yet each breath I draw,*
> *Each dream, each sigh, each heart-beat's ardent throb,*
> *Are dedicate to you until the last,*
> *Oh, Mother, all my life and love are yours!*

General Trepov

When I had finished, the audience applauded franti-
cally. In the interval, or it may have been at the end of the
concert, I saw General Trepov, chief of the police in Moscow, come into the artistes' room. He claimed to be one of
my admirers, and our relations were very cordial. Affable,
well-bred, faintly scented, clad in a magnificent uniform,
General Trepov, whose martial countenance was pitted
with smallpox, twisted the ends of his blond moustache,
and said persuasively:

"Feodor Ivanovitch, why do you sing such controver-
sial stuff? Come to think of it, these high-sounding words
are thoroughly stupid and uninteresting. You've such a
beautiful voice that I should like to hear you sing about
love, or nature. . . ."

He was a sentimentalist, no doubt. . . . And yet, even
as he spoke, I felt that the idea that I had committed a
breach of law and order was at the back of his mind under
cover of his friendly and flattering remarks. . . . I said
that the music was pretty, that I liked the words and
thought them beautiful, and that there was no reason on
earth why I should not sing them. . . . This time I pre-
tended not to hear my interrogator's political objections
and refused to discuss the matter any further.

On another occasion, however, I said to General Trepov:

"I agree that it's very pleasant to love one's mother
country above everything. But you must admit that the
wretched horse-trams in Moscow, besides being most in-
convenient, are a positive eyesore. Abroad they have elec-
tric trams. . . . But I am told that in Moscow their
construction is not allowed. It's the police who refuse permission. In fact, it is *you* who refuse."

This time the General was anything but sentimental.
He began to cough, like a deacon who has swallowed, or
is about to swallow, a glass of vodka, and growled angrily:

"Good God! It's no use talking of other countries!
Abroad they are human beings — our 'citizens' may think

[188]

themselves lucky to have horse-trams — let them make the best of it. . . ."

I am terrified of those in authority. Directly one of them begins to shout at me, I become as dumb as a fish. I was dumb on this occasion. Once in the street, still under Trepov's influence, I looked at the "citizens" with more than usual interest and saw, stumbling towards me, a man with a swelling on his cheek. A dirty bandage was tied clumsily over it, showing a wad of cotton-wool stained with yellow ointment. I said to myself:

" May the devil fly away with you, Mr. ' Citizen ' ! If only you had taken the horse-tram instead of passing under my very nose, I might have answered Trepov more easily. But even a horse-tram's too good for you, my poor man. . . . You are miserably wordless. You take everything too meekly, your toothache and the horse-tram and the head of the police. You only get your deserts. . . ."

But this apparent meekness was only an illusion. It was not long before the man with the bandaged face was protesting noisily. In 1904 it became obvious that the revolutionary movement had gone far deeper than had been thought. The Government, though bolstered up by an imposing array of police officers, tottered and weakened. This weakness proved that its hold on the country was not so strong as had been believed at first, and realization of this fact further roused the people. Disorders became more and more general. The universities were closed owing to anti-Government demonstrations among the students, the factory-hands went on strike, the liberal members of the zemstvos organized banquets at which speakers clamoured with premature audacity for political reform and lower taxation. Presently bombs exploded, blowing up a minister here, a governor there. . . .

At this period of unrest the war with Japan took Russian society by surprise. Moujiks went to war against the Japanese in far-off Korea. In the cabinet there was much speechifying about the high duty that was incumbent on a great power such as Russia, but amongst the masses it was rumoured that the war had been engineered by those influential at court for their own personal profit, so that they might obtain certain forest concessions on the Yalou in which they had an interest. The peasants wept and despaired. They agreed that they could "crush the yellow devils with almond eyes" with their caps, but that there was no need to go so far away to do it.

"After all, they don't come bothering us, they have a right to their own country. What business have we there?"

In the capitals it was said that from time to time wonder-working ikons were being sent to the Far East. . . . Alas! It was soon seen that these ikons could not turn the tide of war. . . . And when the Russian fleet under Admiral Rojdestvenski foundered in foreign waters, Russia was swept by a wave of anguish and despair. I, too, told myself that God no longer watched over my country with the love He had once borne it. . . .

CHAPTER V

*Defeat: The revolutionary movement spreads: Extreme distrust
of provincial administration: The police keep an eye on my tours:
The Kharkov censor and* The Two Grenadiers

ᔓ ᔓ

D ÉBÂCLE!

The revolutionary movement began to spread, and mutter ominously. This time the liberal parties made open
demands for a constitution, and the Socialists, feeling the
crisis approaching, prepared almost overtly for combat.
Changes were inevitable. The Government still held out
and refused to yield to what was officially called a riot, even
though this "riot" had shaken the entire country. Provincial functionaries seethed with energy. Those in favour
of the necessary reforms did their utmost to ameliorate
prevailing conditions, those against them did all that was
possible to sting the people to submission more sharply
than before, like flies in autumn. Their eyes dilated, and
they suspected everyone, without exception, of being a
revolutionary.

More than once at this time I fell under the acute suspicion of provincial administrations. I don't know whether
this attitude was maintained towards all actors as the result
of a general order, or whether it was only I who had incurred their mistrust because I was known to have revolutionary tendencies, was a friend of Gorki's, and was, in a

sense, more "dangerous" than the others on account of my great popularity in the country.

During the course of a tour of the big country towns, I arrived at Tambov very late on the night before my concert. I went to bed with the intention of sleeping late and getting a good rest, but the administration decided otherwise. At eight o'clock the next morning there was a knock at the door. It was the Superintendent of Police. He apologized for his early intrusion very politely and explained that it was due to an official order from the Governor.

"What's the matter?" I asked.

The matter was this: the Governor had been informed that I, Chaliapin, intended to give a political harangue in the middle of my concert!

It was thoroughly absurd, of course, and I hastened to reassure the Governor's emissary as to my intentions. But the gentleman still insisted, politely but firmly, on my handing over my sheets of music for the Governor's scrutiny. There was nothing for it but to hand them over, and they were returned to me the same evening. The Governor of Tambov treated me gently, as you see. But quite a different reception awaited me at Kharkov.

On my arrival in that town, I was informed that the head of the Censorship Department had given orders for me to appear before him. "Given orders," and "appear before him," indeed! Of course, I could have refused to go. He had nothing to do with the matter. The concert had been authorized and the bills posted up. Spurred by curiosity, however, I went. I had never in my life seen a censor in the flesh. I had heard a lot about them and had been told that many of them were intelligent and educated men. I don't know why, but I pictured the Kharkov censor as unkempt and covered with hairy warts. This picture was enough to make me want to see the overseer of political loyalism, and accordingly I went. I was announced and shown into his room.

The Two Grenadiers

The censor had no hairy warts and was in no way unkempt. He was a weak-looking individual with red spots
on his face. At the first sound of his voice, I was aware that
I had to do with a particularly rare specimen of the type.
His voice grated like a Caucasian *arba* whose wheels need
greasing. Most extraordinary of all was the way in which
he addressed me.

" What are you going to sing? "

" My usual repertoire."

" Show me the music."

I showed it to him. With dry, nervous fingers he turned
the pages. Suddenly he started and, ready to give battle,
stared threateningly at me.

" Emperor. . . . What emperor is this? "

I looked. It was *The Two Grenadiers.*

" That's Schumann's celebrated song, Mr. Censor."

He threw me an angry glance, which said plainly:
" None of your Mr. Censors. . . ."

" The words are Heine's, Your Excellency. The song
has been passed by the Board of Censors."

In his grating voice, and with the fixed intention of
crushing me finally, His Excellency read in accusing tones:
" ' The Emperor arises from his tomb.' From what tomb?
And what emperor? "

" A foreign emperor, Your Excellency, Napoleon. . . ."

He contracted the faintly marked brows on his spotty
face.

" I am told that you also sing without music."

" I do, Excellency," I said in the tones of an obedient
subject.

" You are aware that I shall be at the concert? "

" I am extremely flattered, Your Excellency."

" Not only to hear *how* you sing, but also *what* you sing.
And I advise you to be very careful, sir! "

I left him, feeling utterly dumbfounded. If I was not
roused to indignation by his manner of addressing me,

it was because he was too ridiculously petty and had really amused me. What had bitten him? I was never able to elucidate the mystery. To conclude, when I reached Kiev, I learnt that the authorities in Petersburg had sent a warning circular to the provinces to the effect that a close watch was to be kept on my concerts. The Kharkov censor had been seized by panic, and that was why he had " gnashed his teeth " in so stupid and ludicrous a fashion.

CHAPTER VI

A deputation of the workers of Kiev: A paradoxical scheme: A game of cards with the Governor: A confidential police circular

ໜ ໜ

IT WAS AT Kiev in the spring of 1905 that I got my first strong impression of the imminence of revolution. Chance threw me into direct contact with the mass of the workers, and I committed an " offence " which the guardians of law and order found it hard to forgive.

It was at Kiev that I first sang in public the celebrated workers' song *Doubinouchka*. I had come to the town to give several concerts which had been organized by an impresario. When they heard of my arrival, some workers of my acquaintance came to see me and asked me if I would visit them at Dimievka, a slum suburb. I readily accepted, and my friends did their best to give me a good reception. I wandered through the streets with them, I entered their hovels and realized sadly the misery of their existence. Numbers of people are unhappy, I thought, it is impossible to rescue the whole world, and though it is a good thing to help one or two, it has no effect on the general wretchedness. I went home full of these painful impressions.

A few days later the workers came to see me again. They asked if I could give their comrades a chance to hear me sing in the theatre.

If I could have acceded to their request, I should have been only too happy, but it was not so easy as they imagined. They believed that Chaliapin had "only to stand in the square and give tickets away. . . ." But what about the impresario, the theatre, the other singers, the chorus, the orchestra, the various supernumeraries? Was it possible to give tickets away for nothing? But I realized how much the workers wanted to hear me, and longed to gratify them. So I hit upon the following plan:

I would hire the Kroutikov Hall, which seated about 4,500. I would give 4,000 tickets to the workers — they could get up a sweep in the factories, all who drew lucky numbers to have a seat. The remaining 500 tickets I would sell to defray expenses. The workers were delighted with my plan, and I set about organizing the concert.

It was simple enough to hire the hall, and I did that straight away. But I could not appear in public without special permission. In ordinary cases there is no difficulty, permission is granted by the head of the police, but my concert was quite out of the ordinary. . . . The head of the police, I thought, would not take it on himself to grant permission — I should have to apply to the Governor-General of Kiev. I did not particularly like it, but luckily I remembered that I had recently met the Governor's wife, a charming woman who adored artistes — and *vint*[1] as much as she did artistes. "I'll start the campaign," I thought, "with Nadejda Guerasimova" (I think that was her name) "as an ally"; and, with this idea, I succeeded in getting an invitation to play cards at her house.

I played several hands and bided my time. You know how amiable you feel if you make a *chelem*. You grow more and more cordial and good-humoured, everything looks rose-coloured. As soon, then, as she had scooped in all the tricks, I said casually:

"Nadejda Guerasimova, I hate to bother your husband, and yet I fear I must."

"Why, what's the matter?"

---

[1] A card game rather like whist.

"Well, I want to get up a concert for the poor and the workers. It isn't right that everyone but they can hear me sing. We are living in difficult times, you know, there's a widespread unrest. If I don't sing for the workers, they'll be angry. It all depends on your husband whether I give this concert or not. . . . No bid."

Nadejda Guerasimova was in a winning vein. She made another *chelem*.

"Why are you so nervous? My husband's a very kind-hearted man. He's known in Kiev for his goodness and intelligence. He'll be back in half an hour, I expect. You can fix it up with him."

"I can count on you, if necessary, can't I, dear Nadejda Guerasimova?"

"Your songs are so persuasive — they charm everybody. Yes, you may count on me."

An hour later I was in her husband's study. The Governor had indeed a delightful personality. His air was imposing, he had a flowing beard and wore a military uniform with embroidered facings. In a voice as deliberate as his manner, he said slowly, in reply to my request:

"Hm — let me see. . . . Of course. . . . Yes, yes . . . I see . . . a concert for — for the working-classes — it's a very delicate matter. . . . Hm. . . . Yes. . . . It's a very nice idea, of course, and I would give permission with pleasure, but — there is a difficulty — I really cannot explain — but there it is — I haven't the authority. . . ."

I was very much surprised, and involuntarily I spoke in the Governor's tones:

"But — hm — I don't understand, Your Excellency. . . . What do you mean by not having the authority?"

"I'm sorry; it is so. I haven't the authority. . . . But I can trust you, Chaliapin. I have admired you as a singer for a long time. A singer like yourself must necessarily be a good fellow. I'll tell you the trouble, if you'll swear never to breathe a word."

The Governor opened a large file which lay on his desk. He searched through it, drew out a paper, held it out to me, and said:

" Read this."

" It's very indiscreet of me," I thought, when I saw at the head of the sheet the word " Confidential " heavily underlined. In the left-hand corner where the initials M.V.D. (Minister of the Interior, in Russian), beneath which were the words " Department of Police." Then followed the usual text:

" It has come to our notice that the singer Chaliapin has started on a tour of all the towns in the Russian Empire to give a series of concerts and other performances as an excuse for revolutionary propaganda; you are commanded by these presents to keep a particularly careful watch on all concerts given by the said Chaliapin."

I have always believed that the press knew more about my movements than I did myself. Now I realized that the Department of Police knew even more about them than the press! I showed my astonishment. But at the same time I felt that the man before me was not a mere official, but a good sort, and accordingly I began to confide in him. I assured him with the utmost sincerity that I had no intention of spreading revolutionary propaganda, and that I simply wished to give a concert for those people who could not afford to pay, as I had already done several times previously. In addition, I made him see that a refusal to grant permission would have a very painful effect on the workers and would greatly increase their dissatisfaction with the authorities. The General understood, granted me permission, and thought it right to add:

" I have nothing more to do with the affair. It lies now in the hands of the head of the police and the District Commissioner. You must deal with them as best you can."

Breakfast in a bathroom: My free concert for the workers: I set the troops in motion: The concert hall is crowded: I become an acrobat: I sing the Doubinouchka

෨ ෨

THE HEAD OF the police at Kiev showed himself very favourably disposed towards me. He said he had no objection to make on the score of the concert. However, a new difficulty arose, which had to be got over somehow or other. My conversation with the deputation of workers had decided me that it would be better if some of the workers themselves were appointed to keep law and order in the hall. They informed me that the presence of uniformed police might create irritation and cause trouble. It was incumbent on me to see the District Commissioner on this matter, and accordingly I went to his house.

This official was a strange and comical personage. When I rang, a young Ukrainian girl — a servant, no doubt — opened the door, and on my inquiring if I might see the chief, she said she would take in my name.

"Oi think His Honour be in his bath," she said, as she withdrew.

She came back a moment later and informed me that His Honour *was* in his bath, but that he begged me to come into the bathroom. I remembered the famous anecdote about Napoleon and Madame de Staël, and thought

[199]

that the Commissioner must also be of the opinion that genius has no sex. . . . There was nothing for it but to enter the bathroom. You may imagine how fortunate it was for me to find His Honour in such favourable surroundings! I had prepared a summary of my speech . . . alas, I was unable to make use of it. . . .

"Good morning, sir, good morning!" exclaimed His Honour with a strong Ukrainian accent. "I'm damn glad you've come to see me. Shall we drink to your health?"

He was sitting in the bath up to his chest in the water, from which his fat white shoulders emerged. Beneath his mottled nose bristled a mouse-coloured moustache. His eyebrows were so thick and bushy that they would have made half a dozen pairs; a huge, somewhat hoarse laugh issued from the depths of his submerged belly, as he said he would like to drink my health, and he opened his mouth so wide that I could see the gold fillings and the stains on his teeth.

There was a plank across the bath. On this was a bottle of vodka, which had already been seriously reduced, some sort of jelly, and a plate of pickled cucumbers. Although I thought it a most unseasonable hour to drink, I also thought it would be equally unseasonable for me to refuse. . . . I immediately assumed the aspect of a gay dog who loves good living, and sat down on a small stool beside the bath.

"Kvitoki!" shouted His Honour.

The maid appeared, and he ordered her to bring another glass at once.

"And so you've come to see me, eh?" he went on. "Splendid. . . . You know, I'm my own doctor . . . I've never been to a university, but I've got my own ideas. . . . Fancy, they say you shouldn't drink vodka, because it'll burn a hole in your stomach. . . . All right — I soak myself for ten minutes in cold water, and that puts out the flames. . . ."

FEODOR CHALIAPIN

I said that I, too, had not much faith in doctors, and had a weakness for popular remedies.

" It's true, then, that you're one of the people? "

We clinked glasses, emptied them, and ate cucumbers.

" I've come to talk to you about this concert, Your Honour. . . . Pardon me, I didn't quite catch your name? "

I heard something that sounded like " Akakii Ehrisanfovitch." . . .

I explained my business to him.

His Honour raised himself a little higher out of the water and treated me to a perfect view of his hairy chest.

" Yes, but what I want to know is this — why are you giving this concert for the workers, and why free? We have hundreds of thousands of workers. Has the Governor given you permission? "

" Yes, and so has the Chief of the Police. But I was told that I must come to you too," I lied.

His Honour began to hem and haw.

" Well, if the Governor and the Chief of the Police have given their consent, what do you want *me* to do? "

When I had explained exactly what it was I wanted him to do, he stared, began to chew furiously at the piece of cucumber which had been in his mouth for the last five minutes, and sighed heavily; then in tones like dough which has refused to rise he said feebly:

" It isn't nice of you to humbug me like this when we're having such an enjoyable breakfast. . . ." Then, much more firmly, he added in a serious voice: " You must excuse me, but I can't consent to that. The police must be present in the hall. I couldn't have such goings-on. . . ."

I acquiesced, but threw out a suggestion:

" The uniform is the only thing that's a nuisance, Akakii Ehrisanfovitch. Send as many plain-clothes men as you like."

" That's not half a bad idea! For your sake I'll do that with pleasure."

We drank another glass of vodka. His Honour rose in the bath, picked up a small towel, hugged it to his belly, dried his right hand as well as he could, held it out to me, and assured me that he liked all artistes, especially those who had risen from the people. We parted good friends.

I was overjoyed. Everything had gone splendidly! The bills were posted up, all the paying seats had been sold, and the four thousand free tickets had been drawn in the factory sweeps. The night of the concert arrived.

All would have been well if none but the workers who had drawn tickets had turned up. Unfortunately, those who had been unlucky came too. They arrived as if they were going to a concert, and not to a political meeting; that is to say, by ones and twos, not in a crowd. As is usual in Russia, each of them thought that he could manage to squeeze in by hook or by crook — he could find standing-room somewhere. His Honour had been right in saying that there were hundreds of thousands of workers in Kiev, and on this night the streets were black with them, not only the streets in the vicinity of the hall, but all the main roads as well. The authorities were naturally greatly perturbed, and the military made its appearance on the Krechtchatik.

My feelings may be imagined. Now what had I done?

I appealed to the workers' delegates.

" I gave my promise that there should be no disturbances. I hope that for my sake the workers will not betray my trust."

I must do them justice and say that they behaved themselves in an exemplary manner. Order was maintained, but my situation was nevertheless extremely ticklish. It even became tragicomic when I found that it was quite impossible to make my way through the crowd to get into the hall. . . . Who was to sing at the concert, then?

What on earth was I to do?

The Concert for Workers

By good luck, one of the walls of the Hôtel Continental, where I was staying, adjoined that of the hall. Korech-tchenko, my late accompanist, and I opened the corridor window, climbed out on to the slates, and lowered ourselves from the gutter on to the roof of the hall. But the problem was not yet completely solved. It needed another acrobatic feat to get us into the hall itself. We had to squeeze ourselves through the skylight, and this we did.

I do not know what was happening in the streets. What I do know is that the hall was so packed that it presented a most terrifying aspect. Of course the concert did not begin on time.

There was a thunder of applause when I appeared on the platform; the ovation lasted several minutes. When it was possible to make myself heard, I made a short speech to the audience. I reminded them that I had taken on myself the whole responsibility for the evening, and that it had given me great pleasure to organize the concert. I was answerable for whatever might happen, for it was at my request that permission to hold the concert had been granted by upright officials, whom I held in respect. "There are no detachments of police present," I concluded, "so it is up to you, ladies and gentlemen, to see that order is maintained."

Tremendous cheering greeted my remarks, and the concert commenced.

"*Tortured by spiritual thirst,*" [1] I began, and a breath of new life thrilled through the audience. I felt strongly conscious of it.

During the intervals between my songs and the encores, there were exclamations from various parts of the hall. Several girls called out: "Sing us the *Varsovienne!*" There was an insistent shout of "The *Internationale!*" from many hoarse voices. I am perfectly sincere in saying that at that time I did not know these revolutionary songs.

[1] *The Prophet*, words by Poushkin, music by Rimski-Korsakov.

Even today I know nothing about *La Varsovienne*. As to the *Internationale,* although I have not known it very long, I know it only too well. . . .

However, there was a workers' song that I had known since childhood; I had heard it in Kazan on the banks of the Lake of Kaban — it was *Doubinouchka*. I knew that it had a chorus, and that the couplets were sung by one voice — not the voice of one of His Majesty's soloists, needless to say. . . .

It struck me that I could best respond to the requests of the worker-audience by singing this song, and I announced that I would sing *Doubinouchka* if they would join in. There was another thunderous outburst of cheering, and I sang:

> " *I have heard songs that in my country ring;*
> *They do not tell of joy, but grief and pain.*
> *But one is graven deeper on my brain*
> *Than all those songs — the song the workers sing:* "

" *Ei, doubinouchka, oukhniem!* " [1] Five thousand voices wildly took up the refrain. As I had felt at matins on Easter Day, so now I seemed to be lifted out of myself. What was the power in this song? Was it the breath of revolution, or a wild incitement to strength? Was it a glorification of work and happiness and human liberty? I do not know. I was exalted, and sang without a thought as to what might come of it — heaven or hell. I was like a bird with strong white pinions that flies from its nest and soars high above the clouds. Certainly I did not hold, literally or figuratively, the multitude of cudgels raised to strike down the " lords and boyars." But I hailed the death of oppression, and I adored freedom as much then as I do today.

Many years have passed since then. But the memory of that night remains, and will remain with me to the end

[1] The chorus of the song runs: "Ho-la! Let us brandish the cudgel!" *La Doubinouchka* is the cudgel that the people will brandish to avenge itself against its oppressors.

of my life. It was a wonderful success. After the concert the workers went quietly home, two by two, like school-children. Of course my *Doubinouchka* evoked all sorts of comments, and I was promptly classified amongst the revolutionaries of the extreme Left.

The sale of the tickets brought in a net sum of three thousand roubles. Through the intermediary of Lolo-Munstein, the poet, I sent this amount back to the workers of Kiev.

CHAPTER VIII

I am suspect: The revolution of 1905: The barricades: An evening
at Gorki's house: An unsuspected meeting with Lenin

ɷ ɷ

Aᴏғᴛᴇʀ ᴇᴠᴇɴɪɴɢs ʟɪᴋᴇ these, how pleasant to leave for the sparkling blue seas of the South!

Picture me in Italy on the beach at Alassio in a bathing-suit. Warm sunlight makes me blink. Suddenly my wife rushes up in consternation, an Italian paper in her hand.

"What ever shall we do? They're on your track in Russia! They're going to prosecute you for giving money to the revolutionaries. . . ."

I thought she was joking. But no — the Italian paper said plainly: "Chaliapin is wanted."

I had intended to stay in Alassio and return after the season had begun, but this news made me hasten my departure.

I went straight to Moscow, and drove to the Métropole. Munstein came to meet me, quite overcome; he told me that he was in hiding because the police were after him for the Kiev concert "affair." They had read a secret revolutionary pamphlet which said that such and such a concert had brought in three thousand roubles to the funds. "Who could have given a concert that would produce such a sum? Obviously, Chaliapin. . . ."

I wondered what to do, and decided to take the bull by

the horns. I promptly wrote to the police at Kiev, to say that it was I who had given this money, but that I had no idea what use had been made of it — that, moreover, I was not interested in what had been done with it. If money that I give for bread is spent on drink, it's no business of mine!

The authorities evidently agreed with what I said, for I heard no more of being "wanted." The proceedings against Lolo were also dropped.

The result of this affair was a general curiosity about *Doubinouchka.* The audience often clamoured for it at concerts and musical evenings. Sometimes, when the spirit moved me, I sang it, in the capital and in the country, but always on condition that the audience joined in.

One day I sang the *Doubinouchka,* not by request, but because the Tzar had just signed a manifesto promising liberty. I happened to be in the restaurant of the Hôtel Métropole at the time. All Moscow was celebrating. I climbed on to a table and began to sing with overwhelming joy and enthusiasm.

Not every day are men swept together by a surging tide of happiness. . . .

My *Doubinouchka* in Kiev and my *Doubinouchka* in Moscow in some measure enshrine the memorable summer of 1905, so crowded with events and conflicts. The general railway-strike broke out in the autumn. The universities became rendezvous for revolutionary meetings in which all and sundry took part. In the towns, people rebelled openly against the authorities. On October 17 the Government fell. The Tzar's manifesto, granting a new régime, was published. Russia was promised liberty, a constitution, a parliament. Perhaps something might have come of these promises, perhaps Russia might have been capable of reconstruction and peaceful progress. Unfortunately, so it seemed to me, the Socialists and the Government did all they possibly could to ruin every chance of success.

Society split up into countless groups, each of which piped a tune of its own. Some said that too little had been conceded, others that though much had been granted, the Tzar would break his promises. As soon as the strike ended and the country began to settle down, the court believed that the threat of revolution had been imaginary, and that they had been very wrong to " funk "; it was decided to do as the Lefts had predicted they would do — revoke every promise. . . .

In a few days' time, indeed, a new change took place. Joy rapidly subsided, and once more all hearts in the capitals became morose and gloomy. There was an outbreak of pogroms against the Jews and intellectuals. Manifestos inciting the people to these pogroms were printed (as Prince Ouroussov, ex-Vice-Minister of the Interior afterwards revealed in the Douma) by Captain Komissarov of the police, under the ægis of the Police Department and at the expense of the State. . . .

The general unrest soon spread to the peasants. They demanded land and set fire to the *pomiechtchiks'* property. These were merely signs of popular dissatisfaction and were speedily suppressed. But the people of Moscow, still aflame, set themselves to the construction of barricades. . . .

This period of my life is linked in my mind with a recollection which is not without symbolic significance. During this time of unrest I was in Moscow, where Gorki was also living. Every hour was fraught with trouble and danger. Moscow was in mourning for Baumann, the student who had been killed by the police. I knew nothing about this man, but, to judge by the deep sympathy manifested by the revolutionary party, it seemed as though he must have had a remarkable personality and must have known, not only that the earth twirls on its axis, but how the axis (axes) might be twirled in quite a different sense. . . . In reality, Baumann was only a courageous youth who had

fought at the barricades and had fallen at his post. Naturally, the revolutionaries had made a great funeral display.

That night I went to see Gorki with a friend — the
pianist composer Korechtchenko, whom I have already
mentioned, and who was later to starve to death under
the Bolshevik régime. A visit of inspection, possibly even
arrests, were expected in Gorki's apartment, and as no
one intended to yield peaceably, the place was guarded
by a dozen young men, most of them Caucasians, armed
with revolvers and other " instruments." I do not know the
names of these — I play on another kind. . . .

There were one or two Russians among the party. We
shook hands with everyone. They asked me to sing, which
I did with pleasure. Music is beautiful, always and everywhere. It was a truly exquisite evening, in spite of the
uneasiness that pervaded the house and the company.

Many years later, under the Bolshevik régime, I happened to visit Demian Biedny, the poet, at the Kremlin.
Lenin came in. I bowed to him and said how happy I was
to make his acquaintance. The famous leader of the people
looked at me fixedly and said:

" Surely we've met before."

I looked confused, and, seeing this, Lenin explained:

" Don't you remember that on the day of Baumann's
funeral we spent nearly the whole night at Gorki's? " And,
pressing my hand with fervour, he added: " It was a marvellous evening. . . ."

So Lenin was at Gorki's, I thought, and I had noticed
him so little that I had forgotten our meeting! What sacrilege that I, a friend of the Socialists, had paid so little
attention to the great apostle of Socialism! . . .

This slight incident only confirmed my belief that the
three revolutions were but links of a single chain. In 1905
Lenin was already in the ranks and was biding his
time. . . .

The years went by. After the suppression of the revolts

in Moscow, after the submission of the peasants as a result of punitive expeditions, after the stormy period of the first and second Doumas, an apparent calm reigned over the country. The Government appeared to have secured a victory.

People in the know claimed that during these years Russia had grown more prosperous, that industry had greatly developed. The Bourse, anyhow, was very active, and profiteers arrived in the capitals, to dazzle people with a showy display of their recently acquired wealth. Yet amongst the masses, and particularly amongst the peasants, stifled discontent still emitted threatening clouds. A deadly struggle was in progress between the Government and the revolutionary party. Sometimes the latter succeeded in assassinating a minister, sometimes the authorities managed to pounce on a dangerous terrorist and throw him into prison. Nor was liberal opposition in the Douma overcome. On the surface, however, life was more peaceful and equable. Politics no longer obsessed all minds. Men busied themselves with their own affairs.

CHAPTER IX

The pre-war years: With Diaghilev in London in 1914: Sarajevo:
Fateful days in Paris: War!: Back to London, and home to
Russia

∽∾

Dᴜʀɪɴɢ ᴛʜɪs ᴛɪᴍᴇ I was touring in Europe with the
late Diaghilev. Our operas and ballets had a literally phe-
nomenal success. I shall never forget the last night in London. I remember it, not so much because our farewell
performance received an unforgettable ovation from the
English public, as because, by a whim of fate, this performance was the last in the historic week before the outbreak of the Great War. A day or two later the newsboys
were, in fact, shouting the latest sensation: it was reported
that an Austrian Archduke, the heir to the throne, had
been murdered somewhere in Serbia, at Sarajevo. . . .

When I arrived in France from London, rumours of
war were already in the air. I received a truly terrifying
impression during the few days I spent in Paris. The streets
were dense with crowds. Everyone was shouting and shriek-
ing in accents full of enthusiasm and hope, and infinite
fear of the future:

" *Vive la France!* Down with Germany! "

My heart stood still at the thought that all these men
were leaving their homes and families to go to their deaths.

The bankers, however, were still optimistic. One of them

assured me during luncheon that war would be averted, and that I could safely leave for Karlsbad, whither I wanted to go after the end of the season. I took his word, and started. We were going *via* Switzerland, but war took us by surprise in the train not far from Paris. We were told to get out, and that there would be no return train to Paris. . . . I thought of the banker with no particular kindness and made up my mind to get to Paris by hook or by crook, even if I had to go in a wheelbarrow! Unfortunately, I had far too much luggage with me. I suddenly became very generous and began to distribute it amongst perfect strangers! Small change having disappeared like magic, a new field of philanthropy lay open to me. As a matter of fact, I had only notes of fifty and a hundred francs on me. Provincial restaurants' charges were only moderate, it was true, but change was no longer given. Even for a ten-franc bill, fifty or a hundred had to be paid.

In the circumstances I conceived the idea of asking the people who pleased me and who shouted: "*Vive la France!*" to dinner with me. I invited the most sickly and worn-looking amongst them to join me at my table and offered them beefsteak and wine. . . . They said the Russians were "good fellows" at all times, in peace and in war. I heartily agreed, and we drank to France and our common victory.

I got back to Paris and spent several days at La Baule; then I left for London once more, with the idea of getting to Russia *via* Bergen and Finland. It was then more or less dangerous to cross the Channel. The advance guard of the German Army was in the vicinity of Amiens. Passengers to Dieppe were told to lie flat on the floor of the compartment if the train were shelled. Thanks to Providence, nothing did happen, and I reached London in safety.

My English friends advised me not to go to Russia, not to risk my life on the North Sea. They begged me to remain in England until the end of the war — which, of course, would only be of short duration . . . I was offered cottages and country-houses.

I am not home-sick, as a rule. I am too much accustomed to living abroad. But this time I was filled with an indescribable longing for my own country — I could not breathe away from it.

So I thanked my friends and embarked on a ship with the pretentious name of *Sirius,* which, I may say, travelled with far less speed than the wonderful star of that name. This extraordinary vessel carried me safely to Bergen. And thence, thanks to the sovereigns I had brought from London, I very soon reached St. Petersburg. I was back in Russia at last, and the very idea filled me with joy.

CHAPTER X

Life in Petersburg at the outbreak of war: Heroism and banality:
A patriot in the Restaurant Cuba: Varsovia: On the battlefield:
A tragic sight: The French delegates in St. Petersburg: Snow at
dawn, and the grave of the unknown soldier

ॐ ॐ

Back in St. Petersburg, I learnt that the first days of war
had evoked a great burst of patriotic fervour. I was told
what a deep impression had been made by the departure
of the wonderful Imperial Guard for the battlefields. But
at the time of my return I saw no trace of either enthusiasm or depression. Life seemed to have resumed its normal
course. Trade was brisk, carriages rolled along the roads,
and the Morskaia Prospect was brilliantly illuminated.
The theatres were filled to capacity.

Nevertheless, from time to time rumours spread anxiety
among the people. Sometimes there were glowing official
reports of victories, sometimes there were whispers of dis-
asters at the front. It was said that two battalions had been
wiped out in a battle at the Mazourie lakes, that tens of
thousands of soldiers had been killed in the forests, after a
battle that had lasted for two days. . . . The newspapers
slurred over these losses, the thousands of dead were
minimized into hundreds. Tricks were played with the
figure " o." . . .

It was bruited that there was a shortage of munitions,

and that the wretched Russian Army, officers and privates alike, were forced to fight with their bare breasts, in the most literal and tragic sense of the words, in order to check the enemy's advance. . . . It is certain that the Russian armies proved their courage and steadfastness on every front. It is equally certain that war brought out the qualities of charity and self-sacrifice at home. But, as is always the case, a purely verbal patriotism manifested itself in the capitals, a patriotism that ran to sickening flights of rhetoric, too often inspired by drink.

Picture, for instance, one of these " patriots " in the Cuba Restaurant. He is enjoying an excellent dinner, and, having emptied several bottles, his head is none too clear. A band of Roumanian musicians, in red jackets, is playing. Roumania is neutral, and our patriot is roused to a fury of resentment. He springs up suddenly, a cigar between his fingers, and, swaying a little, approaches the platform. Blinking his eyes angrily, he waits, with an air of contempt, for the conclusion of the item, and when the spasmodic applause of the diners has ceased, he inflates his chest, looks owlishly at the conductor, and says in a thick voice, punctuated by hiccups:

" I shay, you — hic — you shwine, when are you — hic — coming — into the war, eh? "

When, later on, the Roumanians had joined the Allied forces and had unfortunately suffered a defeat at the outset, this same gentleman, still hiccuping, still with an owlish eye, varies his patriotic speech to the orchestra:

" Sho you've — hic — come in with us — at last, have you — hic — you shwine? "

Meanwhile the Russian forces had taken Przemysl and Lvov, had lost them, and had again taken the offensive. The war dragged on and on with crushing monotony. From month to month it became only too clear that the Germans were very powerful, and that to obtain victory would be extremely difficult. I often met Russian soldiers

[215]

and talked to them. As a matter of fact, with the idea of
being useful, since I was unable to serve in the trenches,
I had started two hospitals at my own expense, one in
Moscow, one in Petersburg, big enough to care for eighty
men. Doctor friends gave me generous assistance and offered me their services free. During the war-years numbers
of wounded passed through my hospitals; I used to visit
them, and sometimes I would sing to them to distract their
thoughts. From my conversations with them I gained the
sad conviction that at heart they had no idea for what
cause they were fighting, and the dumb resignation with
which they obeyed orders struck me as only the more
pathetic. . . .

The war dragged on and on. In the monotonous grey-
ness of its events, I find it difficult today to say which one
made the deepest impression on me. Yet a tiny episode
lingers in my memory as being the epitome of war's
tragedy.

It was in 1916, I think. I learnt that during a recent
offensive the German planes had dropped a number of
bombs on Varsovia, and that the damage had been considerable, particularly in the slums. A great many tene-
ments had been destroyed, and I had a longing to do
what I could for the poor people. I decided to leave for
Varsovia at once and give a concert for their benefit.
I knew that anything I could do would only be a drop in
the ocean, but it was all that lay in my power. My dear
friends the Kedrovs, who sang quartets then, as they still
do, readily agreed to go with me and take part in the concert. Shells were bursting over the town, but our concert
in the Philharmonic Hall achieved none the less a brilliant
success. The hall was packed; all Polish society, princes and
counts, and, above all, the wonderful Polish actors, gave
us an overwhelming reception. I was particularly moved
when I was given a laurel-wreath tied with streamers in
the Polish national colours. I treasured it for many years

with other souvenirs dear to me. Where are they now, I wonder? I left them in Petersburg. . . .

It was during my stay in Varsovia that I was enabled to visit the Forest of Sakontiansk, where an engagement had taken place in the course of the German offensive. This forest was a few versts away from the town. I went with a lively companion, a Polish chemist. I don't know whether he wanted to celebrate my presence, or whether he was still under the influence of the recent bombardments; anyhow, he insisted on standing on the running-board of the car and firing revolver shots into the air all the way. . . .

The scene of the battle made a tremendous impression on me. Pines had been severed in half, the earth had been ploughed up into gaping holes and chasms by shells. Here and there I saw flayed bodies of horses, and everywhere, amongst the trees, were wooden crosses on new-made graves. On one of these crosses there was a poilu's *chapka* set at a rakish angle, and there was something shattering about this flaunting symbol of careless youth in the cold silence of death. I felt that even the corpse of this soldier would be less terrible to look upon than his *chapka* solitary on the cross. I went up to the grave, bared my head, and knelt down. On the wet ground beside it, I caught sight of a small blue book. I picked it up. It contained his route-directions, together with notes on successful engagements. . . . It was covered with dust and mud and blood. I turned over the leaves, and read:

" In recognition of duty carried out with gallantry and zeal. . . ."

How much there was in those few words! How much suffering had been endured for all this " gallantry and zeal "!

Forced marches, trenches, hellish bombardments, freezing nights, shortage of ammunition, bare-breast attacks. . . . And in the end the last reward — a wooden cross in the Forest of Sakontiansk on the grave of an unknown soldier. . . .

Hour by hour, depression and gloom deepened over Moscow. In order, no doubt, to keep up our morale, France sent us two eminent representatives — René Viviani and Albert Thomas. Petersburg welcomed them with special warmth. Relations between the Government and the people were extremely strained just then. In order to carry the war to victory, there should have been union " between the Tzar and his people," as the saying went. The Douma did its utmost to achieve this union, but in court circles short-sighted and stupid intrigues only widened the rift between the Tzar and his people.

Viviani and Thomas were both members of the French Left wing. Their power in the French Government served to some extent as a lesson to the Russian Imperial court. " France is a united country," was the impression they gave. It was even said in Petersburg, I remember, that one of the objects of these emissaries' visit was to unite Russia's parties in the interest of the war.

Whether this was so or not, the French were enthusiastically received, and amongst other entertainments there was a special banquet at Contan's given in their honour.

M. Maurice Paléologue, the French ambassador, a man of great wit and character, was present at this dinner. I have never forgotten the calm voice in which he asked, at one of the interesting receptions at the Embassy, what I thought of the situation at the front. I knew the extent to which he was tortured by the state of affairs, and could not but admire his diplomatic mask. Here, I thought, is a man who knows how to play his part to perfection!

I have the most pleasant memories of M. Paléologue. I have cherished with gratitude the delightful letter he wrote me to announce my nomination, in the name of President Poincaré, as Officer of the Legion of Honour.

CHALIAPIN
AT THE FRONT

"With Zeal"

The presence of M. Paléologue at the dinner in honour of the French delegates gave it an official character.

Many excellent speeches were made, toasts were drunk to victory, there were handshakes and embraces without number. At the conclusion of dinner I sang the *Marseillaise,* rousing transports of enthusiasm in Russian hosts and French guests. . . .

When I left, at six o'clock in the morning, a pale and lurid light had begun to spread across the sky. St. Petersburg was wrapped in a milk-white, icy mist. I went back to my house in the Kamenny Ostrov, and the events of the night might have remained in my mind as a memory of pure joy, had not the snow made a strange, crackling noise beneath my feet, and had not the crackling snow seemed to say:

" In recognition of duty carried out with *zeal, zeal, zeal.* . . ."

Yes, on this misty morning in Petersburg, the snow brought back to me the picture of a wooden cross on which a poilu's *chapka* hung rakishly aslant.

With zeal, zeal, zeal. . . .

CHAPTER XI

Tragic monotony: Before the storm: Sinister rumours: Rasputin:
A meeting that never materialized: The "treachery" of the Tzar-
ina: Shortage of food: In the Youssoupov Palace: The position
becomes unbearable: The Revolution: The Tzar abdicates

అం అం

Day by day, it became more evident that Russia must
lose the war. Everyone felt the imminence of a storm, but
no one dared to call it revolution, because it did not square
with the carrying-on of the war.

In political circles the resignation of the Government
was openly and uncompromisingly demanded, and the
appeal for the people's right to govern had carried away
the whole country. But, as though it were done deliberately, unpopular ministers were replaced by others still
more unpopular. . . . A rumour was rife amongst the
people that the war was going badly because there were
traitors at court. It was said that Grigori Rasputin, the
Tzarina's strange favourite, was a German spy who was
urging the Tzar to sign a separate peace with Germany.
Resentment was so widespread that even the Tzarina
herself was suspect. The wildest tales about this unhappy
sick woman were bandied about and given credence. They
said, for instance, that she communicated with the Kaiser
over a private line and betrayed state secrets to him. And
at the front the soldiers said that it was unlucky to receive
the Cross of St. George from the hands of the Tzarina —

anyone whom she decorated was sure to stop a German bullet. . . .

One fine day Rasputin's secretary came to my house on behalf of the *staretz*. As I happened to be out, he told my wife that Rasputin wanted to make my acquaintance, and asked me which I should prefer — to go to his house or receive him at my own. I was surprised. What could Rasputin want of me? I could not make it out. No doubt it was unthinkable to him that two such celebrities as himself and I should continue to be unacquainted. . . . As I had heard that the *staretz* was insulting even to persons of high rank, I did not anticipate meeting him with any pleasure. If he said anything unpleasant or insulting to me, I would certainly pay him back in his own coin, and it might end in our coming to blows. Now, noxious as it is to fight without good cause, it is even more noxious to fight with court favourites. I made some excuse not to meet him. . . .

Shortly afterwards, I learnt that a drama had been played out in the Youssoupov Palace; a certain personage had been attacked and had bitten his assailants; he had been sewn into a sack and dropped into the Neva with a stone round his neck. The personage was — Rasputin. . . .

His assassination probably confirmed the people in their belief that treachery was hatching at court. This treason, they argued, had been recognized even by members of the Tzar's *entourage,* hence the act of vengeance. The rumours must have been true! From that time on, events came crowding thick and fast. Food ran short in the capital, and this set a spark to the anger of the people waiting in queues at the shop-doors. There was trouble in the barracks. A private fired on his officer. The entire regiment mutinied. Mutiny immediately spread throughout the Imperial army. A single stone was loosened, and the whole building collapsed. The building was probably unsound. . . .

Revolution

One day, from a window in my house, I saw huge eddies of smoke. The Court of Justice was alight. The Revolution had begun. The people, soldiers, and sailors marched towards the Douma to swell the revolutionary tide. The spirit of revolt ran so high that General Headquarters at the front *insisted* on an interview with the Tzar! The capitals laboured under an extraordinary nervous tension. They were on the brink of chaos. On the Petersburg-Pskov line, in a little station to which some unknown prophet had once given the name of Dno,[1] the Tzar abdicated.

[1] *Dno* means in Russian "The Depths," and also "The Dregs."

CHAPTER XII

Bad actors

৩৩ ৩৩

I HAVE ALREADY SAID that in life, as on the stage, you must have a sense of proportion. This means that you must react emotionally to an event in the exact degree that the event warrants. There is an art of living as well as an art of acting. This is quite comprehensible. The part man plays in life is infinitely more complicated than any part he may play in the theatre.

Difficult as it may be to personate a character on the stage, it is still more difficult, I believe, to play one's own part in life. On the stage I keep myself under control the whole time to see if I have walked or wept in a suitable manner; in the same way, in real life I must have control over my actions. If unsightliness must be made to *appear* beautiful on the stage, all the more must it be made to appear beautiful in life. . . . Hence I am always astonished when I hear a minister, a Grand Duke, or a king utter the wrong words in the wrong tone — like bad actors; make wrong gestures, and — like bad actors — fail to realize that they are acting badly. When I see people like this, I experience a revulsion analogous to the feeling I have when an actress gives a false rendering of hysteria. This insincerity I believe to be responsible for a great many calamities.

Bad Actors

Suppose, for instance, that a *pomiechtchik* wants to converse with his peasants. He may address the moujiks quite sensibly, but, playing his part badly, he will punctuate his sentences so awkwardly, leave such clumsy gaps in the conversation, that, instead of impressing his hearers with his often excellent intentions, he will inspire them with resentment. This *pomiechtchik* actor has not felt the atmosphere, he has not struck the right note. Checkmate. A year later his property is in flames. . . .

A minister takes his seat in parliament, in the Douma, let us say. He mounts the rostrum and holds forth. His listeners are not peasants, but men with a knowledge of punctuation, who know exactly where the speaker should put his commas and full stops. They are instantly aware of any grammatical error. But the minister is a bad actor. Like the *pomiechtchik,* he does not feel the atmosphere, he does not grasp the situation, and errors mount up. One of the members heckles him excitedly, and, like a bad actor who has been given the wrong cue, the speaker loses the thread of his remarks and becomes heated. His voice takes on false intonations, his gestures are no longer in keeping with the cause he has at heart. His thoughts remain unformulated, his plea unaccomplished, and the impression this produces is deplorable. The minister has failed to act his part. Checkmate.

And what about tzars? A tzar must know how to act the tzar. It is a part of the highest importance, of Shaksperian magnitude. It seems to me that he should show that he is a tzar by his mien and bearing. Both must be fraught with majesty. If nature has made me dwarfish and slightly hump-backed, I must, if I am a tzar, create an atmosphere in which, despite my hump, I can convey as great an impression of majesty as a tzar of noble and heroic proportions. Every gesture that I make must evoke from my people a spontaneous cry of:

"There's a tzar, if you like!"

Bad Actors

But if I have not felt the atmosphere, my gesture will be as inappropriate as that of a bad actor, my subjects will be embarrassed, and they will mutter:

" Do you call *him* a tzar? . . ."

I have not felt the atmosphere — checkmate!

And behold — my kingdom is in flames. . . .

CHAPTER XIII

An epidemic of red rosettes: Delusions: Party quarrels and anarchist outbreaks: Gorki and I visit A. F. Kerenski: Gloomy impressions

ᔕᔕ ᔕᔕ

Duᴜʀɪɴɢ ᴛʜᴏꜱᴇ ᴅᴀyꜱ of unrest and disorder a typically Russian phenomenon was to be observed. People believed that the whales would feed on the minnows; to protect themselves against the icebergs which might overwhelm them in the débâcle, they floated with the tide, prudently if not sincerely. As though they had awaited this moment all their lives, they cultivated red roses, every one of the " ists," without exception — symbolists, cubists, artists, and even monarchists.

I admit that I did the same thing myself. The recollection makes me somewhat ashamed, and I feel that I ought not to have acted thus, even though I was genuinely exalted by current events.

I told myself: " The time has come when the gods whom I venerate will take command and make life happy for us all. Life will take on a deep significance and will be lightened by joy and work." But I very soon perceived that no order reigned in the measures taken by the Government, in the minds of politicians, in the behaviour of the populace. On the one hand there were violent party disagreements; on the other, outbreaks of anarchy. You had only to go on the Nevski Prospect to realize to what extent anarchy had unchained the soul of the people. I saw soldiers snatching furiously at posters which other "citizens" were atttempting to put up, and this was enough to provoke bloody battles amongst the crowd. I saw officers being cruelly insulted and mishandled by civilians.

The Soviet of Deputy Workers, supported by the demoralized army and the crazy mob, held the Provisional Government prisoner and kept a close watch on its activities. It suspected all the moderates, even the man who was the "hostage of the Revolution" — A. F. Kerenski. Anarchy was only upheld and strengthened by diarchy.

In the unbridled licence of the Revolution the educated classes in Petersburg entertained serious fears for the safety of works of historical or artistic value. A committee was formed with the object of protecting them. I was nominated a member, and in this capacity I had an opportunity of estimating the spirit of the times.

It was not long before the obsequies of the victims of the Revolution were to take place.

The Soviet of Deputy Workers decided that the dead should be buried in the square outside the Winter Palace, under its very windows — as a lasting reproach to the tzars! It was a ridiculous idea, considering that there was no longer a tzar in the Winter Palace. Several members of our committee proposed to protest against the vandalism of the Soviet. I remember that one of these was N. D. Sokolov, author of the famous *Prikaze No.* 1, which was said to have played such a significant part in the demoralization of the army. Gorki and I undertook to carry our objections to headquarters.

We went first to the president of the Soviet, Tchkheidze, the Social-Democrat (who came to such a tragic end in Paris a few years ago). We laid our arguments before him, but the excitable Caucasian would not even listen to our reasoning. The victims of the Revolution *must* be buried beneath the windows of the despots. . . . We went on to Kerenski, then Minister of Justice. We asked him to use his authority to refuse permission for the interments in the grounds of the Winter Palace. Was it not out of place to set up a cemetery *opposite* a Palace which might be useful to the people? Kerenski agreed with us, and, thanks to the Provisional Government, the decision of the Soviet was overridden. We had succeeded in saving the Winter Palace.

My contact with those in authority enlightened me as to the true and alarming state of affairs. At the time of my visit to Tchkheidze, I was up against a political fanaticism which boded no good.

But Tchkheidze only represented the Centre of the Soviet; what, then, must the fanaticism of the Left wing be like? My talk with Kerenski showed me that in another way the new leaders were struggling under senseless and abnormal conditions.

I saw that these men in whom the power was vested were *worn out,* in the actual sense of the words. They appeared to have no time to eat or sleep. A. F. Kerenski was eternally racing up and down, up and down the long corridors of the Ministry of Justice, and for ever rushing from office to office laden with documents. He was so engrossed that he stared in dazed bewilderment at anyone he met in the course of his peregrinations; he stared with the same abstraction at Gorki and me (it was not until later that I learnt he was short-sighted). A tall, emaciated person, even more harassed than Kerenski himself, was perpetually at his heels with a bottle of milk, waiting for a favourable moment to make him swallow some nourishment, even if it were only a gulp of milk. . . .

We were shown into the office, and a few moments later Kerenski came in, dropping with fatigue. He seated himself in the presidential chair, and his " wet-nurse " sat down beside him. . . . I was struck not only by the milk-bottle, but by the nervy and worn-out condition of the men who were striving to rule Russia in these most critical hours of her history. The conflicting replies of the leaders who were present at our interview revealed how seriously they were at loggerheads amongst themselves. I wondered sadly how it was possible in such circumstances for the Government to keep a tight rein on the affairs of the country. . . . But I realized that this was not the moment to take the ministry to task for its confusion, weariness, and dissension. There were deadly serious causes for it all. . . .

CHAPTER XIV

*The theatres: Soviet speakers lecture the public: I become presi-
dent of the Arts Committee of the Marie Theatre: I call for
serious work: The memory of a painful episode in London: The
"democracy" behind the scenes label me one of the old régime: I
am forced to leave the Marie Theatre: I sing at the Narodny Dom*

∾ ∾

IT WAS NOT very long before the sort of policies we had
witnessed on the Nevski Prospect made their appearance
in the theatres of St. Petersburg. Performances were in-
terrupted by members of the audience — among whom
was Trotski — who held forth from the stalls or the gallery.
They shouted that the time had come to put an end to all
pleasure and futile entertainments; that while people in
the cities were dancing and singing, soldiers were being
killed at the front. Incidentally, the soldiers had already
left the front. The same speeches had been made to the
men in the trenches, only in an inverted sense: "The
people in the cities are dancing and singing, while you are
being killed at the front. . . ."

Disaffection spread to the Imperial Theatres. The old
management, with Teliakovski at its head, had been swept
away by the Provisional Government. The unfortunate
Teliakovski himself was arrested and brought before the
Douma, but was immediately set at liberty, as he was quite
plainly innocent of any crime, and the then leaders of the

Douma were just men. I may say, incidentally, that Teliakovski had been arrested through the machinations of
a spiteful actor in the Alexandrin Theatre, whose claims
he had probably set aside. In spite of all my sympathy and
liking for Teliakovski, who was a thoroughly good sort,
I had to acknowledge that the change in management was
perfectly reasonable. Teliakovski himself admitted it. The
Imperial Theatres were hereafter to be called State Theatres — they were to be transformed into National Theatres.
A management that had been under the ægis of the court
was out of place in the new conditions. Teliakovski felt
that his dismissal was inevitable, and did not take it as a
personal insult. The Provisional Government nominated
a Komissar of the Imperial Theatres in his stead, chose a
new director, and formed an Arts Committee. I became
its president. At that time began the "Calvary" that was
to end in my leaving the Marie Theatre.

The fact was that, side by side with the new management and the Arts Committee, which constituted in some
sort a "provisional government," there had sprung up
behind the scenes a kind of workers' soviet, consisting of
chorus, musicians, and workmen, together with what might
be called the proletariat of the theatre. This proletarian
soviet did not find me to its liking. . . .

My relations with the chorus had always been friendly,
but they had suffered a change on the outbreak of war.
Painful as is the recollection of the unpleasant incident
which I am about to relate, I cannot retract a single word.

It happened in 1913, in London, during the course of a
season with Diaghilev. A lively discussion arose between
the latter and the members of the chorus, who demanded a
bonus to which they were in no way entitled. Diaghilev
refused to accede to their demand; so they decided to play
a nasty trick on him, and also on me, for I had made no
secret of the fact that I sided with Diaghilev.

They had thought out a truly monumental scheme of

revenge in the best Russian manner. . . . There was to be a gala performance of *Boris Godounov,* at which the King and Queen were to be present. Imagine Diaghilev's stupefaction when, a few minutes prior to the raising of the curtain, the entire chorus flatly refused to sing unless their salaries were paid in advance. Sir Thomas Beecham, who happened to be standing behind Diaghilev, was completely taken by surprise. Controlling his indignation, Diaghilev said that in order to avoid a scandal, he would pay them, but the chorus then went on to say that they must be paid in gold, and gold only. There was plenty of gold in England at the time, but ordinary accounts were generally paid by cheque. There were no sovereigns in the theatre, and as it was eight o'clock, all the banks were, of course, closed.

Where could sovereigns be procured? Diaghilev begged the chorus to go on and promised to get some gold and pay them after the end of the first act. But this would not satisfy them. They insisted on having their money at once. The curtain went up on the coronation scene with only the dancers — the chorus refused to come on. . . . I was literally dumbfounded by this incredible insolence. Nothing infuriates me more than lack of respect for the stage and for one's work and career. I voiced my unbounded indignation as soon as I was off the stage, and went to my dressing-room. There I was informed that the chorus held me responsible for the trouble and were hurling insults at me.

Thoroughly upset, I went to the chorus and said:

"Surely it's not true that you are blaming me for this unpleasantness, and abusing me?"

"It's true, right enough," said their spokesman in a pugnacious and sarcastic voice.

I admit that I was unable to keep my temper, and knocked the rash speaker sprawling to the ground. Instantly his sixty companions advanced threateningly on me,

MR. LLOYD GEORGE
CONGRATULATING CHALIAPIN (IN THE RÔLE OF BORIS)

and if an actress had not interposed her body between them and me, I should most probably not be writing these lines now; I was within an inch of a twenty-yard drop through an open trapdoor. . . .

My state of mind during the performance may be imagined. I was ashamed of the chorus, ashamed of myself, ashamed of all Russians. Nor did it lessen my shame when the English stage-hands came to my room directly after the incident, with the kind intention of salving my feelings. In spite of their ignorance of Russian, they had grasped the situation, and through an interpreter they said to me:

" Mr. Chaliapin, we know that the Russian chorus has behaved very badly to you. We saw the whole lot of them go for you. We're not used to that sort of thing in England. You can carry on with the performance in peace — we won't let them harm a hair of your head. We'll kill anyone who attempts to touch you."

At last the opera came to an end. Although I was firmly convinced that I was in the right in this unpleasant incident, I shrank from the thought that I had knocked a man down. I tossed sleeplessly all night. I rose very early and went to the room of this particular member of the chorus. As I entered, I encountered angry and hostile, yet to some extent shamefaced glances from the friends who lived with him; but I apologized so warmly that I believed we were genuinely reconciled. As I went out, I thought once again how good it was to be able to say from one's very heart:

" My friend — or my enemy — forgive me, I lost my temper."

Nevertheless, the chorus, who were entirely to blame for our estrangement in London, kept up a certain grudge against me. I noticed it in the days of " liberty," when demands to be paid " in gold " and " on the spot " became an everyday occurrence. . . .

Moreover, other and more serious causes now interposed to aggravate our half-buried disagreement.

There is a curious proverb that exists, I believe, only in Russia: "*Work is not a bear, it will not escape into the forest.*" I certainly cannot call myself an inexhaustible worker, nor can I deny that there is a streak of Oriental indolence in my nature, but I have always hated this saying. When I became president of the Committee of Arts in the Marie Theatre, I made up my mind to do away with the old bureaucratic time-table of rehearsals — the hours used to be from eleven till one, or from twelve till two, and not one second later. I considered that the actors, who had now become the masters of the National Theatre, ought not to work by time-table, but should follow the dictates of their own artistic consciences. It was incumbent on them all — myself not excepted — to look upon rehearsals, not as a mere matter of duty, but as work to perform with fervour and enthusiasm. In other words, I made it clear that there were to be no fixed hours for rehearsals, but that they were to last until we had mastered our tasks — tasks that were serious and not to be treated lightly. Should it be necessary, we would rehearse from midday till five o'clock. . . .

My new rules provoked an outburst of dissatisfaction. I was called "the General." . . . Just that! But you must remember that at that time many generals had been deprived of their freedom and had been thrown into prison. In the Russian language of the day you spelt "general" and pronounced it "arrest." . . .

I was not arrested, it is true, but it was openly hinted that I was not indispensable to the theatre. The operas could be produced without Chaliapin, and as to rehearsals, his room was preferable to his company. . . . My contract was about to expire, and the new management made no suggestion regarding its renewal. I realized that I must go. Love can never be exacted. . . . I bade a sorrowful farewell to the dear Marie Theatre and went to the Narodny Dom (the People's Theatre), a private enterprise. As the theatre was always within me, I felt very little difference between the Marie Theatre and the Narodny Dom. There was the same repertory, and I sang my usual parts to the selfsame audiences.

The Bolsheviks become bolder: In Madame Krzesinskaia's palace: I feel that I am a "blood-drinker": A dinner at Adjemov's with Maklakov and Stakhovitch: Maklakov's prophetic utterance

லை லை

ALL THIS TIME the Revolution was gaining in strength. The Bolsheviks were daily becoming bolder. The road leading from my house on the Kamenno-Ostrovski Prospect to the Narodny Dom Theatre was close to the Bolshevik headquarters. They had seized upon the palace of Marie Krzesinskaia, the famous Marie Theatre dancer, and had turned its commanding balcony into a revolutionary forum. When I passed the palace, I would sometimes stop and listen to the speakers that followed each other without a break. It was impossible to get close to the balcony owing to the dense crowd, but I could catch bits of the speeches that were shouted at the mob. They ran like this: "These palaces, citizens, belong to you. Exploiters and tyrants have lived in them, but the hour of vengeance has struck. But, comrades, it is not enough that we have possessed ourselves of their domains; no, comrades, a thousand times no! The wretches that have battened on the blood of the people must be exterminated like poisonous vermin!"

When I heard these vociferations, I felt both embarrassed and afraid, for I was wearing a Savile Row suit, and it occurred to me that outwardly, at least, I belonged to the race of blood-drinkers. . . . Those nearest me in the crowd evidently thought so too, for they looked at me furtively and none too amiably. I wisely made myself scarce. . . .

It was plain that the days of the Provisional Government were numbered. Even its most ardent adherents were aware that it was doomed. I recollect a dinner with some friends of mine, when, in spite of my ignorance of politics, I realized to what a pass the situation had come. The dinner had been organized by Deputy M. S. Adjemov, a prospective member of the Cadet party and a supporter of the Provisional Government, in honour of our common friends V. A. Maklakov and M. A. Stakhovitch. They had just been appointed to important diplomatic posts, Maklakov to Paris, Stakhovitch to Madrid. It was a farewell occasion, as they were due to sail next day, and a spirit of cordiality prevailed. Adjemov, who was extremely witty, set the ball rolling. All through dinner we laughed and made jokes at one another's expense, as is our custom among friends. Yet there was an undercurrent of sadness in our mirth. Our jokes were on the melancholy side; we said that the Provisional Government would be thrown into prison, lock, stock, and barrel, by Lenin and Trotski, the threat of which was already rumoured. In my innocence I still tried to maintain that the Revolution would strengthen, renew, and inspire our country, but Maklakov answered me with a bitter phrase. He sighed heavily, and said:

" Not one man — not one — will escape suffering. . . ."

He shook my hand warmly, and the farewell we uttered was affectionate and sorrowful.

I knew that Maklakov, nominated to the most important diplomatic post by the Government, had to leave the country by stealth like a thief in the night. The

Government was aware that if the people heard of the
"imperialist's" departure for Paris, he would be held up
at the station. S. D. Sasonov, ex-Minister for Foreign Affairs, when he was about to start from Finland to return to
the Embassy in London, had already been prevented from
going, by being kept away from the train at the station.
. . . Remembering Sasonov, Maklakov had decided to
travel incognito.

"Not one man will escape suffering!" I murmured,
repeating my friend's words, and I wondered then, as I
wonder today:

"What's the use of the Revolution, then?"

CHAPTER XVI

I sing Philip II in Don Carlos: *Cannonade: Panic: I continue
the performance to the end: The Bolshevik battleship* Aurora
*bombards the Winter Palace and the Provisional Government: I
grope my way home through a hail of shells*

✍ ✍

WHAT'S THE USE of the Revolution?" But there is no
answer, for once revolution is afoot, it waits for nothing.
It annihilates and destroys when and what it pleases.

Clad in a gorgeous purple cloak, a sceptre in my hand,
the crown of King Philip II on my head, I emerge from
the cathedral and proclaim once more to my subjects
that heretics shall be burned, that I am God's anointed,
and that I alone hold sway over the world. As I finish,
there is a sudden mutter of gun-fire from the Neva, quite
close to the Narodny Dom. As a king who brooks no
reply, I listen with stern aspect: is it an answer to my
words? Again the guns boom. From the cathedral steps,
I see my loyal subjects start in fear. A third and a fourth
crash follow almost simultaneously. The stage suddenly
empties — dancers and chorus rush off and, quite oblivious
of heretics, begin to look for safety. Philip II has his work
cut out to convince them that there is nowhere they can
fly to, as it is quite impossible to predict where the next
shell will fall. A minute later, messengers come running
to inform us that the guns are firing in another direction,

and that the danger is over. The performance is resumed, and the audience remain seated, for they also have no idea where else to seek cover.

We asked the commissionaires the meaning of the firing.

"The battleship *Aurora* is bombarding the Winter Palace, where the Provisional Government is sitting," they told us.

By the end of the opera the firing had ceased. My return home, however, was distinctly unpleasant. Sleet was falling, as it often does at the close of autumn in Petersburg. Coming out of the theatre, my wife and I could find no conveyance and had to start on foot through the fog. As we reached the corner of the Kamenno-Ostrovski Prospect, a rain of lead fell about us. The firing had begun again. Shells whistled past us. . . . If my nerves were shaken, you may imagine my poor wife's condition. We ran from doorstep to doorstep in complete darkness — the street-lamps had not been lit — and cowered behind doors until we finally reached our house. I should like to have added "safe and sound," but I remember that Maria Valentinovna, my wife, was so upset by the shock that she was taken seriously ill that night and had to remain in bed for a whole month. I did not sleep; had I done so, I might have said that I awoke the next morning in Communist darkness. . . .

CHAPTER XVII

The Bolsheviks triumph: Assassination of the Liberal ministers Chingarev and Kokochkin: A visit to Komissar Steinberg: Gorki and the Bolsheviks: The Chinese button and Gorki's comparison: The other buttons fall off

இ இ

THE PROVISIONAL GOVERNMENT was overthrown, its ministers were arrested. Vladimir Iliitch Lenin made his solemn entry into the conquered capital.

I had only the vaguest idea of what those men who had become rulers of Russia in a single night stood for. In particular, I knew hardly anything about Lenin. As a rule, I believe that historic "figures" only stand out either when they are sent to the scaffold or when others are sent to the scaffold by them. At this epoch official executions were still unknown, so that to anyone as ignorant of politics as I, the genius of Lenin was still rather shadowy. I knew a good deal more about Trotski. I had seen and heard him often enough in the theatre. From box or circle he would wave his clenched fists and shout contemptuously at the audience: " The blood of the people is running in the gutters, and you, you thickheads and vulgarians, you lower yourselves to listen to the

[241]

stupidities and banalities that a pack of rotten actors spew at you. . . ."

As I had no idea of the sort of man Lenin was, I did not go to the official welcome at the station. Gorki went, although he was at that time, I believe, hostile to the Bolsheviks.

The first chastisement I received from Heaven — probably on account of this sin of omission — was the requisitioning of my car by a band of young men. A car was no good to a Russian who had not made use of it to go and greet the leader of the proletariat. I consoled myself with the thought that my car was very useful to the people. During the first few days of the installation of the new rulers, Petersburg was not quite clear as to what the Bolshevik régime really signified. But the first shock came when a party of sailors invaded the prison and brutally murdered Kokochkin and Chingarev, two "enemies of the people," who had formerly been ministers in the Provisional Government, and prominent members of the intellectual party.

I recollect that Gorki, absolutely staggered by the double assassination, asked me to accompany him to the Ministry of Justice to demand the release of the other members of the Provisional Government. We climbed the stairs to the second floor of a big house, in the Koniouchennaia Road, I think it was, not far from the Neva. We were received by a man with a shaggy head of hair, wearing glasses. This was Steinberg, Minister of Justice. During the interview that ensued, I maintained the modest air of an onlooker — Gorki did the talking. Pale with emotion, he declared that it was abominable to treat human beings as these men had been treated. " I insist," he wound up, " on the immediate release of the members of the Provisional Government. If you refuse, they will probably be murdered, like Chingarev and Kokochkin. It would be a blot on the Revolution."

Steinberg entirely agreed with Gorki, and promised to do the best he could, as soon as he could. I believe that others besides ourselves had taken similar steps for the same purpose by approaching the political Red Cross. Shortly afterwards the ministers were released.

Gorki often intervened in those days on behalf of innocent persons who had been arrested. I might even say that the part he played as interceder took up all his time during the first period of Bolshevism. I often met him, and realized that he felt an overwhelming pity for the class that was threatened with destruction. He was so compassionate that he was not satisfied with securing the liberation of the arrested persons; he gave them money in addition, so that they might escape from the unbridled forces of brutality and live in safety abroad.

Gorki made no secret of his feelings, he openly showed his disgust for Bolshevik rule, and I remember the speech he made in the Michael Theatre. Revolution, he said, is not licence, it is a moral force full of nobility, concentrated in the hands of the workers. It is the triumph of work, the motive power which drives the world. . . .

What a contrast between these wonderful words and some of the other speeches that were made in the same theatre, in squares, and at street-corners — speeches urging the people to bloody massacres!

I soon realized how deeply Gorki was disillusioned by the trend of events and the new leaders of the Revolution.

Once again I must remark on the strangeness and incoherence of the Russian character. Someone has only to exclaim: " So-and-so's a swine! " to set the ball rolling. One and all eagerly echo his words: " So-and-so's a swine! " turning the words over in their mouths as though they were succulent titbits. This is precisely what happened to Gorki. He suffered deeply and devoted himself body and soul to the victims of the Revolution, but this did not prevent the Tartuffes of the capital from spreading the tale that Gorki's one thought was the completion of his art collection, on which, moreover, they added, he spent extravagant sums. Others went further still: they said that Gorki took advantage of the trials and tribulations of the aristocrats and once wealthy families and bought their magnificent art treasures for a mere nothing.

True, Gorki was a great collector. But what did he collect? Old rifles, Chinese buttons, Spanish combs — in short, a heap of odds and ends. . . . In his eyes, all this bric-à-brac was the product of human ingenuity. At teatime he showed us one of these remarkable buttons, and said:

"Look, this is the work of man! To what heights his mind can rise! He has manufactured this button, the use of which we cannot see. How great, then, must be our respect for man, how great our love for a human being!" . . .

By means of this button, which was quite ordinary but for its Chinese ornamentation, Gorki brought home to his listeners the fact that man is indeed "the noblest work of God." . . .

But those who held the power between their hands had a very different conception of man. The Bolshevik leaders buttoned and unbuttoned, sewed on or cut off "buttons" of a very different kind.

The Revolution forged full-steam ahead. . . .

CHAPTER XVIII

The new type of audience: N.C.O.'s and Beethoven: In a box:
The statements of a Komissar: My reply: A heart-to-heart talk
that never materialized: Famine: Dying horses: The knives of
the starving: Misery

ॐ ॐ

LITTLE BY LITTLE, we saw the rich and cultured audiences disappear from the theatre. A new type filled the
auditorium. The change was not sudden; gradually soldiers, workers, and the lower classes in general made up
the bulk of spectators. It was, of course, a matter for
rejoicing that the poor should have an equal chance with
the wealthy of enjoying plays and operas — that, indeed,
was the special object of the National Theatre. In principle
it was an excellent thing that the theatres of the two
capitals should be open to the proletariat. But it would
not be correct to affirm that the Russian people had
sweated blood and tears in order to enjoy the pleasures of
the theatre which had formerly been denied to them, or
that the Revolution had opened the doors against which
they had so long battered in vain.

As a matter of fact, the people neither walked nor ran
to the theatre of their own free will. They went to the
theatre " under orders from headquarters." This or that
society, the hands from this or that factory, were sent to
the theatre. And, incidentally, must it not be very boring

[245]

for an N.C.O. to have to listen to Beethoven at a time when all the grounds of private houses have been thrown open to the public, and where charming "liberated" damsels dance quadrilles to the strains of the accordion played by the famous Jacques L'Éméraude? . . . I quite understand the feelings of the worthy N.C.O., I understand perfectly. When he whirls round with Olympiada Akakievna and presses her close against him in the ardour of the dance, his hand, beneath his partner's right armpit, touches something palpable and tremendously disturbing. What could an N.C.O. feel in the stark music of Beethoven?

Of course, there were exceptions. Not all the people betook themselves to dance in the new public gardens. Some amongst them did listen in silence to Beethoven's music and were moved to tears. But they were greatly in the minority. How much happier would Russia have been had the cases been reversed! . . .

However that may be, theatres and actors were held in a certain amount of favour by the new leaders. Was it due to pure chance that the Office of Public Education was confided to Lounatcharski, who had always felt an interest in the theatre? Whether it was because the Government hoped to make use of the theatre for purposes of propaganda, or because the gay and social life of the theatre was an oasis where the new masters could refresh themselves after their arduous "labours," or because they wanted to prove that the "noble and the beautiful" was not alien to them (is there not an opera-house next door to the gaming-tables at Monte Carlo, and cannot the cries of the Valkyrie be heard simultaneously with exclamations of *"Faites vos jeux, messieurs"*?), the fact remains that the Bolshevik Government was attracted to the theatre and showed it favour. Nevertheless, no actor was allowed to forget that this favour was a condescension, and in this connexion I recall a most significant episode.

[246]

A Revolutionary's Heart

One day I went to see *Don Carlos* at the Conservatoire. I had a stall not far from the box that had once been reserved for wealthy people and which was now at the disposal of the authorities. This night it was occupied by the Communist Ch., who was, to all intents and purposes, Prefect of Police in Petersburg, and some of his friends. Catching sight of me, he asked me to join them and have some tea. I am almost certain that Zinoviev was of the party — Zinoviev, the absolute monarch of the northern capital, once so brilliant.

Enthralled by the excellent interpretation of the play, Ch. suddenly gulped down his tea, and said to me:

"You actors ought really and truly to be suppressed!"

"Why?" I asked, somewhat taken aback by this unpleasing prospect.

"Because you succeed in softening the heart of a revolutionary, which should be as hard as iron."

"But why should it be as hard as iron?" I asked in reply.

"So that his hand may not falter in wiping out his enemy."

I ventured to reply to the Prefect of Police in Petersburg, as I had once replied — but with far less danger! — to the Chief of Police in Moscow, General Trepov:

"Comrade Ch., you are mistaken. I believe, on the contrary, that a revolutionary should be as tender-hearted and as gentle as a child. An ardent mind, a will of steel, but a heart of compassion. Only if he possesses these qualities will he be able to refrain from ripping up an old man or a babe of the enemy class when he meets them in the street. . . ."

The curtain was going up again. Ch. stared at me penetratingly with his prominent eyes and made a totally unexpected remark, which seemed to have no bearing on our conversation:

"It's dull work, drinking tea, isn't it, Chaliapin?" And he added in a low voice so as not to be overheard: "It

[247]

would be far better if we cracked a bottle of wine together. I should like to have a little chat with you."

"Well, let's arrange it," I said.

Ch.'s voice had softened. I got the impression that he
wanted a little chat with me in order to discover what sort
of heart was requisite for a revolutionary. . . . I thought
to myself that there was still confusion in the minds of
those who boasted of the invincible strength of iron.

We shook hands warmly. We met on several occasions
after this — to crack many excellent bottles — but, curious
to relate, he carefully avoided any mention of the Revolution. Contrary to the saying *"In vino veritas,"* the wine
we drank did not move him to speak freely. . . .

The Revolution rushed on its headlong course. The
Bolsheviks had dug themselves in and were now protected
by the army, the civil guard, and the Tcheka, but the life
of the people, both spiritual and material, instead of becoming happier, as had been promised, grew more and
more wretched. The country was going downhill. The
spectre of famine stalked through the towns. Emaciated
horses, abandoned by their masters, were to be seen lying
with their skinny legs bent beneath their bellies. Compassionate citizens found a little hay and held the wisps
beneath their noses, but the poor creatures' eyes were
already glazing, they neither saw nor scented the fodder —
they were in their death-agonies. . . . And later, in the
small hours of the night, men came slinking out of dark
alleys, and cut off chunks of horseflesh with their knives.
The wretched beasts were by then past realizing that the
butchery was done, not only for the good of the people,
but for their own benefit. . . .

CHAPTER XIX

*I am asked to rejoin the Marie Theatre: A touching gift: Many
actors leave Russia: I stand firm: I hesitate to leave my country
in the throes of revolution: Life becomes still harder: I am once
more classed as a "bourgeois": Moskvin, the Governor: Requisitions: My wine and my revolver under inspection: A comical
Komissar who telephones me at three o'clock in the morning to
request the pleasure of drinking my health: His visit: My visit
to Zinoviev*

ᘒ ᘒ

ONE FINE SPRING morning during this period of misery,
a delegation of workers came to me from the Marie Theatre. At its head was E., the manager of the theatre. The
Marie Theatre was doing very badly. As the Government
had no resources, they had abandoned it to its fate. Re-
ceipts had fallen away to nothing. The public had lost
interest in the rank and file of the art — hence a call for
" General " Chaliapin. . . . The cordial invitation and
sincere desire of the delegates to have me once more in
their midst awoke reciprocal feelings in me, and I decided to
rejoin the company which had not long ago plainly shown
me the door. . . . The workers were grateful for my acceptance, and when I appeared for the first time behind
the scenes of the familiar theatre, a most touching surprise
awaited me.

The workers had sawed off a piece of the movable

platform on which, since my first performance as Mephistopheles in 1895, I had risen from hell to Faust's chamber! This piece of wood they now presented to me. Nothing could have touched me more deeply. How much emotion I had felt, how rapidly my heart had throbbed, as the moment approached when I was to appear before Faust on this platform and cry out: " Behold, I come! " Where is it now, this fragment of wood? I left it with all the other souvenirs of my past in the flat in Petersburg, which I quitted in 1922, never to return. . . .

Moments of emotion such as these, however, could not render life easier. Misery held sway, and from day to day existence grew more wretched. Civil war broke out in several parts of the country and increased the dearth in the towns. There were overwhelming difficulties in the theatre. Many actors had fled to the south of Russia, where there was said to be a little less shortage of food. Others had managed to get abroad. At one time I had practically no company left. Yet we had to carry on. Somehow or other we managed to produce this or that opera with the few singers that remained to us of the once considerable company; but this gave me no satisfaction whatever.

I suffered, too, in another way.

The condition of all "citizens," the revolutionaries included, was extremely painful. Every worker received an issue of rations. They were totally inadequate; those of the actors, myself not excepted, were equally insubstantial. However, I was sometimes able to sing in some other theatre here and there, and for this I received flour or other food-stuffs. In this way I lived relatively better than my companions. In the conditions that then prevailed, this caused me some embarrassment — it grieved me to feel that I was in a position of privilege.

Often, I admit, I longed to get away, to escape, no matter where. But at the same time my conscience

CHALIAPIN

ON THE BOWERY, NEW YORK, MAKING A NEW ACQUAINTANCE

pricked me. "You wanted revolution," it said. "You wore a red rose in your buttonhole, you ate revolutionary gruel to sustain your strength, and now that there's no gruel left, only bran, you contemplate flight. You can't do it. . . ."

I say quite sincerely that I should probably have stayed in Russia, I should not have left later on, even, but for certain circumstances that arose, and but that certain facts, at first neither noticed nor suspected, were driven home to me.

Somehow or other, though I suffered materially, I managed to exist. What worried me more than all was the knowledge that my babies often lacked necessary nourishment and had sometimes even to go without milk. Some barbers who had become revolutionaries and were organizing the food-supplies put Pelagia, our good old servant, through a coarse catechism, calling me, in her presence, bourgeois, capitalist — any name that suggested to their minds a black coat and stiff collar. Pelagia had evidently had to deal with ill-mannered brutes, but, unfortunately, persons of this type were to be met at every step, not only amongst inferiors, but in higher spheres too. This reminds me of Comrade Moskvin,[1] who bore some such title as Voievod or Governor of St. Petersburg. One of my impresarios had, without his permission to do so, put up bills of a concert I was to give. It was obviously a slip on his part, but he had not infringed the law; my concerts were always licensed.

At six o'clock on the day of the concert I learnt that it had been stopped. Why? And by whose orders? It appeared that Moskvin, the Governor of St. Petersburg, was responsible. . . . I had already spent half the money I had received in advance for the concert, and had bought bread to keep up my strength. Now the concert was not to be given. What most upset me was the thought that I

[1] Not to be confounded with the well-known actor Moskvin.

must have committed some fault. . . . I called Moskvin
up on the telephone, and said:

"I say, Comrade" (directly I had said "comrade," I
wondered if he would think I meant to make game of
him), "was it you who stopped my concert?"

"Yes, sir, it was I—I did stop it!" cried a sharp and
angry voice in my ear.

"But why?" I asked in more subdued tones.

"Why? To show you that you can't do exactly as you
like! Because you're Chaliapin, you think you can do as
you please."

The Governor's voice was so loud that all my family
heard it, and while I grew whiter and whiter with rage,
my poor wife and children shook with fright. They hung
on to me and in whispers begged me not to answer back.
I myself realized that it would never do to speak to him
as he deserved. And I had to end up on a note of entreaty.

"Don't fine me this once, Comrade Moskvin. Don't
hold up anything against me, don't stop my concert."

"Well, send someone round to me, and I'll see," concluded the Voievod in a condescending tone. . . .

Gentlemen of this sort predominated in the régime, and
the lives of the people, already sufficiently wretched, were
literally poisoned by them.

I was classed as a "bourgeois," then, and, as such, was
subjected to visits of inspection. I don't know what they
expected to find in my house. I suppose they thought I
had cascades of diamonds and mines of gold. They began
by taking up all the carpets. At first I was amused, and
laughed heartily. I was inclined to welcome such diversions in small doses, but the charming members of the
search-parties presently diverted me by their exceeding
perseverance. I had bought fifteen bottles of wine from a
ballet-dancer. I had sampled it with a friend, found it of
inferior quality, and gone to bed. At two o'clock in the
morning, when I was sound asleep, my good Nicolas

(who still called himself my cook, although there was nothing to cook) dashed into my room. He had only had time to slip on his shorts, and he burst out distractedly:

"*They're* here again, sir!"

In came a party of young soldiers with fixed bayonets, accompanied by two civilians.

The latter informed me that they had been commanded by the district revolutionary committee to make a visit of inspection.

"You were here only a few hours ago," I said, "and you've inspected everything."

"That was another agency — not ours."

"Oh, very well, get on with it."

Once more, up came the carpets. Curtains were shaken, pillows were prodded, the back of the fireplace was investigated. Of course, no literature, capitalist or revolutionary, was brought to light.

"Ah! Here are thirteen bottles of wine. . . ."

"Take the wine away!" commanded the leader.

In spite of all my entreaties that my gentle guests should stay and drink the wine with me instead of carrying it off, these virtuous citizens refused to yield to temptation. The bottles were borne away. In the drawer of the card-table they discovered a pack of cards. I confess that I am addicted to this bourgeois form of distraction: I am partial to both preference and bridge. The cards were confiscated.

In a drawer in the bedroom they came across my revolver.

"I have a licence to keep a revolver, comrades — look, here it is."

"That licence, citizen, was made out in another district. As far as we're concerned, it is invalid."

The conduct of the interrogation was not devoid of humour. The examiner was a youth of the lower orders.

"Have you made a note of the cards, Gricha?"

"Yes," said Gricha, gloomily.

"You're sure you've put down all the bottles?"

"Sure — thirteen."

"Next you can put down: 'One revolver, make —' make — oh, Lord, what *is* the make?"

He held it up to the light and tried to decipher the writing on the barrel, but it was in foreign lettering, and he was baffled.

"What's the make of your revolver, citizen?" he inquired.

"It's a Webley-Scott," I said.

"Put down it's a Biblical make, Gricha. . . ."

Everything was written down; the confiscated articles were gathered together and taken away. . . .

Diversions of an even more humorous nature occurred.

One day a Komissar from Archangel, as drunk as a lord, descended on the house about five o'clock in the afternoon, with several pounds of fresh salmon under his arm. I happened to be out, and as he was a great clod of a man, he treated my wife, Maria Valentinovna, somewhat cavalierly. He told her that she must keep a watch over her husband, inspire him with fear and respect, and impress on him that he ought to be at home when a Komissar came to visit him, particularly when the Komissar had come for the purpose of drinking a glass with him and regaling him on salmon just arrived from Archangel. . . .

Whereupon he dumped the fish down because it was too heavy to carry, and remarked that he would leave it until his next visit. Maria Valentinovna, in her confusion, said that she would do her best to carry out his advice and instructions, and the delightful Komissar departed, minus his salmon. What was my surprise, on hearing, at three o'clock in the morning, the shrilling of the telephone!

I unhooked the receiver, and heard:

"Well, you —, are you asleep?"

Quite confounded by this unexpected compliment, I said mechanically:

"Yes, I'm asleep."

"I'm coming round right away."

"But, my dear sir, we're all in bed."

"You don't think I'm going to leave my salmon to go bad, do you?"

It was as much as I could do to get him to postpone his visit until the morning. Finding me out a second time, he took the salmon and departed, after hurling at my unfortunate wife insults that were as picturesque as they were for the most part incomprehensible to her.

After this I made up my mind to put an end, once and for all, to these diversions and interludes. To do so, I had to go to headquarters, which meant to Zinoviev himself. I had to conform to all sorts of regulations before I could obtain an audience at Smolny. At length I received the permits. For there had to be several; it was one of the little weaknesses of the new régime. It was as difficult to get access to a minister or a governor-general as to succeed in visiting a notorious criminal. You had to make your way through dozens of barriers, past crowds of guards and patrols on the *qui-vive*.

In a room on the third floor I was received by a man of middle height; he wore a leather waistcoat, was clean-shaven and intelligent-looking, with the long locks of a provincial musician. He was the type that becomes the idol of the provinces. With a preoccupied air, he asked what I wanted. I told him all that had taken place at my house — the whole story of the cards, the wine, the revolver, the salmon, etc. I said that I in no way doubted the necessity for, and the usefulness of, these requisitioning visits, but that I should be much obliged if they could be arranged at more convenient hours.

"Couldn't they take place, Comrade Zinoviev, say between eight and ten o'clock in the evening?"

Comrade Zinoviev smiled and promised to see to it. As I left him, I remarked casually:

" Comrade, the Soviet of soldiers and sailors at Yalta has drawn nearly two hundred thousand roubles from my current account. Could you not arrange for this sum to be repaid, in view of the money crisis, the food problem, and the shortage of work? "

Zinoviev shrugged his shoulders with an expression of annoyance.

" That, anyhow, has nothing to do with me," he said. " I can't do anything in the matter. . . ."

While I was with him, the telephone bell rang, and I heard him say:

" No need to trouble about them. Treat them with the utmost severity. Shooting's too good for the swine. . . ."

My visit to Zinoviev was not without result. Two days later, to my great surprise, a party of soldiers, this time unarmed, brought back thirteen bottles of excellent wine and my revolver. But the playing-cards were never restored; they served to while away the boring monotony of barrack life. . . .

CHAPTER XX

*Dalski and his anarchism: My friends the Barons Stuart are
arrested: I visit the Tcheka: I receive a promise: My friends are
shot: Gorki goes to Moscow to beg Lenin to spare the lives of the
Grand Dukes: His request is granted: A telephone call: Death of
the Grand Dukes*

ৎৎৎ

MY FRIEND DALSKI, that excellent actor of whom I have
already spoken, professed anarchist beliefs. He maintained
that laws, rulers, and prisons were unnecessary, and that
nearly everything was unnecessary, even keeping the roads
clear of snow. Snow falls at a given time of the year when
the weather is cold, and snow melts at another given time
when the sun begins to shine.

It was said in St. Petersburg that he took part in
anarchist activities. This was not surprising, in view of his
coolness and abundant energy. Whether this was so or
not, Dalski's ideas, which he expounded to me at this time
of my life, struck me as being far preferable to the laws
and conditions which were then determining existence.
And yet, I wondered uneasily, can we entirely dispense
with authority?

" Authority " pleased me less and less. I realized that the
sincerity and simplicity of the old Socialism which had so
impressed me were entirely lacking in the Socialism of
the day. Everything was riddled with falsehood. There

were lies at political meetings, lies in the papers, lies in public departments and organizations. There were lies about trifles, and lies no less when the lives of innocent people were at stake.

Two great friends of mine, the Barons Stuart, were arrested in St. Petersburg almost simultaneously with the Grand Dukes. I had met the Stuarts in 1894 when, as a young man, I was singing in the Panaev theatre. They were about my own age and had just left school. They were charming, well-bred youths. When the Revolution broke out, one of them, Volodya, immediately donned *laptis* and working-kit and got a job as a railway porter. Nicolas, the other brother, who had completed his medical studies at Kharkov University, tried to set up a practice, but his nature inclined much more towards day-dreaming and dramatic art than towards medical and natural science.

The brothers were certainly in no way proletarians, by birth, upbringing, minds, or convictions. But they took no part in politics. Their undoing lay in the fact that they were barons, that their father had been a keeper of records and had acted as consul during the reign of the Tzar. Barons! That was quite enough to render them suspect and to justify their arrest. That Volodya had put on *laptis* and working-clothes to become a labourer only justified their arrest the more. . . .

As I knew the Stuarts inside out, I was able to swear by my own head, anywhere and at any time, that they were absolutely innocent. So I went on their behalf to the Tcheka in Gorokhovaia Street, over and over again. I was very cordially received by a Komissar named Tchoudin, a handsome young man with a magnificent head of hair. He had a pleasant way of looking at you. He greeted me politely and listened to what I had to say. I kept on repeating that the Stuarts were innocent, and begged him to release them as soon as possible. Finally, he asked me to put it all down in writing and send my application to the Tcheka. I did so and waited for my friends to be set at liberty. Unfortunately, it had been decided in high places, just at this moment, that no more political prisoners were to be shot. This decision was about to be ratified. Were those now in prison to be allowed to escape execution? " On no account," decided some satrap of Leningrad. The whole batch were executed in one single night — on the very eve of the promulgation of the generous decree. . . .

And so, for no cause whatsoever, my two dear friends, the Stuart brothers, met their end. . . . I learnt later that Tchoudin had also been shot. In love with an actress, he had helped her to possess herself of confiscated furs or diamonds. It was she herself, it was said, who denounced him.

The Grand Dukes, thrown into the prison in Chpalernaia Street, were executed in the same manner as the Stuarts. Amongst them were Nicolas Mikhailovitch, the famous historian, and the Grand Duke Paul Alexandrovitch. Gorki, who at this time was engrossed in Red Cross work, did his utmost to save them from imminent death. . . .

Attempts to procure the liberation of the Grand Dukes having met with failure in St. Petersburg, Gorki decided to go to Moscow and seek an interview with Lenin himself.

He succeeded in convincing Lenin and obtained from him a written order for the immediate release of the Grand Dukes. He returned joyfully to St. Petersburg with the order . . . but on reaching the station, he learnt from the papers that the Grand Dukes had been executed. The riff-raff of Moscow had had Lenin's order of release telephoned through to St. Petersburg, and the riff-raff of St. Petersburg had promptly shot that night the men who would have been liberated in the morning. . . . Gorki, horror-stricken, became literally ill with the shock.

I heard more and more talk about people who had been

" cancelled out," and the accumulation of horrors weighed more and more heavily upon me. What was the solution? Should I leave Russia? . . .

Maria Valentinovna urged me to this course with growing insistence. " We must escape, we must escape," she repeated. " If we don't, we too may be executed by mistake, like the Stuarts. . . ."

CHAPTER XXI

My wife begs me to leave the country at all costs: Blockade:
Dreams

৩৩

Escape . . . but where? It was easier said than done.
There was the blockade. I was not too clear as to what this
meant, but I knew that it was very difficult to get out of
the country on account of the blockade. I had a premonitory vision of the frontiers, soldiers, guns. It was impossible
to go this way or that. . . .

Directly I realized how difficult it was to escape — I
remember that minute very vividly — I was overwhelmed
with despair. What if the blockade lasts all my life, I
thought. I shall never see the Mediterranean, or the Alps,
or beautiful Switzerland again. I shall have to end my
days beneath the leaden skies of Russia, here, in Perm
Street, with the daily horrors, the intrigues at the theatre,
and the interminable sittings of committees that compli-
cate matters instead of simplifying them.

Yet I felt that if I left my country now, I was leaving
it for ever. How could I give up that country where I had
not only compassed all that one can see and touch, hear
and feel, but where I had dreamed dreams that enshrined
my deepest longings, especially in the years that preceded
the Revolution? How could I give up my dream of a
Castle of Art on Poushkin's Rock in the Crimea?[1] This

[1] I have discussed this scheme in detail in a later chapter.

[261]

tragic division of my inclinations caused me great suffering. My nights became more haunted and sleepless, I lay awake and in agonies. At every moment I caught my breath to listen: was the wagon of the Tcheka stopping at my door? When, worn out with weariness, I fell asleep at last, I had weird and extraordinary dreams; I remember them to this day, for they snatched me for a little space from the vicious circle of my existence. . . .

In these dreams the blockade sometimes appeared to me as a preposterous and prickly hedge, through which I cried to my wife: "How can I get to you? Don't you see me?" Whereupon she would hold out to me a red silk umbrella and say: "Hold on. I'll pull you through." And I would slip through. I was barefooted, though I wore a cloak. . . . Sometimes I dreamed that I was going through a great pine-forest in a troika, whose bells were ringing gaily. I was driving it myself and knew that I was in Switzerland. I felt very happy. But I was disturbed and a little frightened by the noise the bells made — suppose someone were to hear them. . . .

I hastily tear off a bell and stuff it in my pocket, and in my pocket I come across a lump of sugar. I meet a cyclist wearing a peculiar kind of helmet that I have never seen before; he is one of my admirers. He recognizes me and says: "Feodor Ivanovitch, don't go in a troika. Take my bicycle instead, and go by that path. It's picturesque, and quite safe." Half-convinced, I thank him, but want to know what I shall do about the horses. "Don't worry, I'll take them to the theatre," he assures me. "Thank you very much," I say, and mounting the bicycle, away I go down the path. The sun is shining, the grass is emerald-green, there is a lake — how beautiful it all is! And I thought I was never going to see Switzerland again! But here I am, thanks to the cyclist — he is probably a relation of our Pelagia's. . . .

In another dream I see a small Italian town: a tiny

piazza, a fountain in the shape of a Triton, overgrown with moss. I know this little town very well, I once stayed there! I have climbed those stairs without banisters before. Of course; my friend the tailor lives in this house. He used to work with me in the theatre. Was his name Perelli? I am almost sure it was Perelli.

I go in, climb the stairs, and my heart throbs! I am going to see my dear old friend Perelli, whom I have not met for such a long time. He will explain everything: where I am to go and where I can sing. The door of his room is open — I enter, but there is no one there. There is no one in the whole house. Suddenly, from the back balcony, comes an overwhelming fragrance of hot bread, white, newly-baked, French bread! Why, I shall be able to buy some! I step out on to the balcony, and there see dozens of loaves, stacked up like logs of wood. I take one, two, three loaves. . . . The smell goes to my head. . . . But where on earth is Perelli? I must pay him, otherwise I shall feel uncomfortable. Suddenly I am filled with terror. . . . I take my three loaves, dash out of the house, and run madly. . . . The tram! The very thing! It is going to Kamenno-Ostrovski Prospect, where I live. . . . I jump on to the footboard . . . and wake up.

I wake up. The room is as still as death. I see the shadows of night through the windows — the telegraph wires are weighted down with snow. . . . The blockade . . . !

Life becomes hideously "official": All human feeling has disappeared: I fall ill: I am neglected, alone, poverty-stricken: I am surrounded by complete indifference: Escape . . .: My wife is recruited to do hard labour on the Neva in mid-winter: I visit the Komissar: I protest, and flatter him: A visit of inspection: I win my case: Five million roubles are demanded of me: Fresh requisitions: My triggers refuse to catch

⚭ ⚭

As I took no part in politics, was a stranger to all secret agencies, had committed no crime against the authorities, apart from an inner revulsion against the kind of life created by the new régime, I had, one would have thought, no cause to fear pursuit or arrest. Nevertheless, because of my innate timidity, I now began to feel an overwhelming terror. What really appalled me was the absence of friendship, of simple human relations to which I had been accustomed. Formerly when you met others of your kind, you spoke to them spontaneously; if you were sad, they sympathized with you; if they suffered, you condoled with them.

In the madhouse in which I was now living, I found that there was a complete lack of natural feeling. Day by day, life was growing more " official," more arid, more egocentric. Even my own home was becoming a sort of " administrative department," although I do not know how it came about.

I fell seriously ill. As the result of a chill, I had a bad attack of sciatica. I could not move hand or foot, and lay stretched out on my bed. After a week of this enforced idleness, my pecuniary situation became critical. While I was able to sing, I could earn various small sums in addition to my rations, but now these were all that were left to me. There was not enough sugar, flour, or butter in the house. There was no money, either, though that was now worth very little. I collected various gold pieces that I had brought as presents for my daughters from my tours abroad, and showed them to my old business friend, Arsène Nikolaievitch. He looked at them, bent his head on his right shoulder, pulled at the ends of his corkscrew beard, and finally remarked:

"What's the use of such gewgaws, Feodor Ivanovitch? You couldn't buy anything with them. But if you've got a coat or a pair of boots, give them to me, and I'll bring you back flour or sugar or whatever it is you want."

Maria Valentinovna broke into the conversation.

"What's going to become of us?" she said. "We've no money left. We shan't be able to buy anything more."

"Sell what you've got left."

"We haven't anything to sell"—and she made it clear how dangerous it would be to sell diamond ear-rings—we should be accused of hiding them and profiteering.

And no one, not a soul, not a single one of my friends, not a single one of my associates at the theatre, showed any interest, any anxiety—not one asked how I was. My condition was known, and people said: "Chaliapin's ill" with as little feeling as a stone. There was no offer of help, no movement of sympathy, no least little word of human comfort. . . .

I began to believe that X or Y would rejoice to learn that Chaliapin was forgotten and dying of hunger. This blank indifference frightened me more than privation, more than misery, more than any intrigues that might have been on foot against me. It was at this moment that the thought of flight, flight no matter where, insinuated itself into my mind. Escape was essential, not for myself, but for the sake of the children. I kept my decision to myself. Meanwhile we had to live as best we could. . . .

The winter was very severe. Now the District Committee needed workers to unload the cargoes of logs from barges on the Neva. The hardship of such labour, especially in the bitter cold, may easily be imagined. The committee, however, must needs recruit not only men, but women, for this work.

My wife, the housemaid, and the laundress all received orders to report at the Neva dockyard.

Naturally, the order terrified them, for none of them were fit for such work. I went to the committee to protest or intercede on their behalf. I was received by a curly-haired youth with lank, drooping moustaches. When he had heard me out, he said sententiously that each member of a Communist society must help the other.

Finding that I had to deal with a clod, I decided to try a little flattery. I arched my brows with a knowing look and said:

"You're an educated man, Comrade, you've read Marx, Engels, Hegel, and Darwin, too, so of course you must realize that a woman is quite different from a man. She is much too weak to carry logs and splash about in freezing water."

The fool was impressed. He looked at me, smacked his lips, and said:

"Well, then, I'll come to your place tomorrow and see what the ladies can do."

He came. It was ludicrous to see Maria Valentinovna, Pelagia, our housemaid, and Anisia, our laundress, standing at attention in the kitchen.

"To the right — turn!" he shouted.

They turned half-right.

"Right — turn, properly this time!"

They turned right, properly.

The student of Hegel and Darwin remained pensive for an instant, looked down, looked at them once more and — gave in. . . . Not altogether, however, for his revolutionary conscience was in question.

"That'll do. Your orders are temporarily suspended. You certainly don't look as if you could do the work. . . ."

As for me, the bourgeois, although I was not drafted to toil in the water, I was thought capable of pouring a contribution of five million roubles into the Treasury. I received printed demands *ad hoc,* on which the time-limit for payment was set down. I reckoned that I had not earned five million roubles during the whole of my career. How was I going to pay such a sum? Take it from the bank? "The people" had already depleted my account. What was the meaning, then, of this demand? Was it a blunder or a piece of sheer stupidity?

However, armed men came to demand payment, and I went from committee to committee to try to make them see reason.

"Bah — all your kind are swimming in gold!" was all the answer I got.

Of course, I never contributed the money, but I still keep the printed demands as souvenirs.

On another occasion I received an order to "deliver up all my small-arms immediately." As a matter of fact, I did possess a few weapons. They were hung on the walls and consisted of old pistols, rifles, and spears. Most of them were presents from Gorki's collection.

The committee's orders were that I should give up this miscellany within twenty-four hours, failing which I should be arrested. I went to the committee and came across an extraordinary being, who literally enthralled me because he was living entirely outside the "rhythm" of the stormy times. All around him passions were let loose, and strained nerves were snapping asunder, but this personage, as though disgusted by all these manifestations,

went on living peaceably, exactly like " Vanka the Idiot "
in the traditional Russian stories.

Seated at the table, his face cupped in his hands, he
was staring through the window into the courtyard with
an expression of boredom. When I said: " Good morning,
Comrade! " he made no movement, never even turned
his head in my direction. But I knew that he was waiting
to hear what I had to say, so I went on talking.

" You'll have to give them up," the Komissar murmured
dreamily, still without looking at me.

" But . . ."

" There's a law . . ." he continued in the same tone.

" Still . . ."

" You've got to obey."

" But where shall I deliver them? "

" Down there, if you like."

And for the first time during our interview the Komissar made a movement, not with his body, his hand, or his
head; but without a flicker of his lashes, he slowly rolled
his eyes in the direction of the window, as though to draw
my attention to it. In the courtyard, thick with snow, I
saw a medley of " weapons " stacked together — useless
trench-mortars, rifles, old iron, upon which the snow was
falling.

" They'll rust! " I exclaimed, thinking of the armoury
in my study that had taken so long to collect.

" Yes, they'll rust," agreed my man, as imperturbable
as ever.

In my heart I consigned him to the devil and went out
boiling with rage. I decided to go to Peters in person.

" I possess some firearms," I said to the great leader of
the Tcheka. " But they are not in working order; they
don't fire, they don't cut, they don't slash. They were
presents from Gorki."

Peters was good enough to leave me my " armoury "
. . . until a new order should be made. . . .

I go to Moscow to visit Lenin: He helps me to save the treasures of the Marie Theatre: Work in the theatre: No need of art: Triumph of the back-stage Soviet: The actors' rations become too meagre: I visit Trotski: His reply

ᔕ ᔕ

Affairs at the theatre were also a cause of anxiety to me. Although I had been recalled to save the situation, and my advice had at first been followed, the back-stage Soviet soon began to make trouble. I came into conflict with a woman Communist who was directing some theatrical section or other. One day the Marie Theatre received a circular, or, rather, a visit from a functionary, informing us of the latest official decision.

According to this functionary, the former Imperial Theatres suffered from a plethora of costumes and scenery. The provincial theatres, on the other hand, had practically nothing, and since the people in the provinces could not come to the Marie Theatre in pursuit of culture, the costumes and scenery of the Marie Theatre were to be sent to those theatres which possessed none, so that they might carry on.

I protested vehemently against this proposal.

The properties of the Imperial Theatres, unique in their richness and splendour, have a wonderful history and are of enormous artistic value. Were these properties to be allowed to circulate through the provinces, to pass through the hands of those who would ridicule them and their historical interest? . . . I shuddered with indignation at the thought of these precious costumes being crumpled and crammed into travelling-baskets. "No!" I said resolutely, and I remember adding to myself that if it came to fighting for these properties, I would willingly take up any weapon that happened to be handy.

But it was no light matter for a "bourgeois" to struggle against the Communists. The arguments of a non-Communist had no right even to be called arguments. . . . And the authorities were, of course, on the side of the zealous woman Communist.

The manager of the theatre shared my opinion, and we both made up our minds to go to Moscow and inform Lenin himself of what was happening. It was difficult to obtain an audience with him, but not so difficult as I had found it to get access to Zinoviev in Petersburg.

In the Kremlin, in what used to be the Palace of Justice, I believe, I climbed various staircases guarded by armed soldiers. At each step I had to produce my pass. At last I came to a door before which a sentinel was on duty. I was ushered into an empty hall, partitioned off to make one large and one little room. In the middle was a large table littered with papers, and in front of the table was an arm-chair. I had the impression of a very plain and business-like study.

Suddenly a small door in a corner of the room opened, and a man of Tartar features, with high cheek-bones, a small beard, and short hair, came towards me. It was Lenin. We exchanged greetings. He lisped slightly. He asked me very politely to sit down, and inquired what brought me. I began to explain the matter, which was really quite simple, as clearly as I could, but before I had uttered half a dozen sentences, my eloquence was cut short by Vladimir Iliitch.

CHALIAPIN
WITH A NEGRO GROUP

"Quite, quite. I understand perfectly," he said abruptly.

I immediately realized that I was dealing with a man for whom half a word was enough, and that there was no need for me to elaborate. I fell under his spell at once.

"Go back to Petrograd," he said. "Say nothing to anyone, and I will use my influence, if I have any, on behalf of your reasonable anxiety."

I thanked him and we parted. He obviously *had* influence, for the properties remained where they were, and no one dared lay hands on them. I should have been heartbroken if the dear secular dust of the theatre had been swept away by idiotic brooms. . . .

At this same time Communist politicians of the most advanced type, who had once been property-men, began to appear in the theatre. They pulled long faces and pronounced that the art of opera-singers was only a "bourgeois" art, with which the proletariat had no concern, and that it was a sheer waste to give any rations to the actors. From day to day, work became more difficult and unpleasant. The hand that would have raised itself to achieve something would instantly have received a rap across the knuckles. . . .

The theatrical affairs that had led me to demand an audience of Lenin threw me also into contact with another of the revolutionaries — Trotski. In this case the material welfare of the actors was in question.

Civil war was still going on, and our rations had dwindled miserably. We suffered chiefly from lack of fats. When, as happened occasionally, I performed in the Grand Theatre in Moscow, the actors of that capital complained of their reduced rations and begged me to intercede for them.

An opportunity occurred for me to do so. A big Communist gala evening was celebrated in the theatre in the presence of several members of the Government. Trotski was there. He sat in the box that had formerly belonged to the Grand Duke Serge. This box communicated directly with the stage, and as spokesman for my company I approached the Minister for War, who granted me an audience. I had thought him dark, but I now saw that his hair was chestnut-coloured, his goatee beard of a lighter shade, and that he had piercing, compelling eyes that looked at me through glittering eye-glasses. In his attitude — he was sitting on a bench, I think — there was a kind of heavy immobility.

" Good evening, Comrade Trotski," I said.

He did not move, but merely replied:

" Good evening."

" I have come to make a request, not for myself, but for the performers. Their life is very hard — their rations have been reduced, and I am told that this has been done on your orders."

After a minute's silence Trotski, still motionless, said, accentuating each syllable:

" Don't you think I know what it is, Comrade, to be short of bread? But I can't put the soldier in the trenches on the same level as the ballerina who smiles and twirls on the boards."

" Sad, but true," I thought.

I sighed and said: " If you'll excuse me," and slipped silently away.

I notice that you always " slip silently away " when you haven't succeeded in getting your request granted. . . .

CHAPTER XXIV

Lounatcharski: Soldiers sack my flat in Moscow: My visit to Kamenev: A "charming" revolutionary: "War to the palace, peace to the cottage": We talk politics

༄ ༄

Long before the Revolution I met A. V. Lounatcharski at Gorki's house in Capri. We were in the middle of breakfast when we saw a red-headed man with his arms full of pamphlets appear on the terrace; he had eye-glasses and a Henri Quatre beard. He looked like a "nihilist"; he wore a white muslin blouse with black spots, pulled in with a narrow belt, or it might perhaps have been a girdle. He began to discuss with Gorki an article which he had just written, and I recognized the accents of Odessa in his voice. He bore himself modestly and seemed to be full of business, and I found him congenial. I had guessed him to be a journalist, but I asked Gorki who he was. I cannot recollect who happened to be Minister of Education in tzarist Russia at that time, but I was far from thinking that this young man in the white blouse was to succeed him in the future, and that I should one day be in need of his valuable influence in my own Petersburg. . . .

That time was to come, however, and Lounatcharski helped me on several occasions.

He lived the hidden life of a conspirator in Petersburg, and it took me a long while to track him down. Finally I came across him in one of the Lines [1] of Vasilievski Ostrov. I climbed many steep and filthy stairs and found him in a small room, dressed in a long, tattered overcoat, standing before a desk.

"Anatol Vasilievitch, please come to the rescue!" I said. "I have just learnt that soldiers have sacked my flat in Moscow, without authority. They've taken away a trunk full of presents and other things that have been given me. They're supposed to be searching my place for hospital linen because I opened two hospitals during the war. But I gave it all away a long time ago, and now my silver has disappeared, as well as two hundred bottles of excellent French wine."

Lounatcharski wired to Moscow, and my flat was left in peace. As for my vanished wine, I often came across traces of it. Sometimes I caught sight of bottles in a restaurant bearing labels that read: "Special consignment for M. Chaliapin." I drank this wine with pleasure, paying its price and the duty on it for the second time. . . .

My silver still exercised the Government for some time. When I reached Moscow, I received a note from the Soviet headquarters, couched in ingratiating terms, in which I was asked to make an inventory of the silver and send it along to them, when the matter would be taken in hand. I knew that there were no longer any *private* spoons and forks — it had been often and clearly impressed on me that they were the property of the people. Nevertheless, I went to Soviet headquarters with the idea of making out a case that I myself was to some extent the "people." There I made the acquaintance of the "charming and attractive," but also obstinate and harsh L. B. Kamenev, the brother-in-law of Trotski.

Comrade Kamenev received me very pleasantly, quite in the European manner, which did not surprise me, as he

[1] Roads in Vasilievski Ostrov district are called First Line, Second Line, and so on.

was perfectly turned out as a European; but, like all the others, he spoke to me very plainly:

"You can, of course, use your silver, Comrade Chaliapin, but don't forget that if the people happen to need it at any time, they won't make any bones about collecting it."

Like Podkolesin in Gogol's *The Wedding*, I said:

"That's all right. . . . But — but let me assure you, Comrade Kamenev, I won't hide a single spoon or fork, and in case of need I'll give them all to the people. Allow me, however, to dispense with the inventory, because — "

"Because what?"

"Because I have already been visited by comrades, and they have taken most of the silver. If I make an inventory of the remainder, they'll come and take the whole lot. . . ."

The worthy revolutionary looked at me and laughed.

"You're right. There are plenty of thieves about nowadays. . . ."

Kamenev suddenly became very friendly, and for a quarter of an hour he talked to me about the people and their needs. He spoke glibly of their sufferings and declared that a new era was beginning when, not only in Russia, but throughout the world, there would be no more profiteers, imperialists, or rabble of any kind.

He said all this with such amiability that I thought: "Here are revolutionaries who know how to make life happier. If they put you in prison, they'll at least come and shake hands with you through the bars. . . ."

Taking advantage of his mood, I said boldly:

"You've spoken sound sense about the people and the imperialists, but you've inscribed a most inappropriate motto on Soviet headquarters."

"What do you mean?"

"'*War to the palace, peace to the cottage.*' In my opinion, the people are disgusted with cottages! I've travelled a good bit, and for years I've seen the hideous muck-hovels to which peace is declared. . . . It would be much better if the motto ran: 'War to the *cottage,* peace to the *palace*'! "

Kamenev could not find much to say in reply to my sally. " You must understand the *spiritual* significance of the motto," he asserted.

While I was pondering on its spiritual significance, comrades had already descended on my house to make it plain that my pictures also belonged to the people. " Why should you be the only one to enjoy them? " they argued. " The people also appreciate good pictures. . . ."

" Quite true," I thought. But when, later, I came across my pictures exposed for sale in an antique-shop in Berlin, I wondered what people had been meant.

Russian or German? . . .

CHAPTER XXV

My relations with the Bolshevik leaders: The magistrate of Vilno implores me to save his son: Peters, the notorious head of the Tcheka: Dzerjinski: A mysterious encounter that occurs later in Berlin

⟋⟍ ⟋⟍

THE READER WILL have noted that my various encounters with the leaders of the Revolution — ministers, administrators, leaders of the Tcheka — were invariably of a "business" character. To put it more accurately, I always appeared before them as a "pleader" or an intermediary, for myself or my friends. This everlasting necessity for pleading was one of the most salient and unpleasant features of the Soviet régime. The reader will have noted equally, I am sure, that I did not enjoy any particular privilege.

As befell the rest of the unfortunate Russian "citizens," those worldly chattels that could not be hidden were taken away from me. They took possession of my bank-account and of my car. I was treated "*en bourgeois,*" and relieved of my possessions by persons authorized and unauthorized alike. Yet I was in a sense privileged because of my popularity as a singer. Many doors were open to me that would have been hermetically sealed to others.

But how was I forced to use this prestige? For the most part, to protect myself against ridiculous annoyances and petty quarrels. All this was very sordid — the unseasonable requisitioning of a few bottles of wine, some of my plate, useless firearms, forced "contributions." I have set down these details simply because they are more characteristic of the Bolshevik régime than events of importance. If I had to put up with it all, what must a Russian minus friends, influence, or personal prestige (such as the miserable wordless citizen with the swollen cheek) have had to endure? But did not everyone in Russia now have his own particular aches and pains to bear? Did not those whose teeth were formerly sound now feel them loosened and aching?

One summer day I left the Novinski Boulevard to visit Demian Biedny, the poet, in the Kremlin. He was very friendly towards me, and as he had great influence in the Kremlin, he used it for this and that on my behalf. On this occasion I had another request to make him. In Nititska Street, near the Paradise Theatre, a man with a white beard, wearing a large felt hat and a shabby coat with a cape, suddenly knelt down before me and clasped my feet. In my amazement, I stopped dead, thinking I had to do with a madman. But the next minute I realized, by the expression in his blue eyes, his tears, his despairing gestures, and his words of entreaty, that here was a man, perfectly normal, labouring under tremendous stress.

"You are an artist, M. Chaliapin. All parties, whatever political opinions they hold, must love you. You are the only man who can help me in my terrible straits."

I raised the old man and asked him what was the matter. He told me that his only son, who had served as a non-commissioned officer in the war, was under sentence of death. He swore that he was innocent, and wept so pitifully that my heart was wrung. I told him to come to me in two days' time, and said that I would go to the proper quarters and beg, as he himself had begged me, for pardon for his son.

Biedny and Peters

When I reached Demian Biedny, I was so upset that he asked me what had happened.

"You look ill," said a voice, and, turning, I saw a man whom I recognized from having seen him once in Petersburg — it was Peters.[1]

" Peters has come from Kiev to ' set the house in order,' " said Biedny. "Personally, I believe that wherever Peters goes, houses are turned topsyturvy."

"Let him set as many houses in order as he likes," I thought, " it's all one to me." For once I was delighted to see him. I told him of my encounter in Nititska Street.

" I implore you to go into the matter again, Comrade Peters. I am sure the old man was speaking the truth."

Peters promised to do so. Two days later the old man, full of joy, like a Lazarus risen from the grave, came to see me with his son. He was so grateful that he would have laid down his life for me had it been necessary. All thanks to Peters! He has probably committed many crimes, but I shall never forget this act of justice. The young man was a musician — he became conductor of a military band and has, no doubt, from that day to this, often conducted the great *Internationale* on solemn occasions. . . .

Who was the poor friendless old man who had knelt to a stranger in the public streets?

He had once been magistrate of the supreme tribunal in Vilno. . . .

Shortly after my encounter with Peters, I met Felix Dzerjinski, the most notorious of the leaders of the Tcheka. On this occasion it was not I who engineered the meeting, but he who expressed a wish to see me. I believe that he merely wanted to interrogate me, but, out of consideration for me, he elected to do so in the form of a friendly conversation. I have already mentioned Ch., the Communist who deplored the fact that actors were able to " soften his heart," and who had said: " It's dull work drinking tea,

[1] One of the leaders of the famous Tcheka.

[279]

isn't it, Chaliapin?" This same Ch. had become head of a military detachment and had fallen into disgrace. As the result of an inquiry, a sum of fifteen thousand roubles was found to be missing from the regimental funds. I had liked this Communist — he was a good sort, not at all the type of a common thief, and I do not believe that he had intended to steal this money. Probably some pretty actress had "got round him," and as he found it "dull work drinking tea," he had borrowed the money with the idea of paying it back a few days later. Incidentally, he did eventually repay it, probably by borrowing from a friend; but the fact that he had made use of public moneys created a bad impression, and Dzerjinski himself took the matter in hand. As my sympathy for Ch. had not escaped attention, Dzerjinski wished to have a statement from me. So it came about that one afternoon I was invited to tea at the house of an important personage, and that there I found Dzerjinski.

He struck me as impressive, earnest, deadly serious and unshakable in his beliefs. He spoke with a soft Polish slur. "Here," I thought, "is a true revolutionary, a revolutionary fanatic, a man to command respect. In the struggle against the enemies of the Revolution he has neither mother, father, son, nor Holy Ghost." However, he did not strike me as being a mere incarnation of cruelty. Obviously he did not belong to the company of repulsive brutes whose faces had become eternal masks of hate, and who ground their teeth with every movement of their lower jaws. . . .

He conducted the conversation with great tact. I did not at once realize that I was being catechized, not even when he asked me if I knew Ch., what I thought of him, etc., etc. Presently I began to suspect that Dzerjinski had intentionally brought the conversation round to Ch., and so I exaggerated his good qualities. He emerged from the inquiry with flying colours. His career was not ruined, but it was probably directed to another channel. One day, much later, I met Ch. unexpectedly at the Hôtel Bristol in Berlin.

" Why, if it isn't Ch.! " I exclaimed cordially.

Ch. leaned over and whispered in my ear:

" For God's sake, be careful! There's no Ch. here! "

Whereupon he made himself scarce. What had he meant by his words? They remain a mystery to this day.

Demian Biedny, the "pet" of the Kremlin: His apartment the meeting-place of the Soviet leaders: Stalin: A "concert" in General Boudienny's suite in the train: Frounze and Vorochilov: A cavalry squadron frozen to death

᧤ ᧤

Demian Biedny is known as the official poet of Soviet Russia. The following story is told about him. When Petrograd became Leningrad — when the city built by Peter the Great was christened with the name of Lenin, that is to say — Demian Biedny demanded that the works of the great Russian poet Poushkin should now be called "The works of Demian Biedny." . . . This witty anecdote exactly denotes Biedny's position in the Bolshevik "court." Had the works of Poushkin been christened anew, it was precisely the name of Demian Biedny that they would have received. But the story does not quite give point to the high opinion the poet had of himself. One day, I remember, he read us his latest work. It appealed to me very much, and I thought it greatly resembled one of Poushkin's poems. When he had finished reading it, Biedny said in his pleasant voice:

"Say what you like, gentlemen, that's as good as anything Poushkin ever wrote."

His remark shows that Poushkin was his model, but as Biedny could write poems that were "as good as anything

Poushkin ever wrote," what point was there in attributing the earlier poet's works to him?

Biedny[1] is Demian's pseudonym, and one that does not suit him in the least. There is very little of "poor" about Demian, particularly as regards his tastes and habits. He likes to dine well with his friends on good food and good wine — I don't reproach him for that, I have the same partiality myself — and the result is that his bones are well covered with a substantial layer of firm, white flesh. . . . During the cold winter weather he does not stint the best-quality willow logs to keep up the blaze. When I said enviously (the temperature was six degrees in my house) that he was wasting precious material, that it was quite warm enough without putting on any more wood, the dear fellow replied:

"I like to see it blaze — it looks jolly!"

Biedny genuinely believes that he is a hundred-per-cent Communist. But at heart he resembles those queer Russians who, when the time comes to settle a matter of great importance, will attempt (like rapscallions in mediæval times) to obtain the keys of the cellar of the Kremlin from that withered old Communist "witch," Stassova.

Biedny, who was fairly talented, inspired my liking. I have much reason to be grateful to him. I often had recourse to his protection, and was touched by his readiness to help. His apartment in the Kremlin was a kind of club where the grave dignitaries of the régime, anxious and preoccupied, would look in for a few minutes to talk, make plans, or meet their friends.

When I was in Moscow, I would often drop in for a few minutes with him, and his was the only place where I met the Soviet leaders on "non-soliciting" terms.

I must admit that they were all very friendly towards me. I have already said that it was at Biedny's that I first met Lenin (not counting our forgotten meeting at Gorki's

[1] *"Biedny"* means *"poor."*

[283]

in 1905). It was at Biedny's also that I met Lenin's successor, Stalin. I never took part in the political conversations of the guests, nor did I listen to them very attentively. I knew very little about politics, and the little I knew failed to interest me. This, however, did not prevent me from making mental notes about the talkers.

When I saw Stalin for the first time, I little suspected that he would become the master of Russia, " adored " by all around him. I did feel, though, that he was a man apart. He had a pronounced Caucasian accent and spoke very little, but what he said carried weight—perhaps because he never spoke unnecessarily.

" They must stop acting the fool. They must do what they've been told to do a hundred times. . . ."

I gathered from his words, obscure in meaning to me, but spoken with energy, that Stalin was not to be trifled with. With the lightness of the Caucasian gliding noiselessly in felt shoes, he could, if need be, lead the dance, or blow up the Church of St. Saviour, the Post Office, or any other building he chose. You could see it in his gestures, his movements, his eyes; you could hear it in his voice. Not that he was a monster of perversity—he was born with these characteristics.

It was through Demian Biedny, if not at his house, that I met the leaders of the Red Army. One day he suggested that we should do well to visit Boudienny, whose train was at a siding on the Kiev-Voroneje line, not far from Moscow. He led me to understand that the journey might be worth some ten kilos of flour to me—a matter of tremendous importance at that time. It was very tempting to meet a man of whom I had heard so much, and in addition to possess myself of a welcome sack of flour!

General Boudienny, the famous cavalry general, impressed me by his thick, heavy moustache, which looked as though it had been cast in bronze, and by his simple, soldierly face with its prominent cheek-bones. You could see that he was one of those Russian warriors who fear nothing and no one, who do sometimes think of death, but of other people's deaths, never of their own.

Klim Vorochilov, the commander-in-chief of the Red Army, who was also in the compartment, presented a striking contrast. He had a childlike aspect, was puddingy and somewhat flaccid. Of working-class origin, he must certainly have been a workman out of the ordinary. He pleased me by the firmness and warmth of his handshake, as well as by recalling a pleasant memory to me. He told me that before the Revolution he had come to ask me, in the name of his associates, to take part in a concert for the benefit of their sick-funds. He termed himself my fervent admirer and reminded me that he had also begged for free tickets.

I was expecting to meet another leader, Frounze, with Boudienny. I had been told the following story about him under the tzarist régime: During a strike in Kharkov, he had openly knelt in the street and fired on the police. This had made him famous in his party. One day, in the course of a diatribe on the military question, Trotski had ironically remarked that " the military experience of Comrade Frounze was based on the fact that he had once shot a policeman. . . ."

I pictured Frounze as a man with a low forehead, bristling hair, bushy eyebrows, and oblique eyes. This was the only description compatible with a man who had coolly knelt in the road and taken aim. But now Frounze appeared, and my picture collapsed. He had a romantic aspect, accentuated by his white beard. He was quickly roused to anger, but at heart was a man of gentle disposition.

The second-class carriage which had been converted into a sitting-room was as plain as a non-commissioned officer's quarters. *Zakouskis* and vodka were brought in, but everything was unpretentious in the extreme. A woman dressed like a peasant — Boudienny's wife, I believe — set a dish on the table; herrings and potatoes, it might have been, or perhaps roast chicken, I can't remember which. Our modest meal began. We drank vodka, and sang songs, all of us joining in. I was asked to give them a lead, and afterwards to sing alone. I sang the *Doubinouchka* accompanied by the rest, then old Russian melodies such as *Loutchinouchka, Through the forests of willow and pine*, and *Snowflakes*. My audience listened without much response. It was very different from the time when in the prime of my youth I had sung the same songs in an underground *estaminet* at Baku. There, my listeners were escaped convicts who joined in the chorus, and wept. . . .

The leaders said nothing particularly memorable in my presence. The only thing I recall is that one of them spoke of a squadron of cavalry frozen to death near Rostov. I don't know whether they were Reds or Whites, I only know that I visualized the tragic picture: soldiers pressed shoulder to shoulder, stark and cold on their horses. . . . An icy story from the Land of Winter! My thoughts went back to the cross with the *chapka* rakishly aslant on the grave of the unknown soldier.

I remembered the blood-stained note-book, and the words:

" In recognition of services rendered with zeal. . . ."

Always the same — these Russian soldiers, always the same. Whether they fought against the Germans near Varsovia, or against their fellow-Russians near Rostov, they were the same. . . .

The next morning I received a certain quantity of flour and sugar: " A present from a Cossack of the Don."

And so life goes on. . . .

CHAPTER XXVII

Bolshevik "swarms" and the actors: The occupation: My house:
Esthonian vodka takes effect on a Finn: My "friend" Kouklin:
His philosophy and my fist: Overseers: Ladies of the theatre:
"Proletarian art"

ᔬ ᔬ

B Y SENTIMENT, TRADITION, and inclination, the world of
art obviously belonged to the "old world" which was
doomed to destruction.

Artists combined the characteristics of the intelligentsia
and the bourgeoisie; hence they were doubly alien to the
spirit of the proletarian régime. Yet, as I have already
said, the Soviet, for reasons of its own, showed a certain
amount of favour towards the theatre, and consequently
the most ardent Communists could make friends amongst
the actors with impunity. It is a fact that actors are able,
as a rule, to adapt themselves to new conditions and new
people. Perhaps this is because the actor, accustomed to
change of scene and characters on the stage, regards the
most radical revolution in life as a sort of new setting for
new types. Yesterday the actor was impersonating a general;
today, a workman or a drunkard. Yesterday he was playing
in a comedy of manners or a bourgeois drama; today you
behold him in a tragedy.

However that may be, after the Bolshevik *coup d'état,*
all sorts of "promoters" of the Revolution invaded the

Russian theatre like a swarm of flies. With a few exceptions, it was really the "flies" that swarmed. The "elephants" were too weighty, too serious, and too engrossed in work to seek distraction behind the scenes or in visits to the actors. Certain members of the party were in the habit of worrying me, amongst others. Some of them were obviously men with whom it was pleasant to have intercourse — for instance, there was Komissar Ch., who, though decidedly temperamental, was congenial and intelligent. Unfortunately, these were only exceptions. My "swarm" consisted for the most part of half-educated persons who were mentally complete strangers to me, and very often antipathetic.

How had it come about that at the table where Rimski-Korsakov, Sierov, Stasov, Gorki, Rachmaninov, Riepin, and Dalski had once sat, there now lounged all those Kouklins and Rakhyas whom I recall with loathing? I often wonder.

In the conditions of life that prevailed in St. Petersburg during this era, which bore an astonishing resemblance to the occupation of a vanquished city by a mob of shameless rabble, the right to violate everyone's privacy seemed as natural as the victorious officer's right to billet himself on whom he chose. . . . The level of existence had fallen so low that people were resigned when unwelcome guests were thrust upon them, as resigned as they were to the pangs of hunger and the raggedness of their garments. Who, in those days, would have been ashamed of wearing boots that gaped with holes? . . .

But enforced custom did not prevent certain outbreaks of disgust. The gentlemen went a step too far at times, and then dull acceptance turned to violent rage. . . .

Wine and spirits had gone out of general circulation, and the citizens who liked to sustain their courage with a *petit verre* set themselves to distilling their own vodka. I had some Esthonian vodka, made from potatoes. Whether this vodka was of good quality remains to be shown, but I know we all thought it excellent. . . . At all events, my " swarm " found it very much to their taste.

One day several people had gathered at my house. Amongst them were Rakhya, a Finnish Communist, and Kouklin, the Russian Communist, a former corn-chandler, I believe. As long as they were drinking my essence-of-potato, all went well, but when the conversation turned on theatres and actors, Rakhya coolly remarked at the top of his voice that individuals like me ought to have their gullets slit.

Somebody had the curiosity to ask why.

" Because no man should be superior to another — that's why! " shouted Rakhya. " Genius destroys equality."

His comment amused me. " My Esthonian vodka is taking effect on my Finnish friend," I thought. Unfortunately, Kouklin now began to hold forth. He was terribly long-winded. " None but the proletariat must exist," he de-claimed. " If anything else exists, it must be for the good of the proletariat! " Every five minutes he would come out with:

" You actors, have you done anything for the prole-tariat? Yes or no? "

It made me sick. I controlled myself and explained that we actors did what we could for all men, the proletariat included, if they took any interest in what we could do. But he would not budge: nobody knew anything, and I, Chaliapin, knew least of all.

" You don't know anything. Why don't you write some-thing and act it to the proletariat? "

" *You* write something, and *I'll* act it! "

" But you're the actor, so you must write the play. You don't know anything. . . . To begin with, what do you really know about the proletariat? "

Forgetful that I was the host, I felt my temper rising, and, livid with fury, I banged my fist violently on the hospitable board. The blue blood of Ivan the Terrible and Boris began to boil in my veins.

"Get up! And hold your tongue, you rotter! How dare you talk like that? I can't understand you, but who are you, anyway? You're nothing but a brute! I understand Shakspere, but not a dirty swine like you! Say your prayers if you know any, and get ready for the Judgment Day, because I'm going to throw you out of the window. . . ."

Seeing the dangerous turn our conversation had taken, the other guests intervened between Kouklin and myself. They calmed me down, swallowed some more Esthonian vodka, and took their departure.

But things were going from bad to worse in the theatre.

I recollect that in Petersburg in the days of the tzarist régime a man came to see me at the Hôtel du Nord. His hair was cut like a peasant's, he had a reddish moustache, a pock-marked face, and boots as big as canoes. He came in, turned his head stiffly, as though it were impaled on a spike, looked in every corner, caught sight of the ikon, crossed himself, and said:

"Don't you know me, Feodor Ivanovitch?"

"I'm afraid I don't," I admitted.

"I'm the overseer who looked after the building of your villa."

"Oh yes, I remember now. . . ."

"Well, Feodor Ivanovitch, would you be good enough to find me a billet?"

"But what can you do?"

"Do? Why, superintend, of course!" cried my unexpected visitor in surprise.

It's interesting to be an overseer, because he doesn't have to work, he doesn't understand anything and is content to give orders:

"Senka, be careful how you saw that wood!"

And Senka, who is already sweating freely, has to sweat still more as he starts re-sawing.

Ladies of the Theatre

There are many devotees of the amateur cult of " overseer " in our beloved Russia. Specimens of this type rushed
helter-skelter to the theatre in the days of Communism.
During the Revolutionary epoch various ladies who had
absolutely no concern with the theatre took upon themselves to order us all about. My dear friend Teliakovski
had once incurred reproach for acting as manager of the
Imperial Theatre while he was a colonel in the cavalry, but
even in the regimental stables Teliakovski had meditated
on theatrical matters far more deeply than these overseer
ladies had done all their lives. As a matter of fact, they
were Communists or the wives of Communists, and this
was sufficient to turn their pronouncements on art and the
purpose of the theatre for the " people " into law.

I saw more and more clearly that my efforts were useless, and that my work had lost all meaning. The theories
of my " friend " Kouklin triumphed all along the line;
no one but the proletariat had a right to exist, and we,
the actors, knew nothing about anything. Something must
be specially written and acted for the proletariat. . . .
This was the kind of thing that seeped through all the
pores of existence — it was the essence of the Soviet régime.
It froze and deadened our souls, laid waste our hearts, and
sowed the seeds of despair in the minds of all.

CHAPTER XXVIII

The Bolshevik Robot

∽ ∽

Wʜᴀᴛ ᴀʀᴇ ᴡᴇ to think of the men who engendered such
a spirit?

Some classify them as ravening wolves, others as plun-
derers, others as men who were bribed — bribed to destroy
Russia.

Much blood has been shed, hundreds of atrocities have
been committed, and the spirit of destruction has breathed
over the country. But in my heart of hearts I feel it would
be superficial and untrue to dismiss the whole Bolshevik
régime in terms of violence and rapine. It strikes me as
being all very simple, and yet highly complex. In all its
aspects, in all its forms, I see something profoundly Russian, an ugliness essentially Russian in the mixture of folly
and cruelty, of Sodom and Nebuchadnezzar, of which the
Bolshevik régime is compounded.

I should be blind and prejudiced if I did not recognize
that to Lenin and some of his associates the Bolshevik
movement was an attempt to re-create life on a fairer basis.
They were definitely not mere " thieves and brigands."
The tragedy lay in the fact that our Russian architects were
not content to build an ordinary human edifice on a reasonable scale; nothing less than a " tower defying the
heavens " — a Tower of Babel — would do for them. . . .

[292]

They were not satisfied with the steady progress of the man who goes to and fro between his work and his home — they must rush headlong towards the future in seven-league boots. . . .

"Down with the old world!" was the general outcry, and so the old world must needs be swept away, lock, stock, and barrel.

But, above all, our Russian wiseacres claim to *know* everything. They *know* how to transform a cobbler into an Apollo Belvedere; they *know* how to teach a hare to strike a match; they *know* what the hare needs for its well-being, and what will ensure the happiness of its descendants two hundred years hence. . . . There are painters who depict saucepans with ropes, and triangles with hearts and livers, and when asked what their meaning is, will reply: " This is the art of the future. . . ." Our Russian builders have created a similar " art of the future." It is as clear as crystal to them! And so convinced are they of their infallibility that they consider the least deviation from their formula of life sacrilege and mulish obstinacy calling for the strictest severity. . . .

Thus it came about that every human quality, like a medal, showed its reverse side. " Liberty " became tyranny; " fraternity," civil war; " equality " ended in the thrusting down of any head that dared to lift itself above the level of the morass. " Construction " masqueraded as wholesale destruction, and " love " for future humanity manifested itself as an inquisition of hatred against contemporaries.

I love Alexander Blok's poem *The Twelve* — all but the concluding lines, which I cannot grasp. I have never glimpsed " Christ with a crown of white roses " in the Bolshevik procession. The most remarkable thing about Blok's poem is the interweaving of two contrasted musical themes.

There is the hard, mechanical march of the Revolutionary army:

Revolutionaries, mind your step,
The enemy, on the watch, sleeps not. . . .

That is in the spirit of *Das Kapital*—it is Marx,
Lenin. . . .

And simultaneously you hear Russian turbulence,
throbbing with passion and reckless insolence:

Well, so you put on laces gay
And rigged yourself out, stitch by stitch;
And did the officers love you, eh?—
Christ! Come and kiss my lips, you bitch!

———

Catherinette, do you recall
That officer I stripped of all?
You don't? You trollop, you've forgotten;
Like you, your memory is rotten . . .

That is our Jacques L'Éméraude, the accordion-player,
in the once private, now public, garden. . . .

In life under the Bolsheviks, I feel that this second theme
—the natural element—is present with far greater force
than the first, the "official" factor. The practice of Bolshevism has proved far more cruel than its conception.
Perhaps the worst evil lies in the fact that the intolerant
and obtusely arrogant spirit of the "*petit bourgeois*" has
become part and parcel of the régime, in which all the
faults of Russian mentality have their part. We find, not
only Tchekov's Prichibeiev, the non-commissioned officer,
spying on his neighbours' lives, but also Fedia, the con-
vict, with his knife. There is a march past of all the characters in satirical Russian literature, from Fonvizin to
Zochtchenko. They are all there, saluting Vladimir Iliitch
Lenin. . . .

Here they come—provincial registrars, adjutants
spreading syphilis in the suburbs, officials, police, de-
bauched and bankrupt cavalrymen, students unable to

finish their course, quack chemists. Here comes our half-baked intellectual from the country, who, during the boredom of the old régime, sought God knows what escape from the deadliness of his life. He was to be seen at the station where the train was making a short halt, walking up and down the platform and casting reproachful glances at the first-class passengers; he was wont to discourse to his star pupil on the deep impression made on him the day before by the opening chapters of *Das Kapital*. . . .

In the Zemstvo at Kazan, where I was a clerk, there was a minister of public education whom the district teachers used to come and see. They all differed from one another in appearance; each had his own style of dressing and doing his hair; there was great variety in their voices and simple Russian faces. But they all spoke the same language. When I think of them, I am certain that they all thought alike. They felt that the state of affairs that then existed in Russia was worthless, that a day would come when a justice (of which they had but a confused idea) would be established and when there would be a communion of soul between the suffering Russian people and themselves. . . . These were, no doubt, worthy sentiments, but I have a recollection of a woman teacher who burned with love for the people. This love she distilled into venom, as corn is distilled into alcohol — venom at the thought that the Venus de Milo (whom she knew through the works of Ouspenski) dared to be beautiful when the world was full of blind and squinting people; venom at the thought that the Mediterranean dared sparkle under an azure sky (she had read this in Nekrasov) when in Russia there were so many swamps and quagmires. . . . She, too, I am sure, came to do homage at the Kremlin. . . .

Here comes our young highbrow from the capital, whose self-claim to being a "highbrow" consists in his being able to parade Socialist or Marxian quotations at all times and seasons. (He is insincere at bottom, for he ridicules the very words he quotes.) Here comes the old-timer who has suffered tortures in the prisons of the old régime, and is now burning to torture his tormentors.

And, last of all, here comes the famous gas-bag! He takes up his stand and bangs the infernal keys of the calculating-machine. Try to reason with him! No argument on earth will convince him — he has his figures. He has his multiplication table. Capital and interest. He calculates that this, that, and the other can be dispensed with. Why should a man have a home to himself? How bourgeois! So many units can be sheltered in his house. I address him in ordinary human words, but he cannot understand me. He must have figures. When I say "Velasquez," he looks at me strangely and answers: "The people have no use for him. Titian, Mozart, Rembrandt — what's the good of them? No one but a counter-revolutionary or a White Guard would give them a thought." The sum of his requirement is a book-keeper, an automaton, a machine, a *robot* — not a creature of flesh and blood. He needs a robot that has no thought-processes, but is a blind obedience — a robot who with a turn of the hand can do all that the crank in the factory commands him to do. He needs a robot who quotes Lenin, speaks like Stalin, insults Chamberlain, sings the *Internationale,* and, if need be, can batter a man to pulp. . . .

A robot! Russian culture once knew a different kind of robot, a robot conceived by Alexander Poushkin, inspired by the Prophet Isaiah:

> *A six-winged seraph did appear,*
> *Who touched my ears, and I could hear*
> *A myriad sounds — the breathless whir*
> *Of angels' wings in heaven, the stir*
> *Of monsters in the sea below;*
> *I heard the tendrilled vine-shoots grow.*
> *Then bent the seraph down and tore*
> *My lying tongue out evermore,*

The Bolshevik Robot

And twixt my icy lips there sprang
The serpent of all wisdom's fang.
Then with his sword my breast he clove,
Plucked out my beating heart, and drove
A brand that flamed within the chasm,
Till I lay still in deathlike spasm
Within the wilderness. . . .

Does not this suggest a robot? Listen:

The voice of God cried: " Wake, O seer,
Do thou thy will, and see and hear;
Go over land and sea, and reach
The soul of mankind with thy speech."

I hear Comrade Kouklin saying: "You don't understand. The proletariat has no use for six-winged seraphs. What the people want is a six-pounder gun . . . to defend themselves with. . . ."

But, Comrade Kouklin, what I need most of all in life are those things that are *not* necessary. Shakspere is of no use. What use can Poushkin be? What is the good of Mozart? What can you get out of Moussorgski? And of what value was Duse to the proletariat? . . .

Soon I began to feel that the robot would stifle me if I did not tear myself away from his mechanical embraces.

CHAPTER XXIX

A ham! A saviour: The journey to Reval: Koustodiev

ৡ ৡ

THE MONOTONY AND emptiness of life weighed so heavily on me that even tiring and uninteresting tours in the provinces were welcome. At least they broke the everlasting sameness of my existence in Petersburg. The railway journey was in itself a slight diversion. Through the carriage window I saw tramps on the roads, moujiks in the fields, and gained some illusion of liberty. Moreover, these tours were useful from the standpoint of food-supplies.

For instance, two or three days before Christmas a man came from Pskov to see me. With a meaning smile, he laid a large parcel on the table and proceeded to unpack it. It contained two or three smoked sausages, a ham, and three or four pounds of sugar.

"I'm getting up a concert at Pskov next May," said my visitor. "If you will promise to come and sing, I'll leave you all this food for Christmas. I know it's very poor pay for you, but if the takings warrant it, I'll give you a little money as well after the concert."

"Money!" I exclaimed, quite carried away. "A thousand thanks! It was very good of you to have thought of me!"

And in May I sang at the concert I had "eaten" in December!

Visits of this sort were a source of happiness to me and my family, and never shall I forget the intense joy I felt when one spring morning in 1921 an impresario came in person to see me and proposed a tour abroad.

I say "abroad," but this was only a relative term. "Abroad" signified no farther than Reval, once the principal town of a Russian province, but now the capital of Esthonia — a foreign state and a window over Europe. Europe! What was happening in Europe? How were people living there? In our isolation we had no means of telling. "At Reval," I thought, "I shall learn, in the twinkling of an eye, what's going on in Europe proper."

The best of it was that it was no dream — before me, in the flesh, stood a man who was saying in perfectly intelligible Russian that he would take me with him, not to any Pskov, but abroad, to a free country. . . . A doubt flashed across my mind: would I be allowed to go? I remembered the innumerable obstacles I had had to surmount, the time I had spent in various departments, before I had been able to obtain permission for my sick daughter, Marina, to go to a sanatorium in Finland.

"Don't worry about that — I'll get permission," said my visitor.

This he did, and I started on the journey to Reval with Wolf-Israel, the 'cellist, and a musician who had formerly been an engineer, who was to be my accompanist. I managed to take my friend Isaika also.

Is there anything more commonplace than crossing a frontier? It is an ordinary experience for most of us, but I do not believe that Gulliver setting foot for the first time in the kingdom of Lilliput felt a greater thrill than I did when I found myself at the first station across the frontier. We had grown so unused to private enterprise that we marvelled when we discovered a refreshment room where we could buy as much bread as we liked. It was delicious bread, too, baked to a turn and powdered with flour. I was much amused to see Isaika make a rush for it and proceed to cram his mouth as full as he could.

"Stop!" I cried, laughing. "When we get back, I'll denounce you — I'll say that you compromised Russia by making people believe we're dying of hunger. . . ."

But, needless to say, I hastened to follow his example. My impressions of Reval were most enlightening.

To begin with, I learnt that I was labelled a Bolshevik.

I was staying in a delightful old house, to reach which I had to pass the Junkers' school. These young people were Russians. As I drew near, I heard them shouting: "Chaliapin!" and my name was followed by a string of most unflattering epithets. Next came catcalls. I did not in the least regard myself as a Bolshevik; nevertheless I was hurt by the shouting and hooting, and, to obviate any further unpleasantness, I sought for a way home by which I could avoid passing the school. What particularly struck me was the fact that my impresario anticipated trouble at the concert. As I had never experienced any fear, except of authorities, and as I had never been nervous of an audience in my life, I walked quickly and confidently on to the platform. The impresario's anxiety proved groundless. I had a most friendly reception, and the same success attended me which, thanks to Providence, has never left me. . . .

M. Birk, the Minister of Foreign Affairs in Esthonia, asked me to dinner with him at the club on the night after the concert. For reasons of etiquette, he also invited the Soviet representative, a man called Goukovski, who was some years afterwards to poison himself — by order, it was said. I anticipated with delight the thought that I was going to enjoy the pleasure of free human intercourse after so many months of restraint. I took a lot of trouble over dressing and hurried to the club. There disillusion awaited me; dinner was served in a private room. I felt that the Minister for Foreign Affairs did not care to be seen dining in public with the Soviet representative. . . . Was I right?

When I got back to Petersburg, I summed up my impressions of Reval.

1. That life in other countries is infinitely preferable to life in Russia, whatever they tell us to the contrary in Moscow and Petersburg.

2. That the Soviets are not held in any particular esteem outside Russia.

3. That I was taken for a Bolshevik simply because I came from the U.S.S.R.

4. That, in spite of this, I had been a success in Reval.

In short, my first voyage of discovery had been favourable. " If I succeed in getting to Europe," I thought, " I shall be able to work and live there."

The large packing-case full of food that I brought back with me delighted my family. For a time we stopped drinking tea manufactured from carrot-tops by the ladies of the household. With truly idolatrous joy they set about kneading dough with white flour and making pancakes. . . .

My visit to Reval had roused vague hopes in me. I felt lighter-hearted and set to work with renewed ardour on Sierov's opera *La Force ennemie,* which we proposed to produce at the Marie Theatre. I have special reason for remembering the décor, because it brought me into touch with Koustodiev, the artist.

I have met many interesting men in my life, men of talent and innate goodness, but none of them, I believe, lived on the same spiritual level as Koustodiev. His work is familiar to every cultured Russian. His brilliantly coloured pictures of Russian life, full of the gay chime of bells and the sounds of merry-making; his garish booths, merchants, comely, rosy-cheeked girls, handsome vagabonds, and merry rascals, figures typical of Russia, recreated from childhood memories, fill you with delight. Only a passionate love of Russia could have inspired the artist with such pure precision of line, such challenging colour in his portrayal of Russian types. . . . But how

[301]

many people, I wonder, know that Koustodiev, with his joyful flights of fancy, was a hopeless invalid who suffered martyrdoms?

I am unable to think without emotion of his moral courage, for which I can find no other word than heroic.

We decided to ask Koustodiev if he would undertake to do the settings and costumes for *La Force ennemie,* based on Ostrovski's *Live, not as thou desirest, but as God wills.* No one was so well fitted to feel and realize the world of Ostrovski. I went to see him and ask him if he would give us his co-operation.

I felt an overwhelming pity when I saw him lying help-less on a couch. He was paralysed in both legs — I forget what had caused it. He had tried many "cures" and had undergone an operation on his spine, but it was useless.

He asked me to sit down and propelled the couch for-ward with his hands to bring himself nearer to me. Such an affliction evoked pity, but he himself was quite ob-livious of the feelings he awakened. I was struck by the moral courage of this pale, fair-haired man in the forties — there was no trace of melancholy in his face. On the contrary, his eyes sparkled and shone with *joie de vivre.*

I explained my errand.

"I shall be delighted," he said. "I'm only too glad to be of help in this wonderful work. I'll make some sketches for you, and design the costumes. . . . Meanwhile, I'd like to paint you in that cloak — it's so rich, so luxurious."

"You're on rather delicate ground," I remarked. "The cloak is indeed beautiful, but I fear it is stolen property."

"Stolen? You're joking, Feodor Ivanovitch."

"Not at all. Three weeks ago, I received it from one of the State shops, in payment for a concert, so it must have been stolen."

"Tell me all about it."

"Well, I'd been asked to sing at the Marie Theatre for some society or other, and, instead of paying me in

CHALIAPIN

SPEAKING TO INMATES OF SING-SING PRISON

money or flour, they offered me a cloak. I didn't need it, I have a fur one already, but the offer interested me. I went to the State shop and was told to choose what I liked. See what a low bourgeois I am — I didn't pick out the cheapest, I chose the most expensive. . . ."

" I'll immortalize it on canvas," he said. " Just think what a unique subject it will make — actor and cloak-thief combined! "

We burst out laughing and arranged the times for the sittings. Koustodiev painted lying motionless on the couch and inclining the canvas towards him. The portrait was soon finished. So were the sketches and costumes for *La Force ennemie*. I allotted the parts, and rehearsals started. Koustodiev wanted to attend them all. On each occasion I hired a motor-van, and with the help of his son or his friends we carried Koustodiev downstairs on his couch and lifted him into it. He followed the rehearsals with great interest and was much thrilled, I believed, at the dress rehearsal. He was in the manager's box on the first night of the production, and great was his delight when the opera we had all done our best to perfect was enthusiastically received by the audience.

I was to see very little more of this remarkable man. My portrait had been painted during the winter of 1921, and at the beginning of 1922 I left Petersburg. I was profoundly grieved when I heard of his death. I keep my celebrated portrait and all the sketches for *La Force ennemie* in my study in Paris and regard them as priceless treasures.

CHAPTER XXX

A letter from America: I go abroad at my own risk: Riga: A friend from the Marie Theatre: A refreshing shower of offers: A good old tradition

~ ~

MY CONCERT AT Reval had attracted the notice of foreign impresarios. Some journalist had, I suppose, mentioned it in a wire, and shortly afterwards I received a letter from an American impresario. This letter did not come to me straight by post, it was forwarded to me from Moscow by Lounatcharski with a covering note in which he said some quaint impresario was inviting me to come and sing in America. . . . He called him quaint with some reason; the impresario in question had arranged a tour for Pavlova in America and had had the picture of a dancer in the midst of performing a complicated evolution engraved on his note-paper.

The letter filled me with joy. It was a good excuse for asking Lounatcharski if I might negotiate in earnest with this impresario, and if I had any hope of being allowed to leave the country. Lounatcharski promised to see me through.

Before I replied to the impresario, I set to work to try to get permission to leave the country. I had decided to go at any risk, so great was my desire to leave Russia. I obtained a passport fairly soon, but I found that a ticket as far as Riga only would cost me several million roubles. It was more than I could afford. I had the money, but I had to leave enough for the needs of my family while I was away. I also had to carry a certain amount with me. Moreover, I had heard repeatedly that citizens of the Soviet Government, unlike those of capitalist countries, were fortunate enough to receive everything free in exchange for coupons.

I took my courage in both hands and telephoned to Lounatcharski.

" I thought everything was free," I said. " How is it that I've just been asked several million roubles for a ticket? "

Lounatcharski promised to see to the matter, and indeed, a few days later, he telephoned that I could leave for Riga without paying anything.

" Litvinov and other Soviet leaders are going to Riga by special train," he said. " They'll see that you have a seat."

Which they did. When I reached the station, someone came up to me very politely and showed me to a first-class carriage. It was a ministerial suite: there was a drawing-room, a tiny dining-room, and a kitchen at the side. The diplomats were friendly, but at the same time discreet. For my part, I behaved as though I were not very alert and thus avoided any intercourse. We breakfasted and drank coffee. When we stopped at a station, I got out and strolled up and down the platform. It was August, and the weather was fine.

I had a less pleasant experience when we arrived at the Riga station. As we got out, photographers, camera-men, and reporters crowded forward. Litvinov stepped on to the platform, and so did I. There were cries of " Smile, please! " " That's right, thank you! " and " Look, there's Chaliapin, the Bolshevik! "

I book a small room in a quiet, third-class hotel, for I

have not much money. I go to the bank to change my notes. The Lettish clerk smiles.

" I'm sorry, but we don't change that sort of money! " This is cheerful. . . .

I hang my head and return to the hotel. What on earth am I to do? Suddenly I hear someone calling me. It is a friend of mine, a tenor from the Marie Theatre, a Lett by birth. He is young and high-spirited, he grasps my hand to show his delight in seeing me. But why do I look so worried? I explain that I don't know what to do, that I've booked a room in the hotel, but that I'm not sure I have enough money to pay the bill.

" Give a concert! " cries my friend. " And at once! "

He actually organized a concert for me. It brought me success, money, and a welcome shower of unexpected offers. Immediately after this concert in Riga I was visited by a representative of an important gramophone company — M. Gaizberg, who had come purposely from London to ask me to renew my pre-war contract. He put two hundred pounds sterling on the table! Telegrams arrived inviting me to sing in Europe, America, China, Japan, Australia. . . .

I leave the reader to imagine the feast I gave for my friends in Riga. We engaged the whole of the first floor of the Restaurant Schwartz and set to work in earnest; we felt we must spend a quarter of the sum that had, as it were, miraculously fallen from heaven. . . .

After I left Russia, I went to America. I sang in London, and had the honour of remitting the half of my English royalties — about fourteen hundred pounds — to the Soviet ambassador in London, the late M. Krassin. It was in the good old tradition of serfdom: the moujik who went to work outside his village gave the *pomiechtchik,* the master of his life, a part of his earnings.

I have always respected tradition. . . .

CHAPTER XXXI

*I return to Petersburg: I juggle with my conscience: Permission
to go abroad with my family: I bid farewell to Dzerjinski: The*
Internationale

ᔕᔕ

I HAD RETURNED FROM my first tour abroad with a vague
hope of attaining freedom; I returned from the second
with the fixed intention of making my dream come true.
I had become convinced that abroad I should be able to
live more peacefully, more independently, without having
to account to anyone for my actions, without having to put
up my hand, like a schoolboy, for permission to leave the
room. . . .

I did not for a moment contemplate living abroad without my family, but it was far more complicated, of course,
for all of us to get away than for just myself alone. So I
decided, I confess, to juggle a little with my conscience. I
let it be understood that my concerts in foreign countries
benefited and advertised the Soviet Government. Of
course, I did not believe a word of this. Obviously, if I
sing and act fairly well, it is not due to the President of
the Council of Komissars of the People! God made me
thus before the days of Bolshevism. I merely threw out
the suggestion for my own ends.

However, my hints were taken seriously and regarded
with favour, and soon I had the much-longed-for permit
in my pocket, authorizing me to go abroad with my family.

But my married daughter and my first wife were still in Moscow. I did not want to expose them to any annoyances, so I begged Dzerjinski not to draw hasty conclusions from information that might be given about me in the foreign press. An over-zealous reporter might well be capable of publishing a sensational account of an interview that I should never have dreamed of giving him.

Dzerjinski listened to me attentively and said:

"Very well."

Two or three weeks later, on a fine summer morning, a little group of friends and acquaintances assembled on one of the quays of the Neva, not far from the Académie des Beaux-Arts. My family and I were on the bridge of the ship. We waved our handkerchiefs, and my dear old friends and comrades of the Marie Theatre orchestra played marches in our honour.

Just as the ship started, while I was waving my hat to them all — it was a sad moment for me, because I knew it would be long before I saw my country again — they struck up the *Internationale*.

And so the cold and crystal waters of the majestic Neva slowly bore away from his watching friends the figure of Chaliapin, the so-called Bolshevik.

CHAPTER XXXII

I rejoice in the free air of Europe: A Consul of the U.S.S.R. who is also a foreign correspondent: I give him a piece of my mind

დოდ

I BREATHED IN THE free air of Europe with eagerness and joy. After my sad and sordid existence in the Russian capitals everything seemed rich and magnificent to me. The people in the streets looked happy, care-free, and well dressed. I marvelled at the perfectly ordinary displays in shop-windows, where you could buy any goods you liked without difficulty and without coupons. I wanted to forget all that I had left behind me. I was tortured by the least thought of what I had endured. I decided, of course, to keep clear of politics while I was abroad, to devote myself to my work, and to avoid openly expressing my views on the Soviet Government. I am an actor, I thought, politics have nothing to do with me. When I had told Dzerjinski that I would not grant political interviews, I had meant it. Nevertheless, a few days only after my departure from Petersburg I involuntarily made a violent manifestation against the Soviet, simply because a fool recalled to me brutally all I had fled from.

It occurred at Oslo. The U.S.S.R. consul came to greet me, I believe, or else to help me on my journey. Although I did not need his assistance, I appreciated his kindness and thanked him warmly. Now, this consul exercised another official function at Oslo; he was correspondent to the Soviet telegraphic agency. After he had fulfilled his hospitable duty in the capacity of consul, my visitor imperceptibly changed his rôle, took on a very Muscovite expression, and began solemnly to carry out his second official part.

" What do you think of the Soviet Government, Feodor Ivanovitch? "

Simultaneously he produced his pad and prepared to take down my reply.

Where, I wonder, is that famous writing-pad now? Did its owner take it with him in his precipitate flight, or is it still lying on the floor of the hotel in Oslo? The stupid question and the brutal intrusion on my still lacerated spirit made me explode like a bomb. I forgot Dzerjinski and the others and plunged the consul correspondent into mortal terror by brandishing my chair like a mark of interrogation!

" Did they ask my opinion when they took possession of the country? " I thundered. " They did without my opinion then, didn't they? They want to have it now, do they? Clear out! This minute! "

I do not know whether Dzerjinski was informed of the incident, and if so, what he thought about it. On the other hand, unfortunately, I soon learnt what the Russians abroad thought of my attitude to the Bolsheviks. . . . This incident, trifling in itself, is bound up with another problem which has frequently engrossed and worried me. It is this: why are people so ready to see and believe evil in all things?

But here I must make a digression.

CHAPTER XXXIII

A digression: My honorary titles: I refuse a gift from the Tzar:
Soloist to His Majesty: Premier Singer to the Soviet People: I
make a speech: My kind friends label me a Bolshevik: A con-
spiracy of lies: A rat leaves the sinking ship

ᴄᴏ ᴄᴏ

I<small>N THE COURSE</small> of my long artistic career I have often been
given proof of the appreciation of the public, and have
also received official " rewards " from the heads of govern-
ments and states.

As an artiste I have won favour both with the people
and at court. But I assert that I have never sought distinction, for by nature I am not ambitious for fame, still
less am I vain. I have been decorated because it is customary to decorate artistes and I could hardly have been
passed over. Every decoration I have received has come as
a surprise — a very pleasant surprise, moreover.

The first honour bestowed on me under the old régime
was the cause of a curious dilemma, or rather of an incident in which all my difficult nature asserted itself, and
which put my friends, Teliakovski in particular, into a
somewhat awkward situation.

One day I received from a dignitary of the court a case
containing a gold watch, a present from the Tzar. I looked
at the watch, and thought that it did not sufficiently
bear witness to the generosity of an Emperor of Russia.
The gold watch, encrusted with minute emeralds, might

perhaps have rejoiced the heart of a family retainer on his retirement from service. . . . But I had no need of such a watch, as I already possessed far better ones; as for wearing it so that I could boast to strangers: "See what the Tzar's given me!" this would have been futile, for the watch was nothing whatever to boast about. . . . I put it back in its case, and sent it to my dear Teliakovski with a letter in which I clearly explained what had actuated my refusal. It created a "scandal." At that time no one had ever dared to refuse a present from the Tzar, and now I . . .

Teliakovski went to His Majesty's ministers, and, thanks to friends of his amongst them, the matter was settled discreetly. A little later another watch was sent to me — an appropriate watch, this time, and I may add in passing that I still possess it.

It was an equal surprise to me when I was given the title of "Soloist to His Majesty." I was then singing at the Monnai in Brussels, and received a telegram from Teliakovski congratulating me on my new title.

It was only much later that I learnt that Teliakovski had long been pulling strings to obtain me this title. It appeared that the Grand Duke Serge Alexandrovitch, the Tzar's uncle, had opposed my being given this high distinction. He knew that I was a friend of that "good-for-nothing" Gorki, and held me personally to be a "frequenter of bars."

I do not know how Teliakovski managed to convince the Tzar that I should not dishonour this title. Another aspect of the matter interested me. As I was of peasant extraction, my children were also considered peasants; that is to say, subjects of the second grade. They could not, for instance, be admitted to the Lycée Poushkin. I now wondered if the sons of His Majesty's Soloist would be accepted as pupils, and accordingly sounded a high official of the court.

"What am I now?" I asked.

The official explained in nasal tones that the crime of my peasant birth could not be effaced by my honorary title. It was still impossible for my sons to attend the Lycée Poushkin.

"But at any rate, you've got a good excuse to see what can be done about it," he wound up consolingly.

Fate willed that "His Majesty's Soloist" should later become "Premier Singer to the Soviet People." This event — also unexpected — took place in the following circumstances.

At the beginning of the Revolution, when Lounatcharski was Komissar of Public Education, he often visited the opera or the theatres to explain the program to the public. He particularly liked doing this when there was a specially invited audience. Then he would hold forth on the merits and demerits of the play from the Marxian standpoint. In these disquisitions he always did justice to bourgeois culture, but at the same time he would underline its deficiencies and weaknesses. In conclusion he would give his official assurance that the value of the proletarian art of the future, as contrasted with the utter worthlessness of the old forms of art, would soon be clearly demonstrated.

One day, a performance was being given, with my co-operation, at the Marie Theatre for an audience of young Red Army officers. The opera chosen was *The Barber of Seville*. As I did not appear until the second act, I had no need to hurry and so did not reach the theatre until after the commencement of the first act. As I entered, Lounatcharski was still holding forth. In my dressing-room I was informed that he had asked for me, and that I should not have been late for his speech.

I expressed regret and added that I had not been told that there would be any speeches before the performance. . . . At that moment the stage-manager ran in breathlessly, and panted:

"Comrade Lounatcharski requests you to come on to the stage at once."

What could be happening?

I made my way towards the stage, and in the wings I met Lounatcharski, who spoke to me most cordially. He said that it seemed to him right and fitting that I should be given the title of " Premier Singer to the Soviet People " in the presence of the young generation of officers.

Quite overcome, I thanked him, and he led me on to the stage. Striking an attitude, he addressed some very flattering words to my profile and concluded by telling the young officers that he was presenting to them and to all Soviet Russia the "Premier Singer to the Soviet People."

There was tumultuous applause as Lounatcharski ended. In reply to their ovation I said that often in the course of my artistic career I had received presentations from many managements in this or that circumstance, but that this presentation — the title of Premier Singer to the Soviet *People* — was dearer to me than all the rest because it touched my heart as one of the people. "And as I see before me the youth of Russia," I concluded, "I wish it in turn success in life; I hope that each one of you will one day experience the deep satisfaction which I am now feeling."

I spoke sincerely. I did indeed wish with all my heart that these young people should make a success of life. But, be it understood, the thought of politics never entered my head.

Nevertheless, this speech had the effect of classifying me as practically an agent of the G.P.U. A pianist, who had formerly been an intimate friend of mine, told everyone when he went abroad that Chaliapin had sunk very low. And he added: " If ever I got the power in my hands, I wouldn't hesitate to have Chaliapin flogged; I'd choose the rods myself. . . ." A writer, too, who had once been my friend and ardent admirer, and who, in his youth, had made all-night stands in queues in order to get tickets for my concerts, wrote to the papers, to the great delight of the editors of these rags, that in the course of a performance of *Eugene Onegin* at the Marie Theatre Chaliapin, in the rôle of General Gremin, had suddenly torn off his epaulets and thrown them into the orchestra, to the unbridled enthusiasm of the soldiery.

All these reports made the Russian émigrés believe that I was in fact a Bolshevik, or, at any rate, a Bolshevik tool. But why, they wondered, has Chaliapin turned his back on the Government which he likes so much, why has he taken his family abroad?

And when I arrived in Paris, a well-known Russian journalist, airing his views as to the reasons for which I had left Russia, declared sententiously to the Russian reading public:

"Chaliapin's appearance in Paris is significant: rats leave the sinking ship. . . ."

CHAPTER XXXIV

*A strange ecstasy: Despotic love: Gossip and scandal: Heroes
and shopkeepers: Monarchist or Communist?*

✧ ✧

THIS DELICATE COMPLIMENT made me reflect once more
on the strange ecstasy with which the Russian uncrowns
his favourites.

He seems to take a sensual delight in degrading today
the man he exalted yesterday. The degradation is based
on as little reason as was the exaltation. It would appear
that the Russian cannot recognize merit or pay homage to
talent without inwardly burning with resentment. He
hastens to avenge this resentment at the first opportunity.
Perhaps this is an ordinary human characteristic, but I
have seen it especially under its Russian aspect, and it
always astonishes me.

Why do spiteful jokes pass for wit? Why does generous enthusiasm pass for stupidity? Why, for example, was
V. V. Stasov, who was the first to hail modern Russian
music with noble enthusiasm, labelled as "*Vavila Bara-
banov*," "*Nieouva Koryto*," "*Trombone*,"[1] etc., while
Bourenin, who made brutal fun of the sick poet Nadson's
sentimentality, was considered an intellectual? Is wit the
art of seeing ugliness in all things, and stupidity that of
seeing beauty everywhere?

[1] Russian nicknames meaning "Philistine," "lowbrow," etc.

The one desire of Stasov and Nadson had been to see beauty around them. Did not their spiritual greatness lie in the enthusiasm with which they exalted the apparently humblest things of life?

Why is it that Russian love is so despotic and intolerant? "Don't live according to your will," it says, "live as *my* love for you ordains. Believe in *my* conception of beauty. If I love you, you must, at every moment in your life, create yourself in *my* image and *my* likeness. Woe be unto you if you fall away from *my* ideal! "

In the Soukonnaia Sloboda, a young man with curly hair and blue eyes goes to a girl and declares his love with persuasive phrases and quiet dignity. The girl believes in him and returns his love. But after they have exchanged some dozen kisses, the young man with the curly hair and blue eyes remarks that her conduct is unbecoming to a young virgin. "She has made herself cheap. . . ." And if she should dare to whisper timidly that it was *he* who kissed *her,* he will fly into a paroxysm of rage and say inexorably:

"Give me back my letters at once! "

The Russian public *has* loved me — that cannot be denied. Then why did they believe the worst slanders that were spread about me? Why, while they paid homage to my talent, did they credit me with the worst qualities?

I can understand the gossip and scandal relating to my "bouts of drunkenness," although I have never been in any sense a drunkard. The Russian cannot imagine a hero who can stop at one glass — he must swill buckets! I drank very moderately, but since I was a "hero," a glass had to be transformed into a hogshead. . . .

Taking it all in all, this is a compliment: "He's a great lad, this Chaliapin! " The measure of a Russian has often been taken by the quantity of alcohol he could consume with impunity! If he could empty a dozen bottles of champagne without collapsing and succeed in swaying haughtily to the door, people would make way for him with respect and exclaim:

" There goes a man! "

I understand the " drunkenness " ascribed to me — and am flattered. But what I do not understand is why a " hero " should be credited with the actions of a petty shopkeeper.

In this connexion, I recall the following story:

A benefit-night on my behalf had been announced at the Grand Theatre, Moscow. Such evenings always drew a crowd, and I had no need to worry about the sale of tickets. Every seat would be booked. I was told that for a former performance dealers had bought huge numbers of tickets and sold them to the public at ridiculous prices. It displeased me that a performance given for my benefit should be inaccessible to those with slender means — that is, practically all the intelligentsia of Moscow. I put a notice in the papers to the effect that tickets might be had of me direct. It was, of course, a distasteful and wearisome business, but I never refuse to perform what I consider a necessary task. I was very anxious to give pleasure to the intellectuals who were hard up. And what do you think the papers said:

" Chaliapin has set up shop! "

What rumours were not set on foot when I received the title of " Soloist to His Majesty "!

The radicals reproached me both for having been singled out for this distinction and for having accepted it, as, later on, I was reproached for not hurling back in Lounatcharski's face the title of " Premier Singer to the Soviet People." This sort of thing is still going on. If I sit in the Café de la Paix with a Russian general, there is a wagging of tongues in the Russian quarter, rue du Banquier. How long is it since I have become an imperialist, they wonder, or have I always been one? But if I meet my Communist friend Ch. (who is trying to hide from goodness knows whom) in the same café next day and we drink a glass of port together, the entire Russian quarter is thrown into a state of violent excitement. They can't understand it at all:

"Is Chaliapin monarchist or Communist? So-and-so saw him with General D. . . . So-and-so saw him with Ch., the Communist. . . ."

But all this is really only a prelude to the recital of one of the most idiotic and painful incidents of my career. I can speak of it today without anger, but I feel a sense of bitterness when I think of the undeserved suffering which the wretched episode caused me.

The most ridiculous episode of my career: "Kneeling before the Tzar" at the Marie Theatre: The truth of the story

～～

For the first time since the Russo-Japanese War the Tzar Nicholas II had announced his decision to be present at the opera at the Marie Theatre. On the night of the performance the auditorium naturally presented a particularly impressive appearance; it was crowded with cavalry and infantry generals, ministers, dignitaries, and members of the aristocracy. Jewels and orders gleamed and glittered. It was, in short, a super-gala. It was quite an ordinary performance from my point of view, and I was rather displeased; *Boris Godounov* was to be given in a new setting which struck me as being tawdry and ineffectual.

I knew that at this time there was considerable friction between the management and the chorus; they had been making demands for a benefit-night on their behalf, or an increase of salary.

The chorus were thoroughly dissatisfied and had made it plain that if necessary they would go on strike. They had even made the threat in so many words. The chief of the Bureaux of the Imperial Theatres was a hard man, who dealt somewhat harshly with the chorus. Having heard that there was a possibility of a strike, he had had a notice put up to the effect that in the event of any such strike he was prepared to close the theatre for one week, two weeks, a month — as long, in fact, as was necessary to recruit a new chorus. The notice went home, the chorus apparently simmered down, but they still nursed their grievances. When they heard that the Tzar was to be present, they agreed amongst themselves to address him from the stage and present him with something like a petition of their complaints about the management.

I, of course, was entirely unaware of their intention.

Their most favourable moment in *Boris Godounov* came immediately after the prologue, when the singers were being recalled. But our fashionable audience, who all adored *Madame Butterfly*, were unmoved by Moussorgski's wonderful opening music, and there were no encores. In the second scene, that of the cell, the chorus take part, but sing " off." This marvellous scene bored the " super-gala " audience, and again there were no recalls. The chorus could now only count on the coronation scene. " Chaliapin is singing, there are sure to be encores . . ." they thought. But, alas, at the end of this scene the noise in the auditorium had no reference to the opera. . . . People began to gossip and chat. . . .

In the tavern-scene the chorus do not appear, nor do they sing in my scene in the *terem*.[1] They could do nothing.

Sick of waiting, they said to each other: " If the curtain doesn't go up after Chaliapin's scene, it's because the opera's no good and Chaliapin's singing badly; if it *does* go up, that will be the moment to act. At all costs." They hoped, moreover, that the curtain *would* go up. And they were not disappointed. After the hallucination-scene, after the words: " O Lord, have pity on the guilty soul of the Tzar Boris," the curtain fell amidst a tempest of applause and encores. I came back and took my call. And then the unbelievable happened. It was for the moment

[1] The apartments of the Tzarina.

[321]

totally incomprehensible to me. From the centre — *for there were no exits right and left* — the entire chorus came forward, singing the *Boje tsaria khrani*. Led by an actress, they came to the front of the stage and fell on their knees. Hearing the strains of the national anthem, and seeing the entire audience rise to its feet, while the chorus knelt, I could not understand what had happened — the more so as after the exhausting scene which had just come to an end, my heart was beating wildly.

The idea came into my mind that some terrorist outrage had been attempted, or — comical thought — that a lady of high rank had given birth to a child in one of the boxes!

I tried to quit the stage, but, as I have said, there were no exits at the sides, and the crowd was blocking up the centre.

As I attempted to step back, I heard the chorus, with whom I was then on excellent terms, whisper: "Don't desert us, dear Feodor Ivanovitch!" . . . The mystery deepened. The whole thing — my thoughts, my search for an exit, and the rest — lasted only a few seconds. I felt that I was so conspicuous by my height that I could not wander about like a lost soul in front of the kneeling chorus an instant longer. Boris's throne was at hand, and I quickly went down on one knee, leaning against the arms of the throne.

The scene ended, the curtain fell. Dumbfounded, I went into the wings and was instantly surrounded by the chorus, who, in answer to my questions, replied:

"Come upstairs with us, Feodor Ivanovitch, and we'll explain it all."

I followed them, and they told me the reasons for their action. They thanked me fervently for not having deserted them and began to sing *Mnogaia Leita* in my honour, holding me shoulder-high.[1]

---

[1] A Russian custom: The man who is to be honoured is wished "Long life!" and tossed several times into the air in token of enthusiasm.

CHALIAPIN
AS BORIS GODOUNOV

"Kneeling to the Tzar"

When I regained my dressing-room, I found Teliakovski pale and agitated.

"What's the meaning of this, Feodor Ivanovitch? Why
didn't you let me know the chorus were preparing this
manifestation?"

"It's I who am surprised you didn't let *me* know. The
management must have known about it."

"I knew nothing whatever," said Teliakovski, heartbroken. "I wonder what on earth I'm to say to the
Tzar. . . ."

This manifestation, Teliakovski's emotion, and, in general, the whole evening left a very unpleasant impression
on my mind. But I must unhesitatingly assert that I felt
neither shame nor humiliation in having "knelt" thus to
the Tzar. I attached no importance whatever to the incident. Search my conscience as I might, I could find nothing
equivocal or treacherous in my conduct. I did not feel that
I had been undignified or servile. It seemed to me that I
personally had not been involved in the episode. It was
as if a slate had fallen from the roof and, by good luck,
had missed me. . . .

The very next day I left for Monte Carlo.

During the month of January in Petersburg it is delightful to think that in a couple of days' time you will be
seeing bright sunshine and roses in bloom. . . .

Happy and care-free, I set forth for the Riviera.

CHAPTER XXXVI

A campaign of slanders: Gorki's friendship

෴ ෴

Wʜᴀᴛ ᴡᴀs ᴍʏ grief, indignation, and surprise to receive
a letter, a few days after I had arrived in Monte Carlo,
from my friend Sierov, the artist, with a batch of press
cuttings referring to my "monarchist demonstration"!

The *Rousskoie Slovo*, which was edited by my friend
Dorochevitch, published an exceedingly clever cartoon,
depicting me close to the prompter's box, with open mouth
and arms upraised. Underneath was the caption: "A
monarchist demonstration at the Marie Theatre, headed
by Chaliapin." If so much was being said in the papers,
what must not be going the rounds by word of mouth! It
was not surprising that Sierov's postscript ran mournfully:
"How sad it makes me to see you, too, lower yourself like
this! You ought to be ashamed of yourself!"

I wrote and told Sierov that he ought not to have
credited these stupid calumnies, and I reproached him for
having sent me his comments. Nevertheless, the rumour
that I had "betrayed the people" reached as far as the
south of France. Returning to Monte Carlo from Nice by
train one day, I was chatting to a friend in my compartment. Suddenly a party of young people of both sexes —
students, or shop assistants, perhaps — crowded into the
carriage and yelled insults at me:

"Flunkey!"

" Traitor! "

" Blackguard! "

I banged the door of the compartment, and they then stuck a paper on the door, on which they had written in huge letters the word:

LICKSPITTLE

When I tell my Russian friends about this incident and ask why these young people should have insulted me, they always reply:

" Because they were proud of you and loved you! "

It was a strange way of showing their love. . . .

My persecutors were obviously young. Their outrageous behaviour could only be set down to extreme ignorance and lack of education. But how explain the conduct of others, really well-bred people, respected and looked up to by thousands?

A few years prior to this incident I had sung in Monte Carlo. A man entered my dressing-room. He was very much moved, and told me that he was overcome by my singing and acting, and that this one evening was a great event in his life. I should not have paid much attention to these words had not the visitor mentioned his name: Plekhanov.

I had heard of him, of course. He was one of the most cultured and esteemed leaders of the Social-Democratic party in Russia, and, in addition, a gifted journalist. When he said how much he would like to have a chat and a cup of tea with me, I exclaimed with genuine pleasure:

" Do please come to the Hôtel de Paris. I shall be delighted to see you."

" May I bring my wife? "

" Do. I shall be charmed."

The Plekhanovs came. We had tea and talked. While we were chatting, Plekhanov asked me for my photograph. I was glad that he cared to have it, and wrote on it:

"With my sincere good wishes."

A few days subsequent to the incident in the train, I found a big envelope amongst my letters. It contained my photograph, on which I now read two inscriptions: first of all, the one I had written — "*With my sincere good wishes*" — and a second one, just written, by Plekhanov: "*This is now valueless and is returned to the donor.*" . . .

And at the same time a well-known Russian writer sent me a letter full of reproaches and recriminations. I had, it appeared, dragged the name of the Russian intellectual in the mud. I learnt later that this indignant writer had given wide publicity to his intimate feelings; he had sent copies of his letter to the editors of all the papers in Moscow and Petersburg.

So that posterity might know the nobility of his sentiments. . . .

I must confess that this series of affronts caused me deep distress. I tried to find a motive for this extraordinary attitude towards me. In the end I began to wonder if I had not actually committed a terrible crime. Was not the very fact of being connected with an Imperial Theatre a betrayal of the people? I was most anxious to have Gorki's opinion of the incident.

Gorki was then living in Capri, and he kept silent. I had learnt indirectly that many of his visitors had made spiteful allusions to me. At the end of my season, I wrote, saying that I should like to go and see him, but that before doing so I wished to be sure that the contagion had not spread to him. He answered that he had, as a matter of fact, been upset by the rumours that had come to his ears, and he begged me to write and tell him what had really occurred. I did so, and he invited me to come and stay with him at once.

Contrary to his usual custom of awaiting his guests' arrival at the house or at the landing-stage, he took a small boat and came to meet me at the ship's side. This friend, with his sensitive soul, had realized and felt to what an extent I had suffered. I was so touched by this noble gesture that I could not keep back my tears. Gorki soothed me and once more made me understand how justly he estimated the baseness of mankind. . . .

CHAPTER XXXVII

*I refuse to take part in the Romanov tercentenary celebrations: No
one suggests taking away my title of "Soloist to His Majesty":
The Soviet Government does deprive me of my title of "Premier
Singer to the People"*

൙ ൙

THESE WERE ONLY pin-pricks, but they took a long time
to heal. The pain remained, and I made a gesture which
at heart was at variance with my inmost feelings — I refused to take part in the tercentenary celebrations in
honour of the Romanov dynasty. I had no grounds of
conscience for my refusal, although I was hostile to the
existing form of government and desired its overthrow.
But any kind of individual demonstration was, on the
whole, foreign to my nature and outlook on life.

The Romanov dynasty had lasted for three hundred
years. It had produced tzars good, bad, and indifferent.
Some of their actions had been good, some the reverse.
That was the history of Russia. To be the only one who
remains seated when the Tzar appears and the people rise
at the first bars of the anthem which was written hundreds
of years ago — protestations of this sort have always struck
me as paltry. Sincere though they may be, they cannot
affect people, one way or the other. My personal feelings
would certainly have sanctioned my singing at a jubilee
performance in honour of the Romanovs.

But I refused to sing because I was still tormented by the recollection of the attacks on me. The thought that they might be renewed in some form or other made a coward of me.

I was in Germany at the time. I wrote in confidence to Teliakovski saying that I was unable to sing on account of ill-health. I think he realized this was only an excuse. He might easily have construed my pretext into an act of defiance and deprived me of my title of " Soloist to His Majesty," but Teliakovski was a true gentleman and a representative of the old " bourgeois " culture: he breathed no word of my refusal. Nobody thought of taking away my title. To take back a gift that has been made is an idea that could only originate in the minds of representatives of " proletarian " culture. They, in fact, did " take back " my title of " Premier Singer to the Soviet People."

It may not be without interest to record in what circumstances this took place. It will illustrate that " love of the people " of which I have spoken.

As, in my character of " rat," I scurried from country to country looking for a little grain to nibble, I found myself one day in London. Returning from a stroll late one night, the hall-porter told me in mysterious and somewhat anxious tones that two gentlemen were waiting for me. In the middle of the night — who could they be? Those who have favours to ask generally come in the day-time.

" Are they Russians? "

" No, English, I think, sir."

Could they be reporters — at that hour? I was intrigued.

" Tell them I'll see them," I said.

They actually proved to be English reporters. They came to the point at once.

" Is it true, M. Chaliapin, that you have been denationalized by the Soviet Government for having helped the

Whites? According to information we have received, your
return to Russia is formally forbidden."

And they showed me a telegram they had just received,
a telegram similar to the one I had seen at the beginning of
this year saying that I was "pardoned" by the Soviets, that
they were restoring my property, and that I was expected
to sing on February 18, 1932 at the Grand Theatre,
Moscow. . . . Naturally, I was unable to tell the reporters
anything with regard to this sensational news. I could not
understand it. What was the meaning of this nonsense?
What help had I given the Whites?

The reporters were disappointed, but as they were leaving, they put one more question to me:

Where was I going to pitch my tent? Now that I was
denationalized, what country was I going to adopt?

This extraordinary question amused me greatly. I told
them I could not give them an immediate reply, that I
must have at least one night to think it over. I must
calculate which nationality would be most profitable. . . .

That night, in fact, I hardly slept. . . .

What was really in the air, I wondered. . . . A few
days later, letters from my family and from my friends in
Paris explained the matter.

CHAPTER XXXVIII

I settle in my new house in Paris: A Te Deum is sung: I offer Father Spasski money in aid of poor Russian children: Moscow blazes up: The proletariat forbids me the country: I am bidden to the Soviet Embassy in Paris: I am proclaimed a White and an anti-revolutionary: Neither "Soloist to His Majesty" nor "Premier Singer to the Soviet People"—Nothing!

∝∝

AT THIS TIME, thanks to my success in Europe, and my still greater success in America, my financial position was excellent. A few years earlier I had left Russia without a kopek, and now I had been able to acquire a house and furnish it to my taste. We had just moved in, and, in conformity with my religious upbringing, I wanted to celebrate the event with a Te Deum.

I am not religious to the extent of believing that the singing of a Te Deum will strengthen the foundations of my house and assure me of happiness in my new dwelling, but I did feel the need to thank the Supreme Being whom we call God, although we are uncertain whether he exists or no. There is, moreover, a certain luxury in thanksgiving. With this feeling in my heart, I sought a priest. I took a friend with me. We went to the vicarage in the rue Daru and were received by Father George Spasski, a man of great charm and culture. I begged him to come and conduct a service at my house.

[331]

A Te Deum

As we left the vicarage, we saw a group of ragged women with equally ragged children standing on the church steps. The little ones had rickety limbs, and heads covered with sores. The women begged for alms, but unfortunately neither of us had any money with us. How could we tell these poor creatures we had no money? This incident clouded the joy I had felt after my interview with the priest, and that night I was wretched.

Luncheon, of course, followed the celebration of the Te Deum. There was caviar and good wine on the table. But half-way through the meal the words of a song came to my mind:

The tyrant in his palace feasts
And in the wine-cup drowns his care. . . .

My heart was, indeed, heavy with care. God would never accept my gratitude, I thought. Besides, was this Te Deum really necessary?

I thought of the incident of the day before outside the vicarage, and answered my guests at random. It was obviously possible to succour these women. But were there only these few? There must be many more. I rose and said to Father Spasski:

" I saw some destitute women and children yesterday, Father, standing outside your church. You must know of a great many more in your parish. Will you accept five thousand francs, and distribute them as you think best . . . ? "

Father Spasski saw fit to insert a few lines of thanks in a Russian paper printed in Paris for my gift in aid of poor Russian children. And a telegram was straightway dispatched from the rue Grenelle to the Kremlin. . . .

Moscow, which had once been set on fire by a farthing rushlight, blazed up again at the tidings of the farthing gift I had made. The papers said that Chaliapin had joined the anti-revolutionaries. Actors, acrobats, and other mem-

bers of the profession began to protest, saying that Chaliapin was not only a bad citizen, but also a bad singer. As
for the "people," they forbade me to re-enter my country.

Next a telegram was dispatched from the Kremlin to
the rue Grenelle, and one fine day I received a polite mes-
sage (by phone, I think) asking me to present myself at
the Soviet Embassy.

I might, of course, have refused to go, but curiosity
urged me. "Go and hear what they've got to say."

Rakovski, the ambassador, received me very courteously.
He asked me into the dining-room, where I was introduced to his wife, a charming woman who spoke Russian
with a foreign accent. I was offered tea and Russian ciga-
rettes. We discussed various matters, and presently Rakovski said that he had a communication to make me. We
went into his study. He gave me a seat near his desk,
and, nervously fingering some papers, said, in some
embarrassment:

"You see, Comrade Chaliapin, Moscow has charged
me to ask you if it is true that you have given money to
charities organized by the Whites, and if so, whether you
gave it to Captain Dmitrievski" (whose name I now heard
for the first time) "and to Bishop Eulogius?"

And, to my great surprise, he added:

"Is it true, also, that you have spoken publicly against
the Soviet Government at Los Angeles? Forgive my asking
you these questions, but I have received instructions from
Moscow and am obliged to carry them out."

I told Rakovski that I had not assisted the Whites in
any way, that I had no interest in politics, that I was equally
indifferent to both Whites and Reds, that I did not know
Captain Dmitrievski, and that I had not given any money
to Bishop Eulogius. I had given money to Father Spasski
in aid of the children of Russian émigrés but that it
seemed a little difficult to find out which child was White
and which Red.

"Yes, but their education is not the same," pointed out Rakovski.

"As regards my public activities in Los Angeles, all I did was to sing Don Basilio in *The Barber of Seville,* and I must sincerely confess that the Bolsheviks never entered my mind. . . ."

At Rakovski's request I put all this into writing for the information of Moscow. My letter caused much dissatisfaction in the Kremlin, but I really do not know what they did expect.

The Central Executive Committee considered my case, and presently an official announcement was made to the effect that, as I was a White and an anti-revolutionary, I was deprived of my title of "Premier Singer to the Soviet People." . . .

I have said that I still possess the watch given me by the Tzar. I look at it sometimes and say:

"This watch was going when I was Soloist to His Majesty. It was still going when I was Premier Singer to the Soviet People. Now it has stopped. . . ."

And when Chaliapin, deprived of all his titles, gazes into its gleaming gold case, he sees, alas, nothing but — zero!

CHAPTER XXXIX

Gorki

တာ တာ

Throughout my book I have spoken of Alexis Maximovitch Piechkov (Gorki) as a very close friend. All my life I have been very proud of my friendship with this remarkable writer and no less remarkable man. Today our friendship is under a cloud, and I feel that were I to keep silence on the subject that causes me so much grief, I should be suppressing a part of the truth. It is indecent to wear an order when the right to wear it has become doubtful, and so I think it fitting to devote a few pages to my relations with Gorki in this book which is a balance-sheet of assets and liabilities.

I have already told how, at the beginning of this century, a close and warm friendship sprang up between us at Nijni-Novgorod. Although I met Gorki comparatively late in life — both of us had made our names by then — I have always thought of him as a childhood friend, there was so much youth and spontaneity in the relations between us.

Our first years were spent in somewhat similar circumstances, although neither realized the existence of the other. We both came from the sordidness and squalor of a wretched quarter — he from Nijni-Novgorod, I from Kazan — and both of us had followed the same paths in pursuit of fame. It had even chanced that both of us had knocked at the door of the opera-house in Kazan on the same day, in the same hour, and had taken our entrance test as chorus singers at the same time. Gorki had been accepted and I turned down. We often used to laugh about it in later years.

Our paths frequently crossed again in the course of a life that was equally sad and painful for both of us. I was standing in line and passing down watermelons in one of the ports on the Volga, while he was working as a docker and unloading sacks from a boat on the river. When I was working with a shoemaker, Gorki was probably in a baker's shop in the neighbourhood.

Love needs no justification. You love *because* you love. Yet the love I vowed all my life to Gorki was not purely instinctive. He possessed all the qualities which have most appeal for me. I loathe pretentious emptiness as much as I love real, spontaneous genius. I was filled with enthusiasm for his great literary gift. Everything he wrote about Russian life was so close, so familiar, so dear to me that I felt as though I had taken a personal part in the incidents he described.

I admire knowledge in men. Gorki knew so much! I used to see him in the company of artists, philosophers, historians, scholars, engineers, naturalists, and so on. Whenever they conversed with him on their special subject, they discovered in him a kindred soul. On every subject, great or small, Gorki had a store of solid, comprehensive knowledge. If it occurred to me, for instance, to ask him about the habits of bullfinches, he was able to tell me so much about them that if all the bullfinches of a million years had been gathered together, they would not have known as much about themselves. . . .

The good is the beautiful, and the beautiful is the good. In Gorki the two were one. I was enthralled when I saw him dissolve into tears, moved by the beauty of a song or a masterpiece of painting.

[336]

CHALIAPIN

WITH A GROUP INCLUDING GORKI AND H. G. WELLS

I remember his lofty conception of the intellectual's mission in life. I see him as the guest one evening of a Moscow writer who lived in a small house in the Arbat district. After a song by Skitalets, accompanied on the *guzla,* when *zakouskis* and vodka were being served, a discussion arose as to what was really meant by an " intellectual." Many conflicting opinions were expressed. Some contended that it meant a man who had special intellectual gifts, others that it signified a man of a special psychic disposition, etc., etc. Then Gorki gave his definition of an intellectual, and I have never forgotten it.

" An intellectual is a man who is ready at any moment in his life to step forward unarmed in defence of truth, and who is prepared to lay down his very life. . . ."

I cannot guarantee that these were the exact words, but it is the exact sense. I had absolute faith in Gorki's sincerity, and felt that these were no empty phrases. How often have I not seen him step forward unarmed! . . .

Once more I picture him, ill, pale, coughing terribly, being flung by two policemen into a train at the Moscow station. He was being deported somewhere to the south, and we, his friends, went with him as far as Serpoukhov. There the sick man was allowed to rest, to sleep in a bed to his heart's content. In a small hotel, still under the watchful eyes of his warders, we spent a joyful farewell evening with him, joyful because neither physical suffering nor police nor deportation troubled Gorki very much. We had faith in the cause for which he was suffering, and it gave us all courage and confidence. In our hearts these feelings were overshadowed by pity for his illness. But Gorki was not conscious of sadness. How gaily he laughed at the vicissitudes of life, and how little stress we laid on our friend's arrest, for we knew that freedom was within him!

I remember his pale face and his emotion on January 9, 1905, that ill-starred day when, led by Gapon, the people proceeded to the Winter Palace and begged the Tzar on their knees to grant them liberty, and for answer were mowed down by the bullets of the soldiery.

" It's a massacre of the innocents! " he cried in horror.

I was singing at an Assembly of Nobles that night, but I entirely shared Gorki's feelings.

My pride and joy may be imagined when Gorki said to me one day:

" I will never believe any evil that may be said of you, Feodor, and you must never believe any evil of me."

Nor have I forgotten these words:

" If there comes a day when we must follow different roads, I shall still love you as much as I do now. I shall love your Sousanin just the same."

I have indeed had many proofs during my life of his love, devotion, and trust. Gorki kept his word. During the Revolution, when I had scruples about leaving my native country, yet was tortured by the new conditions of life and work — when, after a long inner battle, I had at last decided to go abroad — I did not feel that Gorki was out of sympathy with my decision. I was under the impression that he understood my reasons for leaving Russia.

After I had been abroad for some time, I received a letter from Gorki in which he suggested that I should return to the United States of Soviet Russia. Remembering how difficult it was to live and work there under existing conditions, I could not understand why Gorki had changed his mind, and wrote saying that I did not feel inclined to return to Russia at the moment. I set forth my reasons in all sincerity and sent my letter to Capri.

By that time he had already gone to Russia himself and had probably received the impression that there was a new and positive chance of my being able to work and live there. I admit that I had no faith in this possibility, and so the question of my return and my attitude in this connexion remained temporarily in suspense. Gorki did not mention it again. But later, when I was singing in Rome, I had a conversation with him.

I felt that my first refusal to follow his advice had rather cooled his affection for me. Nevertheless, he repeated, in all friendliness, that my return to Russia was *indispensable*. Again, more resolutely, I refused, saying that I had no desire to go back. Why? Because I did not believe there was a chance for me there to work and live as I understood working and living. I was not afraid of this or that leader, but I was afraid to some extent of the new human relationships under the Soviet régime. . . . The best intention of any of the leaders on my behalf might prove absolutely ineffectual. Any day some party or group might revoke all the promises made to me. Suppose, for instance, that I wanted to go abroad; I should be detained, forced to stop in Russia, and protestations would be useless. It would be impossible for me to get out of the country! If I tried to find out who was responsible for caging the singing-bird, one would tell me it was nothing to do with him; another, that a new law had been passed; a third, the man on whose word I had relied, the man who had promised to safeguard me, would throw up his hands hopelessly and exclaim:

"Good God! There's a revolution on! How can I be held responsible?"

It's true enough that Alexis Maximovitch is continually going in and out of Russia, but he is a figure-head of the Revolution. He is a leader. But what about me? I am neither Communist nor Menshevik nor Socialist-Revolutionary nor imperialist nor one of the Cadet party. . . . If you reply in these terms to those who ask: "What are you?" they will answer:

"It's just because you're neither fish, flesh, nor good red herring, but the devil knows what, that you can stay put in Presnia, you son of a bitch!"

With my wandering nature, I love freedom and cannot bear to take orders from anyone — tzar or komissar!

I felt that my refusal to return had displeased Gorki. When later the Soviet Government adopted a very free and easy attitude towards my rights, both at home and abroad — when I persisted in my decision not to return to Russia and dared to defend my rights — a deep breach was cleft in the friendship that had been so precious to me.

I say openly, and with deep feeling, that of all the losses and severed friendships (not many, happily) that have fallen to my lot in these last years, my estrangement from Gorki has been the most painful and the hardest to bear.

I believe that Gorki, with his sensitive intelligence, might, had he so wished, have understood the motives for my behaviour and shown himself less prejudiced. I am certain that he was not actuated by ignoble feelings; everything my dear friend has said and done during these last years has, I am sure, some explanation characteristic of him, which has escaped myself and others.

What actually happened between us? What happened was that he began to take one view of what was going on in Russia, and I another. I believe that in life, as in art, there are no two truths, but only a single truth. I do not know which of us is in possession of this truth, myself or Alexis Maximovitch. The fact remains that the vision of truth we once held in common is common to us both no longer. I remember, for instance, the joy I experienced when he praised I. D. Sytin to the skies.

"There's a man for you!" he exclaimed with shining eyes. "And to think that he was only a simple moujik! . . . What tact, what wit, what energy! To what heights he has risen!"

And the rise of Sytin had indeed been remarkable from first to last. All these Russian moujiks — Alexeiev, Mamontov, Sapojnikov, Sabachnikov, Tretiakov, Morozov, Chtchoukin — what trumps they were in the national game! But now they are called *koulaks,* they are looked upon as a pestilent brood that must be relentlessly exterminated. . . . Yet I cannot but marvel at their gifts and merits. It grieves me that they are regarded now as enemies of the people who must be wiped out, and that my friend Gorki shares the opinion.

I persist in thinking and feeling that man's liberty in his life and work is the highest good. Happiness must not be imposed by force. No one knows what constitutes another's happiness. I still love that liberty which Gorki and I once so ardently worshipped. . . .

Part III

IN FOREIGN LANDS

CHAPTER I

Memories and Yearnings

っの

DURING THE DARK hours of my life under the Bolshevik
régime, I often dreamed of foreign countries and longed
to escape. I yearned for a free and independent life.

I have attained this life of freedom. But often and often,
my thoughts go back to the past and my dear Russia. I
do not regret the money that the national banks confiscated, my houses in Petersburg and Moscow, or my property in the country. I do not particularly regret our
brilliant capitals or even the Russian theatres, so dear to
my heart. As a Russian, I regret the temporary downfall
of our great country; as a man, I pine for a glimpse of
the Russian country-side, spring in Russia, Russian snows,
Russian lakes and forests. I sometimes suffer from the
home-sickness of the simple peasant, the moujik, who is so
maligned by our fine townsfolk. According to them, he is
greedy, coarse, uncouth, and light-fingered. I recall our
unique and often ludicrous Soukonnaia Sloboda, our
suburbs, which I have often frankly criticized, but where
the lilac blooms in the mud, where the apple-trees bear
fruit, and where little boys eagerly chase the pigeons.

I hardly ever dream of Russia; but often, when I am
wide awake, I think of summer days in the country and
the friends from Moscow who came to stay with us. How
natural and simple it all seemed in those days! Now I see,
as if in miniature, a picture symbolic of life in Russia.

[345]

Memories

I used to own a pretty little cottage with three hundred dessiatins of land in the province of Vladimir. Three of us joined together to build it — Valentin Sierov, Constantin Korovin, and I. We drew the plans and designs for it ourselves, and did all the interior decoration. Tchesnokov, a Vladimir peasant, whom we all liked, was our carpenter. At last the cottage was completed. It was a rambling affair, but was charming and friendly, and, thanks to honest timber-merchants, its pine beams had a sheen like mahogany.

Sometimes, at the end of autumn, I would receive a wire from my friends in Moscow: " Coming. Be there to meet us." I had to start off very early in the morning, when the great pines were as yet wrapped in night's mysterious shadow. I had to get across the stream — the bridge was broken — and the water was still as black as ink. On the opposite bank Emelian and Guerassimus were waiting for me with the two conveyances ordered the day before. . . .

I get up sleepily, dress slowly, wander out on to the lawn, and down to the stream. I step on to a small raft and push off with the boat-hook. . . . On the opposite bank I find a carriage . . . its floor is strewn with sweet-smelling hay. With my collar up to my ears, I reach the station, eight versts away. I pass a great pine-forest. How good it is to be in the carriage, warmly muffled up, instead of in the cold and gloomy forest!

The carriage is drawn by a horse called Machka. Guerassimus urges it on gently.

" Gee-up, gee-up, Machka, none of your nonsense! Don't you start limping! "

Machka trots a little faster and seems to answer with a soft whinny.

The station at daybreak. Dim lamps are still burning here and there. Behind a thin wooden partition, I can occasionally hear the buzz of telegraph wires. Everything

is still shrouded in bluish mist. In the waiting-room people
are lying on the floor, their heads resting on sacks. One
of them is talking in his sleep and murmuring something
indistinguishable. Another turns over and stretches. . . .
Someone comes in or goes out, and the door squeaks pro-
testingly. Suddenly it utters a still louder squeak. A man
with bow-legs, carrying a lantern, comes in fussily, steps
over the sleepers, and goes into the telegraph box. The
words "In six minutes" are audible. . . .

The man with the lantern comes running back, shouting:
"Get up! Get up! The train's coming in! "

The sleepers begin to stir. One gets up, another yawns,
another coughs, somebody sighs: "Oh, Lord Jesus! " . . .
The waiting-room is awake.

Dawn overspreads the sky and casts a sickly pallor
on every face. The travellers' baggage emerges from the
shadows. A far-off whistle is heard. The man with the bow-
legs runs towards the bell.

"Ting-aling-aling! " . . .

Everyone is wide awake now. A man coughs and spits
and begins to mutter his morning prayer.

Outside, the pallid sun streams through the mist which
still hangs low, and in the distance are seen smoke and
sparks from the incoming train.

Here they are, my friends from Moscow, Savva Mamontov in the midst of them. . . .

In no other quarter of the globe have I seen the like of
Guerassimus, of the pine-forest, of the bow-legged porter
at the station. . . . Nor have I ever seen in any foreign
land a station like that Russian wayside station, built of
rotten and splintered wood. In the doorway of the waiting-
room hung an extraordinary wash-basin, sadly awry, and
on the counter of the refreshment room, under a plaited
wire cover, were slices of sausage, and eggs spotted with
black specks and flies, those everlasting flies. . . .

Beloved Russia!

CHAPTER II

Intellectual life in the West: Western music: Mozart and Wagner

ഗ ഗ

IN FOREIGN LANDS — this is the title I have given to the last chapters of my book. . . . I had hardly written the words when I began to wonder if these lands are really " foreign " to me.

For, indeed, the intellectual life of the West is infinitely dear and close to me, both as an artiste and as a Russian. We have all drunk from the same source of beauty and vitality. I love Russian music, and my book bears witness to the ardour of my affection, but I have not meant to imply thereby that Western music is inferior to Russian music. Two things may be equally lovely in different ways.

Though Western music has not, in my opinion, the many-sidedness and mixture of strength and intimacy which is characteristic of Russian music, it contains other qualities no less remarkable. Western music also has varied kinds of beauty. There is the world of Mozart and the world of Wagner. There is no measuring the relative grandeur of either of them. But each of us feels instinctively drawn towards one of them, either Mozart or Wagner. Different as the individual reasons may be for this attraction to one or the other, the most artless of them has its subjective value.

Personally, I am inclined to set forth my conception of

Wagner and Mozart in a more or less paradoxical form. I imagine myself to be a young musical enthusiast, collecting the autographs of my favourite composers. I would sell my soul for the autograph of Wagner or Mozart. I screw up my courage and decide to approach each of them in turn.

I go to Wagner's house. It is an imposing edifice, built of great slabs of granite. The entrance is monumental — heavy oak doors with massive carving. I knock timidly. There is a long silence. At length the door opens slowly. A major-domo, clad in sumptuous livery, appears on the threshold. He looks me haughtily up and down with cold grey eyes deep-set below thick eyebrows.

" *Was wollen Sie?* "

" I've called to see Herr Wagner."

The major-domo disappears. I begin to tremble. I am afraid of being turned away. Nothing of the kind — I am asked to come in. The gloomy grey marble hall is solemn and glacial. Suits of armour standing on pedestals look like skeletons. The inner door is guarded on either side by a stone centaur. I enter Herr Wagner's room. I am overwhelmed by its height and vast proportions. There are statues of knights and goddesses. I have the impression of having suddenly become a pygmy. I feel that I have been terribly daring to come so far. Wagner appears. What eyes! What a brow! With a wave of the hand, he motions me to a chair that looks like a throne.

" *Was wollen Sie?* "

On the point of tears, I say in a quivering voice:

" Here is — an album . . . autographs . . ."

Wagner's smile is like sunlight through a cloud; he takes the album and inscribes his name on one of the pages.

He asks me what I am.

" I'm a musician," I say.

He becomes friendly and offers me some refreshment. An imposing butler hands me a cup of coffee. Wagner makes some memorable remarks about music. . . . Yet when the massive oak door closes heavily behind me, when I see the sky and the quite commonplace people in the streets, I feel buoyant — as though I had shaken off a tremendous weight. . . .

Then I go to Mozart. He lives in a small house, with a tiny strip of garden in front of it. A young man opens the door.

" Can I see Herr Mozart? "

" You're speaking to him. But do come in, and sit down. What do you want me to do? Write my autograph? I'll give it you with pleasure. But I can't see what use it is. . . . Wait a bit, I'll make some coffee. Come into the kitchen while I see to it — we can talk while the grounds are settling. My old servant is out — she's gone to church. How young you are! Are you in love? I'll play you something presently — a little thing I've just composed."

Hours slip by. I ought to go, but I can't tear myself away. I am under a spell. I am held captive by Mozart's flute, which warbles a hymn in praise of the sun in spring to an oread in the forest. . . .

The Battle of the Centaurs in Wagner's music is magnificent, it gives an impression of almost superhuman strength. But I have little liking for the spears that must pierce the heart to draw a few drops of sacred blood. I, who am in love with the music of Rimski-Korsakov, find a more familiar language in the flute that warbles to the oread. . . .

It must not be forgotten, however, that a perfectly legitimate preference for one type of beauty and grandeur need not preclude admiration for another.

CHAPTER III

The European theatre: Its grandeur: The decadence of opera

⌒ ⌒

It is EQUALLY impossible for the European theatre to be "foreign" to a Russian. Its glorious history is the birthright of civilized mankind; it leaves an impression of incomparable grandeur. Its Pantheon is peopled with shades that are held sacred by actors of every country.

I shall never forget that night in Moscow at the Maly Theatre when I saw a great European actor for the first time. This was Tommaso Salvini. I was so overpowered by my emotion that I went into the corridor and shed tears. Since that time into what raptures have I not been thrown by the actors and actresses of Europe! Duse, Sarah Bernhardt, Réjane, Mounet-Sully, Paul Mounet, Lucien Guitry, Novelli, and Feravella, that incomparable Italian comedian, who incarnated the unutterable type of ingenuous and foolish youth in a thousand different ways.

By a trick of fate, I have never seen the great German actors on the stage, but the Meiningen company, that of the Lessing Theatre, those from the Reinhardt and Burg theatres of Vienna, belong *en bloc* to the history of the European stage. Kainz and Barnai in the past, Bassermann and Pallenberg today — these four names in themselves stand for a great theatrical culture.

America, which has only recently begun to develop its

remarkable individuality, has already produced actors of the first rank — it is enough to mention the Barrymore family. . . .

The marvellous Charlie Chaplin, who belongs to both hemispheres, brings my thoughts back to England: Irving, Ellen Terry, Sybil Thorndyke. . . . Every time I respectfully take off my hat to the statue of Irving in London, I feel as though I were greeting all the actors of the world in the person of this one great actor. A statue to an actor in a public square — how rare a sight! A neglected headstone in a deserted churchyard is his customary memorial. . . .

During one of my visits to London I had the great pleasure of meeting some famous English actresses. It was at a luncheon given by Bernard Shaw, who had conceived the idea of inviting none but guests of his own age. Questions were put to me about Russian actors and actresses. I made replies, and cited names, but, alas, I had to qualify each name with: "He is dead." "She is dead."

Upon which the inimitable Shaw remarked with great seriousness:

"How well you manage things in Russia! The famous actor X lived, acted, and died; the famous actress Y lived, acted, and died. But in England —"

And with a significant wave of the hand, he indicated all the old guard of the English stage. . . .

All the magicians of the European theatre possessed the qualities for which I have praised the older generation of Russian actors — the absolute sincerity with which they expressed human emotions, and the fidelity of their dramatic pictures. When Lucien Guitry, for instance, portrayed a father's grief, he showed you the father's very soul. He knew how to express himself without words. He would nervously rearrange his tie, and this one gesture, born of emotion too deep for utterance, conveyed more to the audience than a spate of eloquence.

I recently saw Victor Boucher in the part of a *maître*

d'hôtel. I am sure that everyone who saw him will agree that they never saw a more typical and authentic *maître d'hôtel,* either on the stage or in real life. . . .

Western actors appear to me to possess a quality sometimes lacking in their Russian brethren: a greater sense of restraint and greater ease of gesture. They seem to have a more distinguished stage presence. But, as the French say, each virtue has its vice, each vice its virtue. Russians act more spontaneously and have more temperament.

I must, however, regretfully confess that good opera-singers are as rare abroad as they are in Russia. There are some good, even remarkable singers, but there are no great opera-actors, no opera stars in the true sense of the term.

I recognize the fact that *bel canto,* which calls for great mastery of technique, is more suited to Western music than to Russian. But all music expresses some kind of emotion, and where there is emotion, mere mechanical interpretation produces an impression of monotony. The most sparkling music will sound dull if the singer has not practised the intonation of every phrase and given it colour by putting in the necessary shades of feeling. I have said that in order to give a perfect rendering of Russian music, the singer must be able to express the cadence of a sigh. I realize that this is equally necessary in the interpretation of Western music, even though the latter is far less rich emotionally. In the failure to express these nuances lies the whole condemnation of operatic art.

CHAPTER IV

My dream of a synthetic theatre: Gabriel d' Annunzio: My Castle of Art on Poushkin's Rock: Genuine Rembrandts and bad actors: The day will come

∽ ∽

I HAVE LONG REALIZED this fact. It tormented me for many years while I was still in Russia.

I am playing Holophernes. I do my utmost to realize a character in keeping with Assyrian times. But what about my co-singers? What about the chorus of Assyrians, Babylonians, Jews, and the rest of the crowd that surround Holophernes? They have darkened their skins, put on black beards, and donned period costume, but in spite of this you are fully conscious that they have been eating *chtchi* [1] a few minutes before the performance. I think of all my many seasons; I think of all the parts, comic and tragic, that I have played in opera-houses all over the world. They were all my *rôles*, but a *theatre* of my own I have never had, in any quarter of the globe.

A true theatre is not an individual enterprise, but a collective work which calls for the complete harmony of all its components. In order that Salieri in Rimski-Korsakov's opera may be perfect, the part of Mozart also must be perfectly presented. A production in which Sancho

[1] Cabbage soup.

[354]

Panza is excellent and Don Quixote deplorable cannot be considered a success. Each member of the orchestra and, to a far greater degree, the conductor, have their share in the rendering of an opera. How often I have despaired of my art and believed it to be sterile! Not even fame could compensate me. My own personal experience has taught me the value of fame. I might liken it to a nut which you feel between your teeth, but which you cannot taste. . . . Beyond material wealth and a pleasant titillation of one's self-satisfaction, what is fame productive of in the way of happiness? I have always believed, and still believe, that my talent (which has received such generous appreciation from my contemporaries) has been half hidden under a napkin, and that I have done very little with the gifts God has given me. I have been a good singer. But where is my *theatre?*

It was at the era when these thoughts were assailing me that I met Gabriel d'Annunzio in M. Astruc's office. I was deeply impressed by d'Annunzio's face, with its piercing eyes, expanse of brow, and pointed beard. All his features radiated a keenness that commanded notice. He was then in Paris, writing *The Martyrdom of St. Sebastian* for Madame Ida Rubinstein. I went to see this performed at the Châtelet, and was struck by the originality and power of the dialogue, setting, and whole atmosphere of the production. When I met d'Annunzio for the second time, I began talking to him about my dream of a theatre where anything bordering on the sham would be ruthlessly eradicated and where all the arts would be merged in complete harmony. I was overjoyed by his enthusiastic approval of my conception.

"Next year we'll meet again and try to realize your dream," he said.

This conversation took place in March 1914. . . . In August war broke out. D'Annunzio, that marvellous " soaring spirit," was soon to soar skyward in a real plane towards Fiume, far away from the realization of our peace-time dream. . . . I had been happy to meet so wonderful a poet as d'Annunzio, and felt all the more regret since I knew that our projected collaboration could never take place. Back in Russia, alone this time, I meditated on what I considered to be my life's work. I nursed a dream which was dearer to me than anything in the world of reality. I made up my mind to devote all my earthly possessions and heart and soul to the founding of a centre of dramatic art.

I dreamed of a sequestered spot where, surrounded by a band of earnest and gifted young people, I might inspire them with all my artistic knowledge and fire them with the ardour of my own devotion to the noble cause of the theatre. I wanted to form a group of singers, musicians, and artists, and work with them in peace and solitude, in the creating of an ideal theatre. I wanted to set them down amidst the beauties of nature and give them all the amenities of life.

In the Crimea, on the seashore at Soo-Ook-Soo, there is a lonely rock that bears the name of Poushkin. It was on this rock that I resolved to build my Castle of Art. Yes, a castle. "If kings and knights of old had castles, why should not artists have a castle, too?" I thought. "A castle with battlements, but not for cannon. . . ."

I became the owner of Poushkin's Rock; I commissioned an architect to draw up plans and bought Gobelin tapestries to hang on the walls. . . .

I left my dream in Russia — shattered. . . .

Recently I came across a painful reminder of it. I caught sight of a photograph in a London paper under which were the words: "A gift from the Soviet Government to F. I. Chaliapin." I looked more closely at the picture: it was the projected plan of my Castle of Art. The architect had probably exhibited it somewhere, and it had become "A gift from the Soviet Government." . . .

CHALIAPIN

ON THE BOWERY, STUDYING BOWERY TYPES

Genuine Rembrandts

Sometimes people say to me: "One day a great art-lover will build *your* theatre," whereupon I ask jestingly:

"To what part of the world will he transport Poushkin's Rock?"

Yet I do not speak entirely in jest. My dream is intimately bound up with Russia, with the genius of the coming generation of Russians. A castle built anywhere else — in Ohio, or on the Rhine — would mean practically nothing to me. As to the "noble lovers of art," I could never weary of marvelling at such phenomena! I know of men who spend hundreds of thousands of dollars a year on opera — which is, of course, a proof that they love the theatre deeply and sincerely. . . . Yet their conception of art is deplorably false. From season to season, from year to year, last year as next year, all the productions in their theatres are banal and lifeless. And so it will go on: *Traviata — Traviata ad infinitum.* Bad actors, sham reputation, incongruous settings, and poor singing — the entire absence of talent, and the complete triumph of the commonplace! Yet these same men expend fabulous sums in the acquisition of a genuine Rembrandt; they turn away disgustedly from any canvas that is not unmistakably in the first rank.

To this very day I am at a loss to understand why they insist on originals and masterpieces for their picture-galleries when in their theatres, whose upkeep is just as costly, they are satisfied with reproductions of third-rate works. Can it be because painting, over and above the fact that it is art, is also a sound investment? . . .

And my thoughts go back to Mamontov. He also spent money on the theatre, and died in misery, but what superlative taste he had! What unerring enthusiasm he displayed in the realm of art! Yet he lived in a land of "barbarians" and was a Tartar by birth.

I should not like to end this book, the record of my artistic credits and debits, on a note of sadness and pessimism. To me, Mamontov stands for everything that is inspiring and creative. I have not created my theatre. It does not matter. Others will create it. A day will come. . . .

Art may pass through periods of decadence, but, like Life itself, it endures. . . .